Using Story

Story is everywhere in human lives and cultures and it features strongly in the processes of teaching and learning. Story can be called narrative, case study, critical incident, life history, anecdote, scenario, illustration or example, creative writing, storytelling; it is a unit of communication, it is in the products of the media industries, in therapy and in our daily acts of reflecting. Stories are 'told' in many ways – they are spoken, written, filmed, mimed or acted, presented as cartoons and in new media formats, and through all these, they are associated with both teaching and learning processes but in different ways and at different levels. As a result of growing interest and simultaneous confusion about story, it is timely to untangle the various meanings of story so that we can draw out and extend its value and use.

Using Story aims to clarify what we mean by story, to seek out where story occurs in education and life and to explore the processes by which we learn from story. In this way the book intends to 'bring story into the open' and improve its use. Building on her wealth of experience in the field Jenny Moon explores the theory of story and demonstrates both its current uses and new ways in which to enrich and enliven teaching, learning and research processes.

Ideal for anyone involved in education, personal or professional development or with a more general interest in story, the book begins by considering the range of what is meant by story, and then considers the theory behind the meanings. In the large final part of the book, Jenny provides a rich patchwork of different uses of story in education that cut across forms of story, story activities, disciplines and applications, all of which will aid the use of story.

Jennifer Moon works at the Centre for Excellence in Media Practice at Bournemouth University and as an independent consultant running workshops in higher education and professional development in the UK and internationally.

Using Story

In Higher Education and Professional Development

Jennifer Moon

 Routledge
Taylor & Francis Group

LONDON AND NEW YORK

First edition published 2010
by Routledge
2 Park Square, Milton Park, Abingdon, Oxon OX14 4RN

Simultaneously published in the USA and Canada
by Routledge
270 Madison Avenue, New York, NY 10016

Routledge is an imprint of the Taylor & Francis Group, an informa business

© 2010 Jennifer Moon

Typeset in Galliard by
Taylor & Francis Books
Printed and bound in Great Britain by
TJ International Ltd, Padstow, Cornwall

Library of Congress Cataloging-in-Publication Data
A catalog record has been requested for this book

British Library Cataloguing in Publication Data
Moon, Jennifer A.
   Using story : in higher education and professional development / Jenny
Moon. – 1st ed.
      p. cm.
   Includes bibliographical references and index.
   1. School improvement programs–United States. 2. Educational leadership–
United States. I. Title.
   LB2822.82.M65 2010
   378.1'7–dc22
                            2010001455

ISBN 978-0-415-56468-7 (hbk)
ISBN 978-0-415-56469-4 (pbk)
ISBN 978-0-203-84771-8 (ebk)

Contents

Preface

This is a book about an important aspect of being a human being. We are story-telling and story-listening beings – indeed story, in its universal occurrence, seems important to our humanity. It is a book that endeavours to explore what story is and what it is to us and how we learn from it, create internal story worlds and, on the outside, how it intermingles with the cultures and communities to which we relate. The focus of the book is on the role of story in higher education and in professional development, but it is relevant to all educational situations and I have drawn on broad literature. Anyone who feels that story has no place in education might care to peruse the contents page for this book to see the many areas of educational practice to which story is relevant.

Different parts of the book may appeal to different readers. In writing it, I have drawn from science, the arts and humanities. The introductory and theory parts would be relevant to anyone working with story, whether in disciplinary contexts (e.g. literature), in education or as writers and tellers of story. The large third part of the book consists of a 'treasury' of ways of working with story in education, with a focus on advanced education. It is designed as 'pick and mix', with no specific sequence. The book is not a tidy development of theory that is then applied in later chapters. I wanted it to be like that, but – as I explain in the Chapter 1 – the subject matter dictated otherwise! Story had its own way.

As I wrote, particularly in the theory chapters, I had many insights about story. Submerged in text as they often are, I decided to fish out the insights and put them properly on display in the Chapter 6 – 'Taking stock', which serves to summarise the introductory and theory chapters and as a starting point for the more focused educational chapters that follow. I think that there are other insights that I have missed that can yet emerge from within and across the topics covered. There is much more to be written on story and education and with a fairly extensive reference list, this book can be a useful starting point.

There are, of course, people to thank. I start with Maxine Alterio, whose book *Learning through Storytelling in Higher Education* (McDrury and Alterio, 2003) was a great inspiration for this. I spent time with Maxine discussing joint authorship of a more general book on story in education when I visited her in New Zealand in 2003. However, at that time the publishers would not countenance another book on story and we got on separately with different areas of writing. Then there is John Fowler of De Montfort University, with whom I wrote a paper on story in 2008. John has overtly used story over many years in nurse education (Moon and Fowler, 2008). I would also like to thank those who have been participants in workshops on story and those who have listened in storytelling sessions. They were all important sources of my learning for this book.

I also want to recognise the roles of those around me in supporting my interest in story: my parents – telling and reading those bedtime stories that I, in my sleeplessness, demanded; and my children, Shelley and Kyla, wanting their own bedtime stories (I remember 'Papa's Lemonade' by Eve Rice). But they also wanted made-up stories. Putting down the story book to set off into imagination was both liberating and, at that time of the evening, hard work!

Part I

Some introductory ideas

There are two chapters in this part of the book and they have introductory roles. The first of these contains information about why the book was written and the reasoning behind the manner of its writing – why story is worthy of study. Such reasoning is strongly influenced by the experiences that I, as writer, have brought to this process of writing. It also explores such issues as word use and vocabulary and what the book does and does not cover. It introduces the reader to the twisting journey that I have travelled in seeking the meaning of story and its uses and values. The second of the chapters considers the range of story and introduces various issues such as authenticity that are considered in more detail later. It ends by attempting to draw some boundaries around the meanings of story.

Chapter 1

Introduction

Bringing story into education and professional development

Introduction

I have visited story as a topic again and again in my life and this visit promises to be a big one! All of us – I think it is all of us – visit story all the time, so I will employ the well-used words that 'story is everywhere'. It is the stuff of our entertainments, our day and night dreams; it is in the comfort that we give to others in times of difficulty – 'when this happened to me … ' It is part of the way that people identify themselves and part of the way that communities or cultures are characterised. I see it as related to our inclination to make sense of things – or sense of nothing: as Ben Goldacre says. 'As human beings we have an innate ability to make something out of nothing. We see shapes in the clouds, and a man in the moon' (Goldacre, 2008: 226). Goldacre is talking of how scientific data can be distorted into 'bad science' (Goldacre, n.d.). Perhaps it is distorted particularly when bad science makes good story!

Story is represented throughout the diverse processes of education, both for the teachers and for those who learn, and this is the focus of this book; however, it can meet a solid block of prejudice in the throw-away comment that it is 'only a story or "mere entertainment" and therefore not worthy of attention' (Mar and Oatley, 2008) and in particular not worthy of the attentions of psychological research.

I am only the same as any other human in terms of the story-filled nature of my life, but I have come back to the idea of story again and again because it intrigues me. It is as if a pixie called Story keeps waving to me in the midst of my activities in education and at home, saying, 'Hello, I am here again … ' And Story *is* there again … and again … For example, recently I was writing some curriculum materials on the improvement of group work for undergraduate students, using the principles of academic assertiveness (Moon, 2008a, 2009a; Ireland and Moon, 2008) – and there was Story, waving at me again. Story was present in the manner in which I illustrated academic assertiveness with real-life examples and in the group work scenarios that were presented for discussion in groups of students.

So it is time to make greater sense of this thing. I focus on the role of story in higher education, though the first six chapters are much broader and it is the later chapters which explore the educational uses of story. And it is time to drop the capital letter of Story, though I do not wish to leave behind the notion of play and enjoyment that is so much gathered in the idea of story. We enter the portals of formal advanced education (and within that term I include professional development), but play and enjoyment do not need to be left at these gates. They enhance serious learning and they remain one of the drivers for the writing of this book.

In broad terms the book is an exploration of what is meant by 'story', and why it takes a large role in human existence. I want to understand more about how we learn from stories and how story compares with other forms of expression and about the role of story in advanced education. Like others of my books, this is an act of research and exploration but also a provision of ideas and techniques to enhance education and learning. The enhancement may mean development of deeper understanding – or maybe it could mean that learning is made more enjoyable and there is encouragement towards life-long learning. Story may enhance learning directly or it may influence it through enlivening the act of teaching.

My early thoughts on this project were that it would entail a tidy sequence from a theoretical framework to applications in practice. I thought I had found a framework that would serve as an ordering device for the book (Moon, 2006: chapter 11), but then I found another ten frameworks that story fits or that fit story and I concluded that story is too diverse to be tucked into sequentially related chapters. There would be too much overlapping, so the neat framework idea had to go and now, though the first six chapters follow in a sequence, the next eight, about different uses of story, are not sequenced. Most uses are relevant to most disciplines so these chapters form a sort of patchwork quilt of story – and hopefully the thoughts and ideas add bright and attractive colour to education.

Uses of words

Already I have declared one of my basic understandings of education: that teaching and learning are different. Though of course we would hope that teaching facilitates learning, it may not. Learning is what a learner does. Teaching is the activity of the teacher who hopes to facilitate the learner's learning, but the teacher cannot make the learner learn. She cannot stop the learner's mind from wandering the recalled shores of a Mediterranean beach in a statistics class – she can only provide conditions under which the learning of statistics has, in her view, the best chance of happening. Of course, when the errant learner reads up the topic it is possible that her learning may surpass the content of the teaching. Learning is not dependent on teaching. Story has different roles in the separate activities of teaching and learning and, as a result, sometimes these roles are dealt with separately in this book. The section, for example, on oral storytelling concerns communication, and therefore it is more to do with teaching, though it is also a good technique to help a new teacher to learn to teach or to help students to learn to give presentations.

Another distinction that I will make is between story and storytelling. Many writers now use the term 'storytelling' to imply anything that involves the use of story (e.g. Gabriel, 2000). As an oral storyteller, I am used to using the term 'storytelling' with reference to the oral delivery of story, usually in performance, and I will maintain my use of the term in that context unless I am quoting from the work of others.

I need also to consider the words 'narrative' and 'story'. Both are used in the literature to mean the same or sometimes different things. I am not going to play word games in seeking to differentiate these two because, depending on our habits or disciplinary origins, we have legitimate but differing views on this distinction. For example, Gudmundsdottir (1995), McLeod (1997) and others discuss the words 'narrative' and 'story' in detail, but even then come to different views. For this book, I have drawn on material that is called 'narrative' as well as on that called 'story', but broadly I treat the two words as meaning the same thing, unless I am quoting from others. I will tend to use the word 'story' because of its connotations of play and pleasure, and I do not wish to 'academicise' my approach through use of the more sophisticated term.

I endeavour not to use words, like 'storied' and 'restory', that appear in the literature (e.g. Greenhalgh and Hurwitz, 1998), having some difficulty with comprehension of such terms. However, I do introduce a new word that I will use extensively at times. I use the word 'unspoken' to imply aspects of situation that are perceived or conveyed or operating other than directly through the words spoken. We may or may not be conscious of the unspoken. While this makes it difficult to discuss, I have come to feel that it is an important aspect of story. Some of this unspoken material is affect – emotions – some is imagery (visual, aural, tactile, olfactory and so on) and some combines into what we call 'atmosphere'. I will say that it seems to be a characteristic of story that it carries more information than is present in the spoken words.

That brings us back to language use. I will predominantly use the word 'learner' rather than 'student'. This will make the reading easier for those who use this book for professional development. Somehow also, for me, the term 'student' tends to carry the expectation that a teacher hovers nearby and the student sits as one in of many in staid rows. 'Learner' is a freer word. I will tend to talk of the 'teller' of a story and refer to the 'listener'. Of course, stories may be written and read or depicted in film and watched, but I will still tend to use these words. I also tend to use female-gendered words. As I have said in other books, half of us are male and half are female and it is the turn now of females to have their gender as a primary form of representation ('she', 'her' ...). The common, but grammatically incorrect mechanism of using the plural ('they') to avoid the ungainly 'his/her' or 'he/she', grates!

How I came to write about story and its role in higher education

Story comes into lives in many disguises – often we are not aware of it as story. I have dabbled with writing story for a long time. I have sat in several writers' circles, sometimes with interpersonal dynamics that themselves have been worthy of a story. I have run 'beginning to write' classes, engendering excitement about story-writing. There has also always been something exciting for me about the manner in which story can be a mode of transportation (Gerrig, 1993) away from the present into places of the wildest imaginings – a kind of pleasure-giving magic. There is joy, for me, in having a poem 'on the go'. A poem is likely to be a story with an emphasis on the unspoken material between the words. Having a story or a poem 'on the go' provides somewhere for mental escape.

I worked for some years using hypnosis as an adjunct to counselling. Only recently I have seen that the process was the telling of stories – those of the clients which I heard, those that were generated in my head as I listened, and in hypnotherapy those that I constructed, and through which the clients might mentally wander, hopefully finding ways to work through the tasks or difficulties of their lives (see Parkinson, 2009). In working with hypnosis, I had a number of 'set' stories that enabled me to introduce the appropriate imagery to facilitate relaxation and then appropriate change (Chapter 10). There was a woodland walk to a sandy beach with sandcastles to build and waves in which to paddle under bright sun. There was also a wonderful garden down a flight of ten steps, with a running stream, tall trees and a shed in which problems could be left ('shed') for a while … and then often there were the 'demons' to be confronted and overcome – the cigarettes, the obesity or the world outside in the case of the many agoraphobics whom I saw.

A particularly interesting area of story work that was connected with hypnosis came in the explorations of mind with a group with friends using regression techniques (not therapy). I was always clear that I did now know the origin of the extraordinary story material which could fairly reliably emerge from our minds. I did not designate it as 'past life' material. I came across these methods at first in a battered ex-library book (*Windows of the Mind* (Glaskin, 1974)). Wherever this story material came from, it showed the great mental story-making capacities in many who would not normally call themselves imaginative.

And so story went on touching my life as it touches everyone's life – the delights of encountering children's stories, of the made-up stories at bedtime and more. But now I jump ahead and start to look at how story began to find an educational place in my life. By 2004, I had written two books on reflective learning and one on learning journals (Moon, 1999a, 1999b, 2004), which had brought me nearer to linking my interests in story with thoughts about pedagogy and learning. On a small grant from the Institute for Teaching and Learning I visited and worked with Maxine Alterio in New Zealand, who (with Janice McDrury) had written a book about the use of 'storytelling' in professional and vocational education (McDrury and Alterio, 2003). On my return I approached publishers about a book about the role of story in higher education, but their view was that the topic was not of sufficient interest. The writing of a second edition of my book on learning journals took over but, determined not to be defeated on the story topic, I wrote a chapter on the relationship of story to learning journals and looked forward to delving into the pile of story literature that I had accumulated. Reading through that material brought a revelation. I realised that I was far from clear what I meant by this word 'story'. It seemed that the use of the term 'story' was, in the words of my journal, 'all over the place' – it could be used in so many ways. I therefore endeavoured to pull the idea of story in the educational context into some sort of organised framework to clarify what I was writing. In that chapter I did not get much beyond a framework for story (Moon, 2006: chapter 11). The framework became the basis of some workshops and I learned more then through a chance meeting with John Fowler at De Montfort University, Leicester (UK), who was using various forms of story in his role as nurse educator. The framework became furnished with some examples and a paper followed (Moon and Fowler, 2008).

Since the journal book (2006), I have written two further books, one on critical thinking (Moon, 2008a) and another on what I have called 'academic assertiveness' (Moon, 2009a). Both in their own ways have contributed to my thoughts about the role of story in higher education. I have become more convinced of the importance of the use of examples and illustrations as means of teaching and supporting learning, and these can be in story form. One strand of this thinking relates to the way in which we explain important concepts such as reflective learning and critical thinking. These are difficult concepts to put over and yet are crucial in modern higher education. Some of the problem with such concepts is that they are not easy to explain in language – in other words, there is much that is unspoken about them. To understand these ideas better, I suggest that we need to make use of examples – and these examples may be stories. I have developed the term 'graduated scenarios' for such exercises (see Chapter 7; Moon, 2004, 2009b).

The book on academic assertiveness is written for students (Moon, 2009a). I could have written advice on how to be more assertive as a dry manual but this would have been hard going, and probably a non-starter from the publishing point of view so I used scenarios – stories. The book is full of scenarios – probably numbering a hundred – stories of situations and events to illustrate the points made. Some were from informed imagination, some from talking with students and some based on actual situations. Here is a scenario from that book on academic assertiveness – from a chapter on facing challenges:

> Chen is from mainland China. He has come to the UK to do a degree in Engineering. While he has been studying English for a long time in China, it seems different here and he is finding day to day life very difficult. He has gone into a supermarket to buy some rice and he cannot find it on the shelves. There is a girl stacking shelves. He knows that at home, he would ask her where the rice is (though he would be embarrassed not to know …) but – well – she might not understand him and then he would feel foolish. He imagines her screwing up her face at him. Then again, he might not understand her and he might have to pretend to understand and he might walk away in the wrong direction. Then he would feel even more foolish. He

goes on looking and not asking and feeling more bewildered about how he will ever fit in here.

(Moon, 2009a: 9)

In another part of my current life, I am an oral storyteller. I tell stories in schools, care homes, festivals and folk clubs. In the course of storytelling, I have to decide which stories will 'work' and learn them for retelling, and I then have to put them over in a manner that will entertain an audience. In a whole book of stories, often it is only one story that feels 'right'. What is the attraction? Why am I disinterested in Greek and Viking myth and yet I like American and Australian aboriginal stories and those from old China? Beyond length and complexity, what makes a story worth telling or 'engaging' (Chapter 4)? I feel that it needs to have something that I am going to call 'magic'. I make no apologies for the use of such a word. I have said above that there are many unspoken ideas around story – and this is another.

I see oral storytelling as closely related to the process of teaching. To tell a story satisfactorily – perhaps in a crowded pub – there must be engagement of the teller with the audience. Teaching does not facilitate learning if there is no engagement with learners. I think we would do well to educate new teachers in the art of storytelling because in that is the essence of the art of engaging audience. And as I have said, oral storytelling is similarly useful in helping learners with the art of presenting (Moon 2010a; 2010b).

Beyond the story influences on my life-before-this-book, there is the role of the research for this book itself. I have never before accessed so much information on one topic – but it becomes evident that story is far from one topic (Parkinson, 2009). It spreads out across disciplines and areas of interest – and any may have relevance to higher education. Story is overtly significant in disciplines like literature, creative writing, law, history, education, drama, media subjects, sociology, religious studies, ethnography and heritage and folklore studies. There is often a strong role of story in art and design disciplines, psychology, psychotherapy and counselling, in areas of business in anthropology and in the literature of professional learning, where story is used in medical, nurse, teacher and social work education. Story is represented in other disciplines too – a valuable source was written by a computer scientist in his work on the development of computer 'language' (Schank, 1995). Story is there in sciences, but perhaps it is hidden because the ethos of science is so 'anti-rhetoric'. I have, though, mentioned 'bad science' – is story which adversely affects the public understandings of science, for example the health myths that lurk behind advertisements that are created to support particular diets, and here, science has to counter the compelling story. Story is also central to the relatively new activity of reflecting on personal and professional development that is represented in many disciplines now. It comes into the way in which teachers teach and it plays a large part in qualitative research methods – and it is part of the day-to-day life and communication associated with many professional lives.

There are some books and papers that have been particularly influential on my work for different reasons. Among many such texts I would note Field (1952) and her alternative name, Milner (1957, 1987), Progoff (1975), Schank (1995), Gough (1993), Donaldson (1992), Bruner (1986, 1990), Phillips (1995), Greenhalgh and Hurwitz (1998), Richardson (2000), Sparkes (2002), McDrury and Alterio (2003), Laming (2004), Denning (2004), Gabriel (2000), Ryan (2008) and Morpurgo (2006), and a series of papers from a research group at the University of Toronto (summarised in Oatley, 2008a). So it is perhaps not surprising, with all those areas to cover, that the pile of literature of which I want to make sense and from which I intend to develop ideas about story in higher education is of a height whereby it is very likely to topple over and flood my living room floor – and it still grows!

This book: what it does and does not do

I come to this book with three tasks in mind. First, I want to get closer to knowing what story is. The second task follows the reasoning that 'story' is a widely used word in general social interaction. The word may mean story in the manner of the meaning that I write, but sometimes it is used as a substitute for other words like reason (for doing something) or a belief system, a description, report or account (see Chapter 2). The word is 'fluffy' from overuse and is coming to have a buzz-word quality which ensures its broader 'mis'-use. Overuse of a word is a problem if the idea behind the word is important, and I believe that the notion of story is important in educational and other human processes. There are many situations in which story is used as a method of communication but is going unrecognised. Before it is too late, I want to capture the concept of story in all its diversity and richness and explore its relationship to higher education and professional development. If we can recognise the manner in which we are using story as teachers, learners and researchers we can make better uses of it. In taking this line I encounter the view that 'story' is not a proper content for advanced education and I wish to oppose this. (I note, incidentally, that one way in which 'story' does seem to creep into educational situations is under the name of 'narrative', which seems to improve its academic respectability.)

The third task is that I want to explore the thinking that lies behind the assertions that it is not just chance that story plays such a part in the lives of humans, but that human brains have a predisposition to organise thought and communication processes into story for expression or a personal explanation of the world. There are many iterations of this observation, but Hardy (1977), in her chapter entitled 'Narrative as a primary act of mind', perhaps is the most eloquent. Others who have made similar comments are Fuller (1982), Mattingly (1990); Clandinin and Connelly (1990), Lanzara (1990), Rowland et al. (1990), Boje (1991, 2002), McEwan and Egan (1995), McLeod (1997), Claxton (1999), Fulford (1999), Gabriel (2000), Denning (2004) and Parkinson (2009). Some questions are associated with this idea that story is linked to being human: what drives us to tell stories, sometimes over and over again? Why do we listen more closely when someone says, 'I'll tell you a story'? What does it mean to be engaged in listening to a story? What is the relationship between the story and memory? And again, how do these observations relate to educational situations?

The fourth aspect of story that I intend to explore is the role of what we call 'fiction' in learning and higher education. This is another way in which, again, I counter higher education thinking which eschews the value of story and fiction; saying that is not 'true' has no place in education. But what is truth? And anyway, we do use fiction in education in case study and other examples and I want to explore these uses and other possible roles for fiction.

In following those four tasks, I will be covering a great deal more material as well.

I have said already that one thing that this book does not do is to pull the idea of story into a neat framework from which, in some logical manner, I derive the subject matter of the rest of the book. Story is too diverse for this treatment. Following from that, nor do I feel that there is one form of pedagogy, or one theory about what story is. I do I think that there is a great potential for the uses of story in higher education and that my exploration in this book is a dipping of the big toe in the pool of potential uses and conceptions of story. I hope to make this field of thinking more easily penetrable by others in terms of the enrichment of their practice or their theoretical or research activities. But then I begin to question my metaphor ' … a pool of water … ' It is wrong. I see the relationship between story, humans and education is more like a rainforest, with bright ideas that flit through the canopy this way and that. The writing of the book has been something of a process of flitting around. As soon as I have put ideas down (like, for example, that of the framework), new ideas have emerged that have added to or changed my thinking. The process of writing this book has been one of accumulation and change. It has been a process of research far more than most of the other writing that I have done – and I do not see the completed book as an end-point.

I need to say also that I am not going to be dealing with story as a subject of study – such as studies of English literature and creative writing. That job belongs to specialists in those disciplines. Most of what I am going to be saying in this book is not specific to particular disciplines. I want to share ideas around – picking up some of the practices in the use of story in one discipline and showing how they can be used in other disciplinary areas. There are word limits to what I can do on this, but there are not word limits to the further thinking of readers!

The content of this book

The book consists of three parts. Part I is introductory, covering this chapter and the next, which explores the range of story. In it I explore views of what story is, its purposes, and come to identify some of the boundaries for the meaning of story. Part II of the book concerns theory – and in writing it, I found that it formed into three chapters of ideas and one in which I review the ideas. The three sequenced 'ideas' chapters cover matters of learning and understanding of stories, the way in which meaning works in stories and a chapter on the broader uses of story in culture and communication. Then there is the review chapter – 'taking stock'. The chapters in Part III of the book are not sequenced by meaning. They cover a range of roles of story in education, summarising how story is used and providing a collection of ideas that hopefully can inspire and encourage greater use of story in education.

Thinkpoint

So that is where I am at the moment – a sense that there are huge numbers of ideas about story in many different places. I think that there are principles to be extracted, but it is going to be a difficult job.

This was a note to myself in the journal I used in researching story on 18th December 2007, as I started to write the book.

Chapter 2

The multiple dimensions of story

Introduction

There are many meanings to the word 'story' and while I do not intend to engage in literary theory, it is important to tie down what I am going to choose to mean by story in the educational context, as that is the focus of this book. In particular this is preparation for the chapters on theory and the educational aspects of the relationships between humans and their story activities. In exploring the range and meaning of story, first I note the vastness of the topic and look at some of the more obvious distinctions between different types of story and the ways in which story is communicated (p. 12). There is a section introducing issues of authenticity (p. 14) and then a large section exploring the purposes of story (p. 16). The sheer number of purposes for telling stories was one of the surprises in writing this book. Then I look at the literature – at what others have considered to be definitions of story, and follow with considerations from my own angle, though I have chosen to focus on where the boundaries of story and what is not story might lie, rather than constraining this slippery concept in definitions. This chapter inevitably scans many topics that are elaborated further in later chapters.

The vastness of the topic of story

Once I thought that 'story' meant story and a carefully considered definition would yield a simple framework which would structure the book. Those were the easy days. But, despite the complexity that I now recognise, I do need to tie down some meaning for story or I would be including the meaning of 'throw-away' phrases like 'That's your story is it?' and 'It's the story of my life!' or 'Our products tell their own story', as advertisers might say. In its overuse, 'story' graduates towards meaninglessness. Gabriel (2000) is similarly concerned 'about the increasing tendency to view every sign, every snippet of conversation, every image and every cliché as either being a story or telling a story' (p. 3). In attributing the word to everything, we lose its potential for recognition or further development of story as an educational tool.

However, it is difficult to find a stable meaning for story (Moon and Fowler, 2008). To take some examples – Mar and Oatley (2008) use the term story (or narrative) for fiction writing. McDrury and Alterio (2003) discuss the broad heading of 'story in higher education' and then focus on the personally experienced stories of learners in professional development or vocational education. In a similar professional context, Connelly and Clandinin (1990) talk of 'narratives' and Mortiboys (2005) talks of 'storytelling'. Others, often, but not always in the professional field, use the term 'critical incident analysis' (e.g. Brookfield, 1987; Cowan, 1998). Another view of story that is also relevant to higher education is that of McKee (1999), writing about story in the context of screenwriting – then story is an entity that 'will excite audiences' (p. 3). McKee considers that good story-writing can be taught and that the 'storyteller is a life poet, an artist who transforms day to day living, inner life and outer life, dream and actuality into a poem whose rhymes scheme is events rather than words' (p. 25). In other educational situations there is a general use of case study material that may be constructed from someone's real experience (Fowler, 1981, 1995) and such use may coincide with the 'scenarios' (e.g. Moon, 2009a). Case studies, critical incidents and scenarios, whether experienced or fiction, are often stories. 'Story' as a term is also used in research, educational and therapeutic activities (e.g. Bolton, 1994, 1999) and Sparkes (2002) uses 'telling tales' for a wide range of activities that constitute qualitative research activities on the lives of sports people). These 'tales' are fiction as well as accounts of real experience. In other words, there is a large vocabulary around story even within the educational context – and the terms are used inconsistently.

Some initial parameters of story

In this section I demonstrate some different dimensions of story beyond terminology.

Stories are presented in different media. Sometimes the characteristics of the medium determine the nature of the story that can be told – a story that is based largely on the nuances of language might be difficult to represent graphically. Some of the media that may carry story are:

- sound: the vocal telling of a story; we listen or lip-read;
- drama and dance: the acting out of story (that may or may not include sound);
- the written word: a story is read with eyes or fingers (Braille);
- graphic representation: comic strip, cartoon sequence, storyboard, photographic journalism; other forms of imagery, etc.;
- music: e.g. the music of Peter and the Wolf tells a story;
- touch: story can emanate from a tableaux or sculpture as well as inspiring its construction;
- mime;
- and the brain constructs stories in various 'altered states' (dreams, daydreams, meditative or hypnotic states), which may be in pre-linguistic form; these are sometimes remembered and translated into conscious imagery, and language (Damasio, 2000).

A story may often be portrayed by a mixture of these media. This book largely focuses on story as told or presented in written form, but most of what I will say will relate to most of the other media most of the time. What we do with a story when it gets inside our heads probably may differ from person to person, according to the literature of 'learning styles' and multiple intelligences, and subject to our psychological preferences or aptitudes (Gardner, 1983). It is interesting to note, for example, that there are different ways in which storytellers choose to learn stories to tell orally. Some learn a story on the basis of the sequence of scenes from the story, which are then recalled in sequence, while others rely on the linguistic sequence of a story (Chapter 13). I need also to acknowledge the differences in experience between listening to a story that is read, that is told, and reading a story for oneself. An oral storyteller can respond directly to an audience; whereas someone reading a story is less able to do this and television story cannot do it (Harrett, 2008; Rosen, 2009). Mar and Oatley (2008) contrast responses to film, theatre, television and other multisensory presentations, with responses to reading.

There are different activities associated with story and this is often ignored in literature that purports to define story. Some activities associated with story are as follows:

- constructing a story (fiction or non-fiction);
- selecting an appropriate story to tell in a given context;
- the telling of story – not necessarily a story constructed by the teller;
- listening to a story;
- perceiving, memorising and reconstructing a story for retelling;
- adapting a story from one medium to another;
- researching story or stories in qualitative research.

This list links with the purposes for story later in this chapter and the place of story in the activities of teaching or learning.

A first look at issues of authenticity ('fact' and fiction)

This section comprises some basic comments on authenticity to aid the discussion of the range of story (see Chapter 4 for detail). It demonstrates that the common ideas of the authenticity of a story, fact and fiction, reality and unreality, are somewhat leaky concepts. I shall take 'authenticity' of a story to relate to its relationship to events purported to be 'real' or experienced as 'true'. This brings in issues about the purpose of the story, who tells it and the meaning of words such as reality, fact and fiction.

To deal with authenticity I refer to the work with Fowler (Moon and Fowler, 2008). We presented a framework for story which was meant to capture the range of types of story and some important relationships between some of them. We conceived of story as fitting into the following categories – I have modified the headings to broaden their relevance:

- Personal story: the description and maybe reflection on personally experienced events that have sufficient unity and coherence to be identified as stories and that are made public to at least one other. The material might be reflective writing in a journal or blog, oral or in other format.
- 'Known' story told in a communal setting: these are the stories told among people who share experiences, such as those working within a common profession, workplace, or as learners on an educational programme. The stories are about events or experiences within the common interests of the tellers or listeners. They may be presented and used as case studies, case histories, scenarios or critical incidents or they may be part of an action research work (Carr and Kemmis, 1986).
- Non-fiction but 'not personally known' story: these are stories in the media – stories that are at a distance from individuals, but that are taken to be 'true' or authentic accounts within a real experience or context (e.g. of shared profession, workplace, etc.). They may be the generalised material of case history and study, scenario and critical incident, or from research. They form the basis of much learning in humanities disciplines.
- Fiction and fantasy: fictitious stories are those that are accounts of events that the listener cannot be sure have happened. However, fiction and fantasy is made up of elements of experience that are interpreted and reimagined by the presenter of the story – and reinterpreted by the listener in relation to elements of her own experience.

The issue for authenticity is that one person's 'personal' story becomes another's 'known story' when the first person communicates her story to the other. Correspondingly, another's 'known story', when it is communicated to another individual or group, becomes the new individual's or group's non-fiction – not known and not personal stories. And, taking it one step further, a mix of personal, known and non-fiction becomes fiction when it is remixed with someone's capacities for imagination. It may also be interpreted by the listener in relation to her known experiences. An example of such a situation in professional studies might be where known stories of one group of professionals are communicated to another group as a series of case studies. To this latter group, whether the case studies were 'made up' (i.e. fiction) or were originally based on real-life situations probably does not matter.

There is a tendency to consider 'fact and fiction' as distinctive opposites – but it is far from as clear as that. As a further example, a learning journal entry about a specific incident may seem to be 'fact', but if journals are to be seen by tutors, then strategic or perceptive students will modify their accounts of observed events to suit what they perceive to be the criteria for assessment (or perceived tutor preferences – Salisbury, 1994). 'Modification' is fictionalisation.

Taking this further, we make sense of the world in relation to what we know already. Knowing is a constructive process (Chapter 3), a form of fiction which is generated on the basis of a selection of prior experiences. In reading a story, we make meaning by matching read words to our prior experiences. The attribution of meaning, even to a word, has come about through experience. The processes of representation of an idea, of retelling it and of reading or hearing a story are further processes of interpretation or reshaping (Lamarque, 1990). 'Reshaping', 'interpreting' and even listening are acts of fiction (Lawton, 2007).

The purposes of story

In this section I am concerned with the purposes of story in all situations – formal and informal – and I include all of the activities of story – creating, telling, listening, and researching and using story as a form of communication. I accumulated these 'purposes' of story in separate lists over several years. When I consolidated the list in preparation for this book I was amazed at the number of purposes that there were for story. I include the list in full because I think it is important to show just how wide is the use of story as background for the rest of the book. For the list, I have taken a broad meaning of the word 'purpose'. Sometimes the delivery of a story is central to the purpose and sometimes the story is incidental and is not used consciously as a story. There are many overlaps between items in the list and there is no particular significance in the sequencing of the list. Where purposes relate obviously to the material of later chapters I add the chapter reference, and occasionally I have added references, but generally I have left them until later.

Reading this section word for word is not important for the casual reader – observation of the headings and a flick through the elaborations of headings will be sufficient. The list demonstrates the vast role of stories in human lives.

Story as a form of communication

- We use stories to surprise others or to convey the unexpected or 'news'. This can be a source of satisfaction (e.g. as in gossip) or it can also be covert power-play – raising self-esteem by knowing the most surprising or 'newest' news or through demonstrating inside knowledge.
- Stories can change meanings or stabilise them and reflect them more clearly to others. Wizardry has taken on a particular image after Harry Potter (e.g. Rowling, 2000)!
- The stories we deliberately choose to tell can transmit information about our own identities and values. Deliberately choosing to make reference to bible stories or to war stories or specific personal experiences (e.g. 'name dropping') conveys personality and personal values.
- The sharing of stories between professions or groups can promote the development of understandings and the recognition of points of view that may differ. Stories can demonstrate the legitimacy of having those different perspectives or ways of interpreting the same event (Chapter 8).
- The telling of a story in a teaching situation can encourage engagement and capture flagging attention. In a lecture people may refocus and attend when someone says, 'Let me tell you a story about this.' Change in pace or style of speech may emphasise 'story mode' (Chapter 13).

Story as a means of facilitating learning from experience

- Story can be used as a means of learning from vicarious 'experiences' (e.g. 'What would you do in this situation?').
- Listening to, constructing or telling a story can provide a means of making sense of an experience for the teller or others (Chapter 7).
- Story is used because it can encompass a 'bigger picture' about a topic, including affect and other unspoken material (Chapter 3).
- Story can encompass affective material overtly or covertly. Stories consist of more than would be apparent from the 'sum of' the words (Chapter 3). They can convey a 'bigger picture' or more holistic information than other communication. This is an important characteristic of story (Chapters 3 and 4).
- Stories convey information about experiences when the experiences cannot be accessed directly by the listener (e.g. stories about historical characters or far-off travel) (Chapter 9).
- Story is used in the spread of 'soft' or local social knowledge or accumulated wisdom within groups in society such as organisations. It may be called 'gossip' or rumour (Chapter 4).
- Stories can indicate a sense of 'how we got here' in the thinking behind history, arts, social sciences, sciences or other disciplines.
- Stories told about an event or person tend to associate them with explicit and implicit qualities that steer us towards particular ways of organising and memorising experiences. In other words, stories tend to influence the listener's subsequent interpretation of the subject (not necessarily consciously) (Chapter 4).
- Stories illustrate ideas that are to be presented, provide metaphor, analogy, enhance a point being made.

Story as a medium for the development of skills (storytelling)

- The practice of oral storytelling enables learning of communication skills. It is a presentation skill that can be practised and developed (Chapter 13).
- Listening to oral story can improve listening skills.
- Development of stories is practised in the context of learning to engage in creative writing.
- Stories can convey information on how to do something (e.g. The Swiss Family Robinson was written to convey practical information (Seelye, 2007)).

Stories and learning about the nature of knowledge

- Stories may be used to demonstrate and explore ambiguity and uncertainty (e.g. Zen and the Art of Motorcycle Maintenance by Robert Pirsig (1974)).
- Story is a way of helping listeners to learn more about the nature of knowledge (Chapter 4). A story can explore different ways of characterising or

representing an object or event or situation. The same object/event/situation might be explored from different perspectives, or different aspects of the same object etc. can be explored (e.g. novels and non-fiction of Ann Oakley (1984, 1989, 1992)).

- A story can be a container for the activity of informal theorising whether a story is fiction or non-fiction and whether listened to or told. Learning to engage in informal theorising is important in much professional practice – and is part of reflective practice. Many of Iris Murdoch's books explore ideas through story – e.g. The Message to the Planet (Murdoch 1989).

The construction of story as an aid to learning communication skills

- Writing a story can aid in the development of writing skills.
- Use of story can develop writing and communication skills in the study of new languages. Storytelling can be used with language students (Heathfield, 2005) (Chapter 13).

A story makes an event distinctive or creates connotations

- The construction of a story around a topic makes an idea more distinctive and memorable. One can 'return' to it in memory more easily if the storyline has been 'developed' – though the return might be to the story and not the original (Chapter 5).
- Stories assign meaning to ideas and knowledge. This can be in the form of bias and maybe a negative influence (Chapter 5).

Story and its effect on the listener

- Stories entertain.
- Stories provide a means to entertainment in computer or interactive games (Chapter 14).
- Stories can bring about emotional learning and insight for the listener (many parables are designed to do this) (Chapter 3).
- Stories can stimulate catharsis (e.g. horror stories, romance, thrillers, etc.).
- Stories are used in social situations to engineer the attitudes of others; e.g. the rewritten stories of the brothers Grimm were designed to elicit nationalistic feelings (Grimm and Grimm, n.d.).
- Stories can encourage people to form identities that may be transient or longer term. This is relevant to the concerns about the use of violent characters in interactive games, film, television and other media. Bettelheim (1976) suggested that fairy tales frame the thinking of children.
- Stories may be therapeutic – consciously or unconsciously. They are widely used in therapy – overtly in narrative therapy or covertly in other forms of therapy and counselling (Chapter 10).

Story and its role in social behaviour

- The telling of stories seems to create a sense of commonality and comfort among a group of people who are facing a common experience or adversity. In adverse situations people tell stories to each other, e.g. when the train breaks down – 'I remember when ... '
- Listening to a story can create a link between personal experience and the broader experience of others or another ('Ah, I am not the only one to experience that then').
- Telling a story is a way of influencing others, e.g. making a point more strongly by illustrating it with a story. Preachers use story or parable to this effect.
- Story can covertly encourage change of attitude and thereby change in groups or society (e.g. through rumour) (Chapter 5). Leaders of opinion and others have often endeavoured to influence the literature available to populations in order to reframe their views. For example, the play Cathy Come Home (Sandford, 1966) was used to raise the issue of homelessness.
- Sharing stories around a theme is a means of sharing experiences and, at the same time, developing empathy and understanding within a group, improving cohesion and teamwork. Telling stories provides a way of getting to know others through the stories that they tell (McDrury and Alterio, 2003; Denning, 2004).
- Story, in the context of book clubs, can be the focus and starter for the development of social groups. Book clubs may be used to facilitate socialisation of students or other communities.
- People use stories to make themselves noticed in a group.

Story and its effect on the teller

- People often tell stories when there has been a personally traumatic event. The telling, often over and over again, seems to have important therapeutic or normalising effects on the teller (Chapter 10).
- Stories are used to transport the self to a pleasant fantasy (usually with emotional associations). This may be for pleasure or for 'escape' from other situations that tend to 'worry'. Such deliberate relaxation methods may be used to help students to manage workload and examination stresses.
- The construction or telling of stories can stimulate or develop 'bright ideas', imagination and creativity. The effect may be the actual story or the shift out of the 'everyday' modes of thinking. Some stories, particularly with strong visual content, engender a feeling of excitement in the teller.
- Personal story is central in the construction of personal identity and therefore in personal development. It is often used in this way in journal writing, blogging, and sometimes in counselling and therapy (Chapters 8 and 10).
- Work with personal story can stimulate development of a sense of well-being and having a place in society (e.g. in its use in reminiscence work in gerontology).

Progoff (1975) used personal story to help unemployed youth to value their lives. There are other examples in Moon (2006) (Chapter 10).

Story as a way of stimulating thought in the listener

- Listening to a story can stimulate personal reflection or review (Siddhartha by Hermann Hesse (1974) is inspiring for me).
- Story is a covert means of presenting ideas and exerting influence when direct telling or presentation of the material is resisted by the listener (e.g. in organisational change, in forms of therapy and in parable, etc. – Chapter 10).
- They provide material for examination (such as critical incidents). In this respect, they can stimulate and enable the development of critical thinking or the making of judgements (e.g. Laming, 2004) (Chapter 9).
- Stories can broaden or deepen thinking, or stimulate understanding (Chapter 7).
- They can be a starting point for discussions (e.g. in educational contexts or informally).

Story as a subject or means of research in academic or professional learning

- Stories are a means of inquiry within a group of people, where interpretations can be compared and researched (Chapter 11).
- Story is a means of learning about the ways in which other people think or act under different circumstances. Such learning may emerge from fiction or from working with case studies (Chapter 9).
- Stories can be used to develop understanding of the manner in which ideas can be processed. They can demonstrate ideas that could not be explained in words (Chapter 7).
- Stories in the form of graduated scenarios, by their incorporation of a process of comparison, can enable learning of skills (e.g. clinical reasoning, patient care skills – Chapter 7) (Moon, 2009a).
- The use of story is a method of inquiry in itself in ethnography (e.g. Connelly and Clandinin 1990) (Chapter 11).
- Stories of lives are a subject of study in sociology, psychology and other disciplines, particularly when a constructivist view is taken (e.g. Clough, 2002 – Chapter 11).
- Narrative is a subject of study itself in English. A range of arts disciplines are associated with story (drama, writing, song and poetry, etc.).
- History and sociology and other disciplines are constructed partly on the bases of stories.

Use of story as a means of clarifying a complex or difficult situation

- Stories can be the starting point for discussion of a difficult topic. The story may be directly or indirectly relevant (e.g. metaphor etc.; McDrury and Alterio, 2003) (Chapter 8).

- There may be reinterpretation of a story in dramatic form to reflect a situation back to an audience or an individual, with the idea of eliciting response, learning or reinterpretation and change (Playback Theatre, n.d.; Boal 1995) (Chapter 10).
- Story is used in problem-solving. A story may facilitate movement towards a solution – for example by working with an absurd story as explanation before considering more 'sensible' interpretations. The absurd quite often holds the 'answer' (Chapter 7).

Story as a means of constructing new knowledge

- Stories are a means of constructing new knowledge. Fiction can be a 'container' for trying out new ideas; 'what ifs' (e.g. science fiction).
- Related to the previous point, in the context of research, stories may aid the generation of new hypotheses (Chapter 11).
- Story is important as a means of transmission of knowledge, particularly to young children or those with relatively little formal education when abstract thought is unfamiliar (Bettelheim, 1976).

Story as a form of transmission of traditional culture

- Stories can preserve and convey the non-verbal aspects of tradition and culture in the development of ideas or in a community (Chapter 5).
- They can preserve and convey the verbal aspects of tradition and culture in the development of ideas or in a community. These sometimes might be in the form of 'guiding myths' or attitudes.
- Stories can convey accumulated wisdom that is not or cannot be specifically be verbalised (unspoken) (Estes, 1992).
- Stories convey historical forms and uses of language (Carter, 1991).

Story and its role in belief systems

- Story has a profound role in some disciplines – as an indicator of belief and cultural concomitants (e.g. in religion and works such as the Bible).

I make a few observations on this list. Compiling it reiterated the importance of story in human life – and it emphasised story's large and considerably unrecognised role in education. It also enabled me to see the substantial use of story in everyday interactions and to consider how and how much people use story in conversation. Those who do not use story tend to have a staid and dry style and they have difficulty with humour. Others use story too much and they can be tedious. There are some who are not good at selecting the right story for the occasion. Schank (1995) links the good use of story with a concept of intelligence. Over the course of writing this book I have come to agree with him. In writing this list I also realised that the purpose for telling stories may either be that of the teller or to benefit the listener. Sometimes their purposes are complementary – not always!

What is story?: seeking some defining boundaries

So far in this chapter I have added more and more dimensions to the concept of story – it grows like the spreading branches of a tree. It is time to start to pull this thing into a more organised form. To continue the metaphor, I need now to find the trunk and the roots that support the branches and this is the task for the rest of the chapter. First, I review material from other writers and then plot out some defining ideas about story, drawing on this whole chapter and Chapter 1. I will then attempt to trace some of what I will call the 'boundaries' that seem to me to be important in the concepts of story.

What is story?: the views of other writers

In looking at the definitions of story used by others, my main endeavour is to seek out what I consider to be useful ideas for the purpose of this book – rather than engaging in a general survey of the literature on the definition of story. If the latter were my task, I would dip into literary resources (Koch, 1998), which I am not doing. I have considered the purposes for story in advance of these sections because they demonstrate the great breadth of story, its diversity, and demonstrate that most of the definitions in the literature do not encompass the whole field, though few acknowledge their limitations. Exceptions to this are Stein and Policastro (1984), who say that the variety of purposes for story made it difficult to find a 'stable' concept. Denning (2004) agrees with Polkinghorne, a significant theorist in this field, who comments that 'story is a large tent with many usages under that tent' (Polkinghorne, 1988: 156).

Other writers go to some lengths to discuss definition of story. Gabriel (2000), considering story in organisations, says that story 'may be a product of fantasy or experience' and that the plots of stories entail 'conflicts, predicaments, trials, coincidences and crises that call for choices, decisions or actions and interactions' (p. 239). He talks of story as having a role in explanation, interpretation and sense-making in complex and multi-causal situations, with which science cannot always help us, with its more stringent methods. We cope with these situations by using story to attribute 'motive, agency or purpose' to situations. This latter point, not usually recognised in connection with definition of story, touches on the different roles of story for teller and listener.

Some writers use the word story as if its meaning is immediately obvious. An example is Fuller (1982), who questions whether the concept of story is the elusive 'engram' – but does not tell us what he means by story. McDrury and Alterio (2003), in their book on professional education and development, do not attempt to define story, but consider 'storytelling'; they define that as an 'experience that enables us to convey, though the language of words, aspects of ourselves and others and the worlds, real or imagined, that we inhabit' (p. 3). They summarise it as 'making sense of experience' (p. 9). Whereas Gabriel's focus is on story as a concept in itself, that of McDrury and Alterio is on the manner in which it is or can be used in educational contexts. Others expand on the relationship of story to experience – for example Connelly and Clandinin (1990), who, in the context of research on teaching, say that 'Narrative is a way of characterising the phenomena of human experience'. It is 'a study of the ways humans experience the world'.

In these definitions that refer to experience and story, so far experience is treated as actually lived experience. Engel's (1995) definition broadens this. In the context of her work with children, she says that stories 'give us a new way to experience life … a second world, beyond the world of immediate action', and that the ability to live in both worlds is a characteristic of being human. Using language, humans can 'shift back and forth in this double world, each world shaping the other, their stories organising their perceptions of actions and objects, their perceptions of actions and objects informing their stories' (p. 6). This is similar to the line taken by Mar et al. (2006), whose focus is entirely on fiction. They say: 'What makes literary fiction unique is how stories enable us to be "transported" into an imagined world (Gerrig, 1993), offering a form of cognitive simulation of the social world with absorbing emotional consequences for the reader'. Phillips (1995), arguing the case for the use of fictitious story in organisations, makes a similar comment: story 'creates a space for the representation of the life-world within which individuals find themselves'. I return to this idea of stories as 'creating a space' later. Ryan (2008) in a more generic approach extends these latter ideas to say that 'aspects of reality are linked with associative memories and fantasies and put together to communicate an understanding of the world or of ourselves'.

In the context of organisation and management studies, Taylor et al. (2002) elaborate on the social role of experience in story and raise the issue of what makes a story worth listening to. They agree with Boje's definition of story as oral or written performance 'involving two or more people interpreting past or anticipated experience' (Boje, 1991: 111). Taylor et al. focus on the meaning-making functions of story through social construction. They see a 'good' story as creating a context that enables others to examine what is happening in the story. They say that the story needs to be 'engaging' – and this is achieved variously through use of the 'chronological sequence, a link between the exceptional and the ordinary, dramatic quality, poetic quality, imagery, exuberance, the use of tropes or figures of speech, concrete language, an interesting setting, central characters and terseness'. They suggest that two more holistic characteristics of an engaging story are that the story 'tells us something about what it is to be human' – and that the story is enjoyable. Ryan also mentions the playful aspect of story.

McLeod (1997) writes as a psychotherapist and he says something of the consequences of the delivery of a story, which he sees as a description of an event – story can bring order and completion to experiences, solve problems, and it enables the development of a sense of perspective with regard to the event. He notes that story also communicates useful information about the teller and her intentions, for example why she chose this story to tell in the (therapeutic) context, her expectations of the world, her feelings and morality. Story demonstrates what sorts of events are unusual or unexpected to the teller. Temple and Gillet (1989) make a similar point, seeing stories as 'explanatory devices that help us to make sense of the random and inexplicable happenings of everyday life' (p. 136). Day (1991) sees the subject of story as a break in what is normal. He says that 'people tell stories when their lives press forward against some blockage or breakdown … we struggle to make sense' (pp. 78–79).

Like McLeod, Plummer (1995), in his work on sexual stories, sees the telling of story as providing information about the teller and her sociological context. While Plummer does not define story as such, he works around sociological issues in personal story – the need to write, the writer, the listener, the power politics that governs the telling of personal story and the impact on the listener. He brings out many issues that relate to the broader definition of story and a particularly helpful summary statement is:

> Whatever else a story is, it is not simply the lived life. It speaks all around the life: it provides routes into a life, lays down maps for lives to follow, suggests links between a life and a culture. It may, indeed, be one of the most important tools we have for understanding lives and the wider cultures they are part of.
>
> (Plummer, 1995: 168)

An important element of story that seems to be missing from many of the definitions above is the role of emotion (affect/feeling). I briefly referred to it as an unspoken aspect of story in Chapter 1 and return to it in Chapter 3. Gabriel (2000) does introduce this idea, saying that stories generate emotion in the teller and listener 'through a poetic elaboration of symbolic material' (p. 239). The series of papers written by the University of Toronto research group (e.g. Oatley, 2008a; Mar and Oatley, 2008; Dijikic *et al.*, 2009) view the reading of fiction as a process of involvement in a simulation of an aspect of life which entails emotional engagement and empathy with the characters. Their research suggests that people who read more fiction are 'better primed for social relations'. I explore their ideas more later.

Now I come to some writers who have used similar kinds of definition of story to that which I have chosen – a list of points that plot the boundaries of story and which distinguish it from description and report and other expressions that seem not to be story. Ricoeur (1984), for example, talks of stories 'grasping together' ideas. Fulford as a journalist, defines story as more than just an experience:

> A story has shape, outlines, limits … an experience blurs at the edges and tends to merge imperceptibly with related experiences … Stories, in order to become stories must be simplified, stripped of extraneous detail and vagrant

feeling. We find it easier to do this with the lives of others – though from time to time, we may apply the same technique to our own history.

(Fulford, 1999: 4)

Fulford (1999) goes on to say that 'stories survive partly because they remind us of what we know and partly because they call us back to what we consider significant' (p. 7). In their work on story in medical clinical practice, Greenhalgh and Hurwitz (1998) take a fairly similar line to that of Fulford. They start with an excerpt from the opening of The House at Pooh Corner (Milne, 1974) and from this they draw five qualities of narrative. First, stories have a beginning, 'a series of unfolding events' and an end. Second, the relationship between the teller and the listener can influence the viewpoints expressed in the story. Third, the actors in the story are 'characters'. This implies that they have relevant emotional lives as well as performing action. Fourth, narratives may include information that is beyond the events of the story. The extent of this extra information is the choice of the narrator, who might be influenced by the curiosity of the listener. Lastly, Greenhalgh and Hurwitz (1998) say, a narrative is engaging and 'invites an interpretation' (pp. 3–4).

Finally I turn last to the work of Bruner (1986, 1990, 2002), to whose definition of story reference is frequently made. Bruner (1990), an educationalist and psychologist, explores story as a human phenomenon. Using the term 'narrative', he describes narrative as a 'way of using language' (p. 59) which employs a special set of linguistic tools and techniques, such as metaphor, to enhance meaning. Bruner says first that a 'principal property' (p. 43) of narrative is that it is composed of a distinct sequence of events, mental states and happenings that involve actors. These are the 'constituents of story'. The meaning of the narrative is derived from the pattern of the whole sequence, which is the 'plot'. The 'interpreter' of a story has both to 'grasp the … configuring plot' and to make sense of the roles of the constituent elements of the narrative in that plot. I would suggest that another part of the process is the distinction of the pattern of the plot against its greater background or context – the recognition of when a story is being told. I come back to this idea in Chapters 3 and 4.

A second feature of Bruner's definition is that the 'power' of story material is not dependent on whether it is fact or fiction. It is judged in terms of how it works internally – the veracity within the story. Stories are units with the elements working in relationship to each other more than to elements outside the story. This notion of Bruner's works, in my view, for some stories, but the power of other stories may depend on external realities and the purpose for telling. If I am telling the story of an incident at a job interview, its veracity in relation to external events is important and it relates, presumably, to the purpose for telling. In contrast, if I am entertaining in a storytelling session at a folk club, the audience will not be surprised if I tell them that an old man is turned into a fine white stallion through drinking a magic potion.

Bruner (1990) says (third) that narrative 'specializes in forging the links between the exceptional and the ordinary … when you encounter an exception to the ordinary, and ask someone what is happening, the person you ask will virtually always tell a story' (p. 49). The story is likely to explain the exceptional through a reasoning process – which is the content of the story. As in the previous of Bruner's points, I suggest that this may only relate to some forms of story. It seems to me that Bruner describes stories where the 'exceptional' – the surprise or twist is – within the story. However, sometimes the whole story represents the exceptional. Broadcast 'news' stories are usually exceptions or additions to the normal, but the exceptional element is in contrast to their broader context, and does not appear within the story. For example, the news that a five-year-old child is nearly two metres tall and cannot get school clothes is in contrast to knowledge of usual human height. The contrast that demonstrates normality here is between the story and its context and not within the story, as Bruner seems to suggest it should be to constitute story.

There are another two points that Bruner makes about the nature of narrative. He says that 'well formed' narrative cuts between the inner lives of the actors, the events of the story and the actors' responses to the events (their interpretations of what is happening, for example). Narratives may be open to variable interpretations – so that one reader's understanding legitimately could vary from that of another – thus potentially setting up negotiation stances. This would form some of the working content of the study of literature.

Before I set my own boundaries round story in the last section of this chapter, I return to the work of Phillips (1995) and his typology of some aspects of story. Phillips examines types of story in a two-by-two table. He examines non-fiction and fiction against non-narrative and narrative. In fiction that is non-narrative, he includes theories, mathematical models and typologies – 'different kinds of fictions that we find useful in thinking about the world of organisations'. The non-fiction non-narrative cell includes survey data, laboratory data and content analysis. In terms of narrative fiction, he includes biographies, case studies and ethnographies, but leaves a question mark in the cell for narrative that is fiction – and within the text of his paper (as I have said previously), argues for the value of such stories in organisational contexts. Phillips' typology is useful in my discussion of boundaries because he deals with what is not story as well as what is story. With such a widespread and diverse phenomenon as story, to be explicit about what comes outside the term is as helpful as endeavouring to say what it is that is inside.

What is story?: setting some boundaries

One approach to story definition is to be clear what kind of story is being defined and to define only that – so if fiction is the focus, then the definition is for fiction only. However, I endeavour to explore all of what we call story. To come to my set of boundaries for story, I draw on the ideas of others, but have 'played around' with ideas beyond this. I listed words that seemed to come within the boundary of story and then words that were not story (like Phillips) and then looked at how I felt they were or were not story. The process reminded me of the use of repertory grids (Kelly, 1955). In this way, I came face to face with an issue that had bothered me throughout my considerations: that I wanted to define what I came to call a 'strong-form' story – the kind with a beginning, middle and end and a twist (the kind mostly used for entertainment) – and another form, which at first I called 'weak-form', later renamed 'broad-form', story (such stories are not weak but neither are they 'strong form').

Here are the 'workings' of my repertory-grid-type of exercise. I do not claim that the lists are 'complete' and there is some overlapping.

Words usually associated with story in the strong-form sense of the word

- Story, narrative, anecdote, metaphor, parable, tale, legend, myth, saga, epic, allegory, fairy tale, yarn, libretto, play or film-script, gossip, short story, novella, play, 50-word story, novel, some jokes, narrative poem, mime.

Words associated more often with 'broad-form' story

- Case history, scenario, critical incident, recounting of an event, autobiography, biography, expose, 'piece'.

Forms of communication that may include strong-form or broad-form story

- Novel, history, comic, play/film-script, memoir, life story, news, patchwork text (see Chapter 7).

Forms of communication that are not story (though they may include story elements)

- Essay, monograph, account, report, speech, presentation, lesson, lecture, description, statement, history, chronicle, diary, journal, blog, article, thesis, sermon, editorial, discourse, critique, review, notice, riddle, exposition, message, letter.

From the lists, and bearing in mind the definitions of story from others, I listed what seemed to be general features of story. I use the term 'listener' to represent the person to whom the story is communicated. The listener may be a reader or viewer for non-verbal material. I elaborate on many points mentioned below in later chapters.

General features of story

- story is a form of representation of the products of human mental functioning;
- there may or may not be a 'listener' – in other words, story can be told for the satisfaction of the teller (e.g. as a means of making personal sense of something) or an imagined audience;

- there is evident coherence and structure to a story which is usually recognisable to the listener;
- a story stands out as a coherent unit from its context by virtue of contrasts with the context and/or its internal unity or theme;
- there is usually a purpose for telling a story that may be overt or covert for listener and/or teller;
- a story may be told for the benefit of the teller or the listener – or both;
- there is an obvious progression in causal links or organisation in the expression of ideas in a story;
- story may be fiction or non-fiction or indeterminable – these distinctions are labile;
- there is a difference between reports or 'chronicles' and story (Gabriel, 2000) – a chronicle is usually a report;
- in the act of listening to story, we may temporarily suspend judgement or requirements of reality;
- there are distinguishing features of what I have called a strong-form story and broad-form story.

Features of strong-form story

- strong-form story has the general features of story (above);
- it has a beginning, middle and end structure;
- there is something within the story that is out of the ordinary or contrasts with normality that makes the story worth telling;
- something is resolved or transformed between the beginning and end of the strong-form story;
- there is likely to be considerable unspoken content – the story could be said deliberately to convey a 'bigger picture' than is conveyed by the meanings of the words themselves;
- there is usually an intention to engage the listener and the teller works to achieve this through expression, imagery, building of suspense, interest, alluding, understating and use of other devices;
- the listener is encouraged to suspend judgement or disbelief as she listens (Gabriel, 2000).

Features of broad-form story that distinguish it form strong-form story

- broad-form story has the general features of story (above);
- it is often personal story – or it is the account of an event and then it may be called a case study/case history, scenario or critical incident;
- it may be used to illustrate or illuminate something;
- the ideas expressed in the broad-form story are likely to be fairly explicit and the information is likely to be fairly overt;
- the purpose for this kind of story will often be to make a point or give an example or news;

- the broad-form story is more likely to be told for the teller's benefit, in contrast with the strong-form story, which is more likely to be told for the listener's benefit;
- the engagement of the listener may be less important than the conveying of the information contained; alternatively engagement is sought through the content rather than the devices in the telling of the story (e.g. in telling 'news').

There are certainly points on which others may wish to argue in the lists of boundary features of story. We are, after all, working with constructed terms.

Thinkpoint

Stories are often, though not always, made of words, and in using words in a story we try to make the words describe experience. Ted Hughes points out some of the difficulties that are to be encountered with words. When words multiply to stories, issues are compounded!

> A word is its own little solar system of meanings. Yet we are wanting it to carry some part of our meaning, of the meaning of our experience, and the meaning of our experience is finally unfathomable, it reaches into our toes and back to before we were born and into the atom, with vague shadows and changing features, and elements that no expression of any kind can take hold of. And this is true even of the simplest of experiences.
>
> (Hughes, 1967: 119)

Part II

Theory

Story and human functioning

How can the theory around story and its relationship to human functioning be anything other than complex with so many different forms and purposes for story observed (Chapter 2)? If story is not one thing to us, then its relationship to human functioning is unlikely to be described by just one area of theory. Indeed the impossibility of one-theory-for-all is further substantiated when I indicate the range of disciplines that can contribute to our understanding of story – disciplines that include neurology, psychology, sociology anthropology, education, philosophy, studies of folklore and literature. I cannot summarise all of this in a few theory chapters, so there is considerable summarising and focusing.

The driving idea for this theory section is how we learn from story, how story might be related to our humanity, and how story relates also to the communities and communications that are also part of human ways of being. These ideas, together with the questions posed in Chapter 1 (see p. 12) underpin these theory chapters and lead on to all the chapters in Part III.

I have wrestled long and hard with a substantial pile of literature on story in order to find a logical sequence through which to convey the sense that I make of the theory of story. In my rough notes there are around 30 pages of plans and concept maps, drawn and redrawn. What comes out of that are three main sections. These are:

- learning and the understanding of story;
- the deployment of meaning in story;
- social, cultural and communication functions of story.

In these chapters (Chapters 3, 4 and 5) there is a progression from focus on the individual's brain mechanisms (which include emotional factors) to the broader processes of making meaning from story, and this includes consideration of the mechanisms of story itself; and then I progress to the wider social, cultural and communications functions of story. There are overlaps, and some ideas could fit into more than one place. Because of the complexity and length of these chapters, I added a summary chapter to this part of the book (Chapter 6), which I have called:

- Taking stock: reflecting on insights and the educational roles of story.

Chapter 3

Learning and the understanding of stories

Introduction

This chapter is the first of the three chapters that explore the relationships of story to human functioning and it consists of two distinct discussions. I look at the process of learning from story and then I consider the role of what I call the unspoken in story. In the first part, on learning (p. 33), there is considerable space devoted to a description of how I have come to see the process of learning. I start from the beginning with the material on learning because it lies at the heart of human work with story. The ideas provide a background particularly for Chapters 4 and 5 and more generally for Part III.

In the second part of the chapter (p. 46), I consider in more detail the unspoken aspects of story. This is based on the idea that important aspects of a story, told or listened to, may be implied by language but are not addressed in language. A reason why humans use story might be because stories are effective containers for information – much more than an 'account' or report. The unspoken element includes emotion, spirituality, past, present and future implications of the story, its context, atmosphere and other such implicit factors.

Learning and learning from story

To relate learning to story, I describe something of the complexity of learning. I reiterate some of the material from previous books, in particular from those in 2004, 2006 and 2008. For writing this material, I originally drew substantially on Marton and Booth (1997) and Bowden and Marton (1998).

Models of the process of learning: two stances on learning

I start by distinguishing between two models of the process of learning. Both are models that attempt to describe what we observe and neither ever purported to be necessarily 'right' – they are ways of organising our thought processes around the topic of learning. The first model that I describe is the popular conceptualisation of learning and it has the effect of tending to mislead our thinking. It treats learning as a process of the accumulation of knowledge. Knowledge is seen as being 'taken in' and built up like a brick wall. A teacher may be seen as the supplier of the 'bricks of knowledge' and in this role she needs to know what the learner knows already in order to 'lay' the correct knowledge in the 'correct' order (according to her sense of order). If a brick is 'incorrect', it is replaced. Learning is more than this, and the model does not work well for the complexity of material in story form – nor does it make room for emotional factors (affect). Stories tend not to present clear items of knowledge – ideas in a story are enmeshed in context and are not distinctive bricks.

The second model on learning is a constructivist model. The metaphor that it uses for knowledge is a flexible and shifting network of ideas and feelings, some being more closely linked than others. The term 'cognitive structure' is helpful as a description of this notional network (Ausubel and Robinson, 1969; West and Pines, 1985; McAlpine and Weston, 2002). The cognitive structure is our 'internal experience' of the world, what we know, understand and feel at a given time (Marton and Booth, 1997). This model allows for the conceptualisation of a complex view of learning which includes affect.

At this point I add some vocabulary. First is the term 'material of learning', a term for the new idea that is potentially to be learned by the learner (and in contrast to this term, 'material of teaching' is what it is that the teacher teaches). On the constructivist view, new material of learning may be rejected or linked into the network of the cognitive structure in the process of assimilation (Piaget, 1971; Lauritzen and Jaeger, 1997). In assimilation:

- the idea may either be directly linked into the cognitive structure as it exists – so it adds to what is known already;
- the new idea may be modified – or conceived of differently – in order to fit existing knowledge represented in the cognitive structure;
- the new idea may stimulate modification of the existing cognitive structure itself – so a change in understanding is prompted.

The new material of learning that presents for learning is 'external experience' (Marton and Booth, 1997), another term which I will use in contrast to 'internal experience' or the contents of cognitive structure. The two-way process of modification that is implied in the bullet points above is called accommodation (Piaget, 1971). Applying this to an example, a learner is exposed to new material of learning about a steamship built by Brunel, a nineteenth-century engineer – the SS Great Britain. The learner may reject the information as not of interest or known already, or she may use the new information to expand her current knowledge of the SS Great Britain and of historical ships generally. Or the new ideas might cause her to modify her view of ships in the 1800s. Perhaps she had the view that there were no steamships until more recently and she needs to modify her understanding of the history of maritime trade (steamships were much faster) and, thence, perhaps the history of seamanship and the implications for the lives of sailors and so on.

In the conception of the processes of assimilation and accommodation, this constructivist model has gone well beyond simple accumulation of knowledge, to seeing knowing as a process of change. The cognitive structure or internal experience changes and since the cognitive structure is the essence of the person as a learner, the person changes as she changes her state of knowing or understanding (Marton and Booth, 1997).

Some processes of cognitive structure of relevance to story

There are five further points about the functioning of cognitive structure that, in different ways, relate to story. The first point is that it is the state of the cognitive structure that guides the processes of assimilation and accommodation. What we learn is guided by what we already know. The cognitive structure guides the focusing of attention, what we choose to learn and how we make meanings from the material of learning. It also guides the accommodation of existing cognitive structure in response to it. I illustrate this. A chemistry lecturer tells an anecdote about how the bright blue (fictitious) element, indium was first found in caves on the Starland Hills. For most learners the new idea enhances their view of indium – as was intended by the lecturer. However, Tom saw the famous patches of indium when he visited Starland last year. He is transported mentally to the scene and how he slipped over, and he muses on the consequences of his damaged ankle, and not the indium as intended by the lecturer.

So new learning is guided by what the learner knows and what she chooses to pay attention to. 'What we know' may be prior knowledge, but in a story it may be the context of a story that has been set up – what has just happened and what we are led to expect in the story. Story, by its nature, provides a rich context of ideas and expectations that can guide the processing or further input of ideas. By the time Snow White meets the seven dwarfs, we know a lot about her and her predicament and the nature of the story probably leads us to expect that things are about to change (she bites the apple brought by her stepmother).

The second point is that the cognitive structure may change or may be stimulated to change without the involvement of new material of learning. This is reflective learning and we can learn from the process of reflecting on what we know already without new external experience (Moon, 2004). I draw on the wisdom of J.K. Rowling in the form of story, to illustrate it very beautifully in a Harry Potter story:

> Harry stared at the stone basin. The contents had returned to their original silvery white state, swirling and rippling beneath his gaze.
> 'What is it?' Harry asked shakily.
> 'This? It is called a pensieve,' said Dumbledore. 'I sometimes find, and I am sure that you know the feeling, that I simply have too many thoughts and memories crammed into my mind.'
> 'Er,' said Harry, who couldn't truthfully say that he had ever felt anything of the sort.

'At these times,' said Dumbledore, indicating the stone basin, 'I use the pensieve. One simply siphons the excess thoughts from one's mind, pours them into the basin, and examines them at one's leisure. It becomes easier to spot patterns and links, you understand, when they are in this form.'

(Rowling, 2000: 518–519)

The third point is that we also learn from the process of representing what we have learned. The process of learning is invisible to others. We can only know what someone has learned when we ask that person to talk about the new knowledge or write about it or draw a picture and other forms of representation. It is possible that I may be excellent at learning, but poor at representing that learning in one or other form. Dyslexic people may be seriously handicapped in academic assessment for this reason. When we 'assess learning', it is an assessment of both learning and the process of representing that learning – two processes. The important point for this chapter is that the process of representing what we know is a further way of learning. If I read a story and learn the essence of it then tell it, I learn more from the process of telling it. I have to reorganise it in my own words and learn as I do this. If I were to mime the story I would learn, but I would learn different ideas about the story than the representation in language. We learn differently from different forms of representation.

The fourth of these points is that the process of learning to learn can be considered in the same way as the process of learning knowledge. In other words, I suggest that we use the cognitive structure that we have developed with regard to the processing of knowledge in order to learn to learn in a more effective or efficient manner, and this is likely to include affect as well. Many of the ideas that are associated with this are derived from the literature on approaches to learning and epistemological development (Chapter 4). It seems that real improvement of the ability to manage knowledge develops mainly when the learner confronts learning challenges such as engaging in a course or needing to deal with complex material for understanding.

On this constructivist model, learning is thus a matter of relating and balancing existing knowledge and new material of learning. The fifth point is that other factors are important in influencing the assimilation and accommodation of new ideas. One is simple choice. The learner who went off into a daydream about his trip to Starland (p. 35) had the choice to listen to the lecture or to daydream. Another factor is trust in the source of the new material of learning. A motivated student who trusts the material of teaching and knows that the new ideas can benefit her, may allow, without question, the change of her cognitive structure in response to the material. Another learner, confronted by the same ideas told to her in the bar by a fellow student, may be more cynical, choosing, perhaps, to perceive the material as nonsense and not allowing it to change her cognitive structure. On later reflection, she may realise that she is confused and unsure of what to believe. Fictitious or 'real-life' material can have this confusing effect. I refer to literature of this sort later in the chapter. Most of what we learn in formal educational situations is relatively in accordance with our expectations and is probably trustworthy, so relatively uncritical processes of assimilation and accommodation can operate and the cognitive structure is changed in the process of learning. However, the real world is full of dissonant messages and we need practice in managing them and to develop the ability to think critically (Moon, 2008a). Cognitive dissonance is a term for these situations (Festinger, 1957; Lauritzen and Jaeger, 1997). Dissonance can be uncomfortable but it is the kind of challenge to the learner that serves to improve the process of learning to learn. Complex material where there are few absolutes, such as that in ethics, philosophy and religion, is unlikely to be simply accepted or rejected because ideas are usually enmeshed in networks of other ideas. For example, faiths are associated with behaviours of prayer and worship, clothing, child-rearing and practical issues such as sending children to a particular school. If there is a change in faith, it might take time for all the various areas of related knowledge and action to become consistent with the new beliefs.

Many stories, particularly strong stories, rely on the production of cognitive dissonance for part of their effect. Because, by their nature, they carry much context with them, and because they tend to 'lull' us towards a 'suspension of disbelief' (Gerrig, 1993), the 'surprise' or 'news' aspect of them is in the form of a challenge to our existing cognitive structure. Dissonance is produced which may or may not be resolved in the story. The plot is the container for the dissonant messages.

'Meaning' and its attribution

Meaning is a central concept in the processes of learning and story. However, there can be confusions about the meaning of 'meaning' itself. Ausubel and Robinson (1969), though proponents of meaningful learning, saw meaningfulness as a quality of the material of teaching – saying that a teacher decides what concepts are meaningful for her students to learn. In the constructivist model the significant meaning in the process of learning is that construed by the learner. A new concept is meaningful to me as a learner if, in my process of accommodation of the new material of learning, it either fits in with existing cognitive structure or stimulates a shift in my cognitive structure about which I feel comfortable. Since the attribution of meaningfulness is based on the patterns of my individual cognitive structure, the meaning that I make of a concept may differ from the meaning that someone else makes of it. However, humans must agree on many meanings or we could not live in communities. Without this commonality we would exist as if we followed different reality and were demented. Greatly helping us to co-ordinate the meanings that we attribute to things is the fact that the tools and practices that operate in the process of making sense have been developed as a social process (Lave and Wenger, 1991; Wilkes, 1997). Children do not learn everything from 'new', but use the cultural accumulation of ideas encompassed in language in order to interpret the world and attain meaning. Language is a socially developed tool and where a word does not exist for something, the idea does not usually exist in public terms, though it may be implied in an unspoken manner.

The following list summarises some of the ways – beyond content – in which learning is affected by its social context:

- the manner in which understandings have been constructed in past social situations;
- the tools used in order to develop those understandings (e.g. language);
- the conventions associated with the knowledge (e.g. the different views of different disciplines and their ways of working with knowledge);
- the manner in which learning is expressed (e.g. in speech/written conventions/ in action, etc. – there are social conventions governing these);
- and therefore the manner in which there is learning from the representation of learning (see p. 36).

Learning and experience

One use of story in education is where sharing stories helps students to learn from their experiences (e.g. from a professional placement) and hence it is important to build on the ideas about learning above to explore the process of learning from experience. As I see it, all learning is learning from experience but some-times the experience is mediated. Mediation can mean it is interpreted, simplified and reorganised into what is assumed to be a more comprehensible sequence, usually for the benefit of a learner. Teaching is an act of mediation. Mediated experience is still experience. The experience of being taught in a lecture may be made up of the (uncomfortable?) sitting, the (croaky?) voice of the lecturer, as well as the meanings that the material stimulates for the learner. The most important learning for the student may be about not sitting in that area of the lecture theatre again because of the cold draught. Learning in a lecture theatre is no less learning from experience than is learning in a field situation. I do not see experiential learning as 'special' in the manner in which it is often presented – because all learning is experiential. I will say more of that later.

Processes in learning and story illustrated through use of a story

I have said that we build meanings by working with experience. We learn from new material of learning in relationship to our present and prior experience since the prior experience makes up the state of the cognitive structure and guides how we respond to a present experience. I have said that the nature of experience is individual in the sense that it is an individual who experiences it, but social in that all experience is mediated by the social surroundings. Both are illustrated in the following story. It is about a field trip for adult students who are enrolled on a Geology programme. The (part-time) students are in the second level of study.

There is a type of limestone quarried at Beer in Devon (UK) that has long been valued because it is easy to quarry and to saw into shape. In the open atmosphere it hardens to form an excellent building stone and it has been used for construction of many famous major buildings. A learner, Alice, sees on the programme noticeboard that that she will go on a field trip to Beer to visit the old underground quarries and to learn about the geology of the site. She has not heard of Beer or of Beer stone. Beer is, of course, a word and a place name. The word might initially trigger associations with the drink, but this link will probably fade as the meaningfulness of Beer as a place gains ascendancy. The notion of Beer stone might be relatively meaningless at present. There is a lecture on limestone and Alice reads about its chemical structure and compares this new material of learning with her direct experience of other kinds of stone and she begins to furnish her concept of the stone with meaning.

Georgio, another student on this module, by chance went to Beer on holiday last year and saw the quarries and so he has a more meaningful concept of Beer stone. The meaning is associated with seeing and touching the material but also with the anecdotes told of the history of the quarrymen by the guide on the trip around the quarries.

Before the trip the Alice asks Georgio about Beer and Georgio expresses his response in the form of a story of his visit, what they did and his memories of the quarries and the appearance of the stone and he mentions the signatures of the seventeenth-century quarrymen on the walls that were pointed out on the quarry tour. The story triggers prior experiences in Alice's mind – of trying (years ago) to inscribe her boyfriend's name on a slab of limestone.

The study of limestone, of course, could be part of biology in that limestone is developed from animal shells, or maritime studies (since it was formed under the sea), or engineering because it is a construction material. The frames of reference for each discipline are different and different meanings would emerge for the same material. The geological approach means that any practical investigation will be geological, and any reports written will use geological format and terminology. Geology, like other disciplines, is a constructed discipline, and influences how we construe knowledge in the context of that discipline.

Alice and Georgio and their colleagues go on the field trip. They see and touch the stone, smell the dampness of the quarries and in other ways experience Beer stone. Alice can accommodate her prior knowledge (gained from various sources prior to the visit) to the new and now personal experiences of the stone. The concept of Beer stone might then be said to be more meaningful to her. One could say that from her conversation with Georgio and the lecture, Alice had a number of experiences that created a 'slot' in her cognitive structure for the greater meaning of Beer stone (expectations). Her prior experiences and the expectations that had been set up will have influenced the manner in which she received the new information. However, Alice may have had uncertainties about some of the meanings that she has made. She might remember that a feature of the stone is that once dried, it is so hard that it cannot be scratched; but then how does this relate to Georgio's story about the quarrymen's signatures – were they scratched or marked with something or was he talking about some other stone? This is cognitive dissonance. She might think, 'I can wait to resolve it' or 'I have to get this right' or 'it is unimportant – but supposing the issue comes up in the short questions that the tutor is apt to use as assessment … ' Cognitive dissonance can be disturbing.

Other features of meaning

There are other aspects of the development of meaning. I have suggested above that meaning can change with the physical experiencing of an object, but it may change with alterations in the experience of other objects that are related to the first object. I return to the story of Alice and her experiences. After her visit to Beer, Alice learns more about the chemistry involved in fossilisation. Beer stone itself was not mentioned, but the broader knowledge invested more meanings in the concept of Beer stone itself. Alice also sees a television programme about a cathedral built of limestone in the thirteenth century and when she tells a fellow student the next day, he jokes that the secret of Beer stone is really that they paint it with beer to harden it but that 'they don't tell you this'. These further ideas enrich Alice's concept. She incorporates some ideas into a bedtime story for her son and she writes poetry. She was moved by the marks of the quarrymen and writes a poem about it. The meanings brought out in the story and poem are different from those in her assignment for the module. They have more emotional content and allude to ideas and experiences without being verbally explicit (using the unspoken). In these processes, Alice has been learning from the representation of her learning.

Some time later, Alice rereads her poem and this brings back a broad range of memories of beer stone – more than the words in the poem. This is the process of appresentation (Marton and Booth, 1997) – a partial representation of something that is perceived as external experience can stimulate a more complete internal experience of the 'whole' of that thing. For example, the face depicted on a video-conference screen triggers an internal experience of the known person and it is with the perception of the whole person that communication is made. Internal experience can therefore be much richer than external experience and we will tend to respond in behavioural terms to the appresentation of the object in internal experience, instead of the thinner information 'of that moment' from the external experience of it. In the context of writing about story, Bruner (1986) summarises this, saying that humans 'take whatever scraps they can extract from the stimulus input, and if these conform to expectancy … read the rest from the model in their head' (p. 47). One of the ways in which poetry and story work is by alluding to concepts rather than spelling them out, and the listener supplies and develops a rich set of perceptions in her own way. Two people, reading exactly the same story with the same words, may create different meanings out of the story because of the nature of their prior experiences and hence the internal experience in their cognitive structures. This may or may not matter. It will probably not matter in the context of entertainment but it does matter for two stories in a court case. Meaning resides with the learner and, as Gabriel has said,

'The truth of a story lies not in the facts, but in the meaning' (Gabriel, 2000: 4), though the word 'truth' is also contentious (Laming, 2004). I return to issues of truth and 'reality' in Chapter 4.

Figure and ground and the role of frames of reference in learning from story

A further phenomenon in the processes of learning is the distinction of figure from ground (Marton and Booth, 1997). This process is fundamental to learning and to listening to stories. I have said that the existing internal experience in cognitive structure guides the process of learning from external experience. To learn something, we have to be able to distinguish that which we have selected to learn from the context, from surrounding ideas and from other material. The process is going on all the time, with constant development of figures and grounds within figures and grounds – for the moment I will illustrate the process in a simplistic manner by going back to the story of a trip to Beer, but it is another story. It is the next year, and another trip is set up, this time for first-year students, partly to help them to get to know each other and as a start to their first geology module. Unfortunately Gordon Wheelwright, the tutor who planned the trip and was to do a briefing for it, is ill and no one has been available to tell the learners how they should focus their attention on the trip. All they know is that there will be reference to limestone in their lectures. On the trip, Tom is fascinated by the social history of quarrying and listens attentively to stories about the lives of those involved, imagining them walking along the miles of tunnels with their candles in an environment of damp dark and dust. Saul is intrigued by the structure of the caves, and how they reflect the different historical periods of the development in the form of the quarrying. Phil is anxious that there will be an examination question related to Beer stone, and he focuses his attention on all that he can learn of the physical and commercial qualities of the stone. For Danielle, the trip is social. Without a briefing, they lack the frame of reference that would enable them to select figures for 'appropriate' learning from their perception of what is essentially the same ground – the trip. As a result, they will probably develop different concepts. This may not matter at this stage of their programme but if they are to be assessed on their knowledge of Beer stone, then it will be unfortunate if their knowledge is largely of the social history of the quarry. The briefing that should have happened would have guided the learning. It would have indicated what was important – and which 'figure' material they should focus on. Of course, it is tempting to suggest that Gordon Wheelwright would have 'supplied' the frame of reference, but he could not do that – the frame of reference is constructed on the learners' understandings of the trip, which may or may not have coincided with the intentions of Gordon Wheelwright.

In learning, we can use the guidance of others (e.g. in a briefing), the context and our internal experience to frame our processes of distinguishing what we intend to learn from what is not needed for the current sense-making. This is an ongoing process. As we learn more, we have more internal experience with which to guide the further framing and distinguishing of figure from ground processes. The frame of reference could be said to be a guide and to act as a driver of the system of internal and external experiences in learning so that we learn what it is that we want to learn in an appropriate manner. It enables the learner to focus on relevant aspects of the external experience (Marton and Booth, 1997). The effective operation of the figure ground comparisons has much to do with effective learning and the development of sophistication as a learner. I come back to this in Chapter 4.

What I have said above is of course a vastly simplified description of learning. Learning in a field situation is immensely complex. There will be constant distinctions being made between figure and ground within probably changing frames of reference. This is an important issue when it comes to the development of situations in which students are expected to learn the complexities of real life from stories or from field experience. Such situations are an excellent background to learning, but if the situation is too complex in relation to the learning that is expected, the learning may feel superficial and descriptive in relation to a broad sense of context.

Variation

There is one more concept that almost inevitably follows from the notion of figure and ground processes. Going back to the example of the Alice's field trip: Alice learnt about the beer stone the first time, but supposing she returns to the quarry a week later, one could perhaps say that there is no more learning to do about the rock – there are now no differences between her internal and external experiences. In order for there to be new learning there needs to be variation between selected figures in external experience and the internal experiences. Learning, on this basis, is a process of experiencing variation and choosing whether or not to accommodate to that variation – and change the internal experience (Marton and Booth, 1997).

It is easy to see that the variation in the external experience leads to a potential for learning. However, variation can also occur when there are changes in the internal experience, while the figures in external experience remain notionally the same. I take a new example to illustrate this. This example is of Joelle, who is learning how to change a car wheel. She has not done this before. She is learning by watching an instructional DVD. On the basis that variation is essential for learning, I could say that a learner wanting to learn about how to change a car wheel by watching the same DVD of the procedure twenty times will probably have ceased to learn after the first few viewings. However, it is likely that the learning will continue to be enhanced in further viewings because the learner creates her own variation by changing the aspects of figure and ground to which she attends. In other words she changes her frame of reference in order to perceive new aspects of the process. Initially the focus might be on the technical use of the equipment required for changing the wheel (e.g. fitting the jack etc.), and then it could be the safety aspects, all of which are dealt with continuously through the DVD. The learner is creating variation by altering her frame of reference and therefore the internal experience that she uses to guide her learning. She might actively interact with the process by identifying questions to herself while she is viewing. The questions create variation by refocusing the frame of reference. So variation may not only be in a change of the external experience, but through the learner changing the frames of reference and the internal experience to which reference is made. This whole process of changing frames of reference in order to learn in appropriate detail is associated with taking a deep approach to learning (Marton *et al.*, 1997).

I have suggested that learning occurs in response to variation in the external experience as well as through changes in frame of reference that enable the learner to see something differently in the same situation. There seem to be at least two other ways in a learning situation that variation can occur and so lead to more learning. Both of these involve active change of the internal experience by the learner in a process of reflection. Going back to the example, Joelle may only watch the DVD once or twice, but then she reflects on its content, relating it to other knowledge and understandings and bringing that to bear on this situation and thereby varying aspects of the her internal experience. There is no contact with the actual material of learning in external experience, but the learner is using the ideas that she can summon from her cognitive structure to enhance the learning process. This was discussed earlier in this chapter.

The other manner of creating variation without change in the learning situation is through the representation of the learning. Joelle may have seen the DVD twice, and she may now be asked to put the learning into practice by changing a wheel in the manner demonstrated. As I have said, learners can learn through the representation of their learning. As she goes through the process of changing a wheel Joelle will be working with the learning from the DVD and with the practical experiences from the practice of wheel changing. There will be variation between her 'educated' internal experience and the new learning from the doing of the task – what works and what does not work in her efforts. There may also be emotional influences that facilitate or inhibit the process. Difficulties or success in the practice of changing the wheel may discourage or encourage her.

I summarise the concept of variation: learners learn from variation in learning situations. There are at least four forms of variation. They are when:

- there is change in the external experience in the material of learning;
- with the same material of learning, the learner changes her frame of reference and perceives different details, thereby changing her external experience;
- the learner works with her internal experience and relates it to other prior experience and learns more as a result;
- the learner represents her learning and learns from comparison of the variation of the external experience between practices.

All of these forms of learning are relevant to learning from a story, though the context of the story may interfere with learning more general principles that can be applied elsewhere.

Story, learning and emotion

I see emotion as present in and influencing every activity of human mental and physical life, not as a system separate from what we call 'rational' activities (Damasio, 2000). I see it as having multiple relationships with human activities such as learning and there are many different ways in which emotion interrelates with our involvement with stories. In a story about a fragile young romance, for example, I can feel upset by the interference of the parents, excited by the love between the couple and disturbed by something the story reminds me of in my own life.

In terms of the roles of emotion in stories, first, stories can be told with emotion as their central theme – it is the subject matter. They may explore the emotional life of a person – the self in autobiography; the emotional life of others in biography. They may also concern the management of emotion of others – for example a fictitious story about a single mother and her struggles to manage her disruptive child. Second, stories may deliberately generate emotion. Ghost and horror stories are designed to stimulate feelings of fear. Within limits, people appear to enjoy the generation of such emotion, but they also enjoy the lust or love in romantic or sexual stories. Many stories work because they generate curiosity and an urge towards resolution of dissonance that has been set up within the story. Third, emotion is a by-product of some stories for some listeners. This by-product may not be planned by the teller. 'Babes in the Wood' might remind me of an unpleasant personal experience in deep woods. I may remember the actual event or I may experience discomfort when I hear the story. Similarly a character in a novel may remind me of someone in whose company I have felt relaxed – and relaxation might be an outcome of the story. Fourth, emotion is involved in the processes of telling and of listening. If I feel bad tempered as I tell a story, it is likely that something of my mood will influence my style of telling, for example in my language or expression. Or if, as a listener, I feel happy, I might be more likely to interpret the story optimistically. In a related manner (fifth), emotion can inhibit or facilitate the telling of or the listening to a story. Censorship is usually argued on grounds of rationality, but can be more to do with emotional response to material. Stories are told or not told in conversational or social situations in relation to the feeling that the teller has about her audience. I might not tell an amusing story to someone who I perceive to be in a negative mood for (my) fear that the story would 'fall flat'.

A sixth relationship between stories and emotion is where emotions trigger the telling of stories. When a group of people experience stress they often start to tell stories to each other in a kind of mutual comforting – 'When this happened to me the last time … ' – though this may not happen when the individuals are in a competitive relationship, such as waiting for an interview.

The seventh relationship between story, learning and emotion I have called 'emotional insight' (Moon, 2008a). It is when suddenly one's perspective on the world changes in a substantial manner and there is a sense that something is different. There may not be words to describe it. A story can trigger such a change. We talk of 'life-changing' books. I see as a form of emotional insight the learning that seems to be implied in Donaldson (1992) and in various papers in Mezirow (1991).

Lastly (eighth) there is a sense of a satisfying 'emotional kick' when one has expressed ideas effectively in language in prose or poetry or told a good story that is 'right' for its context and has had an impact on listeners.

The role of emotion in story seems to be dealt with somewhat variably in the literature. Many hardly mention it, but Oatley and his team in Canada have produced a series of papers in which the role of emotion in fiction (specifically) is explored. Oatley says:

> Emotions are at the centre of literature because they signal situations that are personally important but that might be either inchoate or just beyond the edge of easy understanding … [Fiction] can allow people to find out more about the intimate implications of their emotions. [Fiction offers] a laboratory space that, relative to real life, is safe and can make the relations of emotions to goals easier to understand.
>
> (Oatley 1999)

In an experimental situation, Oatley (1999) showed that the emotions evoked by the same fiction material were different for different people, and he used this to reinforce his argument that fiction is constructed by the listener/reader. This position of course, supports the constructive stance of this text.

Learning from story: a summary and a reflection

This is a pause to pull ideas together in a long and complex chapter.

We learn from story through the interplay of external and internal experiences and processes of elaboration from the flow of meaning in the story. Stories may play with our processes of establishing internal experience by the deliberate creation of dissonance, where external experience is put into conflict with current internal experience.

Variation and framing are central to learning from story and they are ongoing since the developing context of the story and what has already just been assimilated become part of the internal experience that guides the learning of the ongoing flow of new external experience in the story. The potential guidance from what has just been learned may be strong or less strong. Story can provide strong guidance for learning, because it is a flow of meaning that is designed to engage. In this sense a story is a frame of reference, but there will be other frames of reference within it (Chapter 4).

The teller of a story manages the flow of potential external experience in order to influence the processes of assimilation and accommodation of the story material in the listener. However, the teller cannot make the listener follow the direction – she can only make that direction compelling or engaging for the listener. It is possible that an element in the story may trigger the listener's thoughts into a completely separate realm of meaning from the ongoing story. While the teller manages the storyline, stories usually rely also on the generation of broad associations in the listener, invoking imagery and emotion. Apperception means that a teller may provide a few descriptive words about, for example, a meadow in spring, but will rely on the listener filling out the idea with her own images (sight, sound, smell, etc.). There are more extreme examples of this – story may be used to stimulate the listener to think of her own version of a given story in therapy or organisational change (e.g. McLeod, 1997; Denning, 2001, 2004, 2008) (Chapter 10).

I have shown that there are many ways in which emotion interacts with learning and with the generation or telling of story. There is much that is relevant to this in the next section, since emotion is an important aspect of the unspoken in story.

The unspoken and its role in story

The unspoken is the topic of the second half of this chapter.

In the literature on story it is not surprising that there is a focus on the explicit language in story but I have come increasingly to recognise the limitations of explicit language and the extent of what goes on in human communication that is not explicit. I have come to see this as an important characteristic of story, particularly strong-form story. I use the term 'unspoken' to include the imagery, emotion, past and present contexts of story, the internal experiences of the teller and listener that contribute to meaning, whether consciously or unconsciously, the implicit expectations of story structure and any sense of spirituality for teller and listener. However, there is nothing coherent about this list except the importance of these elements to the sense of story. However, there are issues here for learning from story that will emerge later.

I begin with some general references to the unspoken in story that make the case for its importance and then I consider the elements of it in some more detail.

The unspoken: some general references in the literature

Here is an observation. When I am half asleep and particularly when I am ill, my mind drifts and sequences of images float past. These are not in language or vision, but pre-verbal 'wordless stories' (Damasio, 2000). They are often sufficiently coherent to be story but I notice that if the images are left in this form, I cannot remember them. If, in a waking state, I describe the images in language, while I sense that the language may often be a poor translation of something richer, I can retain the images and think about them. If I represent the images graphically I seem to be able to maintain a greater sense of the feeling that was associated with the original images. Milner's (formerly Field) work expands these ideas on working with imagery (Field, 1952; Milner, 1957, 1987).

The importance of the unspoken has been long acknowledged. McKee (1999) refers to Plato's argument for the exiling of poets and storytellers from Athens in 388 BC on the basis that they were dealing with ideas concealed 'inside the seductive emotions of art' instead of being explicit as the philosophers (McKee, 1999: 129). Ironically, those who argue for the greater use of story in medicine (for example) often do so on the basis that story can communicate a more comprehensive picture of the patient's experience. They accept the value of the unspoken and do not demand that it becomes explicit (Dittrich, 2001; Greenhalgh and Hurwitz, 1998).

Oatley (1999) alludes to the unspoken in story (fiction) in a consideration of how real conversation cannot be properly depicted in fiction. He notes that the writer has to add information about the motivations and emotions of the actors which would normally be passed between them by facial expression, tone, posture and other non-verbal elements of communication or display. Story has to convey these in a way that elicits the unspoken elements for the reader/listener. He talks of providing the context to enable the reader 'to understand the elliptical'. Fiction offers 'the context of characters' goals and plans. It gives a sense of how actions lead to vicissitudes. It allows ... the reader to experience something of emotions that can arise'. He says that 'all of these are omitted from a faithful ... copy of real life' (Oatley, 1999: 108). He gives examples of a real-life conversation around a photocopying machine and contrasts it with a fictionalised version.

There is considerable variation in the literature as to how much account is taken of the unspoken in the study of narrative or story. Theorists at times refer to the unspoken but appear not to deem it a major element in the conveying of meaning. Polkinghorne (1988) stresses the role of language: 'Linguistic forms have as much reality as the material objects of the physical realm ... they filter and organise information from the physical and cultural realms and transform it into the meanings that make up human knowledge and experience' (p. 158). Polkinghorne does acknowledge that much that builds human experience 'is hidden from awareness' (p. 159). Bruner (1986) also talks relatively little of the unspoken. 'Language', he says, 'not only transmits, it creates or constitutes knowledge or "reality"' (p. 132).

I have turned many times to Donaldson's (1992) work on 'human minds', feeling that it relates well to the views of learning, reflective learning and critical thinking that I hold. I do so again in relation to the unspoken. In her model of the functioning of the mind, apart from intellectual learning and information gathering functions, Donaldson suggests a non-linguistic mode that she calls the 'value-sensing mode' (p. 150). It develops in parallel with intellectual capacities, but in Westerners, at least, she suggests that it is usually developed to a lesser extent than in, for example, many eastern cultures. In a different context, Shotter (2001) describes a similar capacity that he also argues is under-utilised in Western cultures. Again, but directly in relation to story, Taylor et al. (2002) talk of the 'felt meaning of a story' that derives from what they view as a form of 'aesthetic perspective ... a particular type of knowledge ... of sensation and feeling'. They suggest that this meaning 'is not mediated by inductive or deductive reason ... but rather is characterised by abductive reasoning (Pierce 1957)'. They suggest that the quality of this meaning distinguishes between effective and less effective stories in management and organisation research. In a similar context Nymark (2000) argues the value of work on story in organisational research, saying that story has 'the capacity to tap into the unconscious qualitative phenomena that pervade organisations' (p. 54). Adding to this, Mattingly (1990) observes the manner in which stories 'point toward deep beliefs and assumptions that people often cannot tell in propositional or denotative form, the "practical theories" and deeply held images that guide their actions' (p. 236). She relates this to the ideas of professional education developed by Schon (1983, 1987). Coffield (2000) seems to support this when he draws on Geertz (1973) to talk of the 'thick' tacit versions of personal knowledge in practical work situations as opposed to 'thin' explicit description that is used to describe and justify that work practice (p. 29) (Polyani, 1969). Swap *et al.* (2004) and Snowden (2004) also mention the role of tacit material in stories told in organisational contexts. It is particularly important to consider the role of story in organisations because many of the stories that circulate are negative. The unspoken in stories can thereby provide a pool of hidden negativity (Gabriel, 2000).

In the context of nursing, Koch (1998) alludes to the unspoken, saying that story provides not necessarily the answers to the questions in practice, but 'the rich data. ... which illuminate the questions'. She talks of using story to 'get to know' what it is like for patients on the ward. The non-language-based experiences that are enmeshed in these kinds of story or case study forms, however, may need to be interpreted into 'pedagogical discourse' in order that the '"nuggets" of knowledge are obtained' (Usher and Soloman, 1999). In the translation processes there may be losses in the quality of the meaning because it is essentially not language based – and often we do not value the unspoken. I would assume also that much that Atkinson and Claxton (2000) call 'intuition' – with a semi-respectable ring about it – is an element of what I call the unspoken.

In their work on story in various therapeutic situations Gersie and King (1990) have less investment in being explicit. They see 'the unspoken' as part of an 'inner world' 'of great delicacy, spun out of the threads of human experience and dreams, whatever the age of the spinner' (p. 35). For them, the use of story as a method provides a 'point of embarkation' (p. 35), and a way of gaining access to the internal mind – without necessarily making it explicit. Holmes and Gregory (1998) and Richardson (2000) apply similar ideas to the use of poetry to 'get at' unspoken aspects of nursing. Richardson uses the term the term 'evocative representation' for this process and says that poetry provides a 'a striking way of seeing through and beyond social scientific naturalisms'. In all these cases, I suggest that attaching a word to the unspoken, as I have done, may enable us to value it.

I conclude this section by returning to Damasio (2000), who relates the 'naturalness' of wordless story' directly to aspects of brain function. He says:

> The imagetic representation of sequences of brain events which occurs in brains simpler than ours, is the stuff of which stories are made. A natural preverbal occurrence of storytelling may well be the reason why we ended up creating drama and eventually books ... Telling stories precedes language since, it is, in

fact, a condition for language and it is not just based in the cerebral cortex, but elsewhere in the brain and in the right hemisphere as well as the left.

(Damasio, 2000: 188, 189)

From this it seems that the unspoken represents a shape of story before it is interpreted as language and that this is represented in the feeling that we 'know' something before language is attached to it. I feel that in many areas of academia there is too much assumption that we can put all worthwhile knowledge into words (Moon, 2009a).

The unspoken and story: a more systematic approach

The section above suggests that there are references to the unspoken in the literature, but they tend to be scattered and unsystematic. I endeavour, in this section, to link the unspoken with story more systematically, endeavouring not to lose the essence of meaning. It is important, first, to note that the way in which unspoken material operates will not necessarily be the same for the teller and the listener. The teller can only offer a story in the same way that a teacher can only offer material of teaching. She cannot make the listener attend or comprehend the story as she has intended. Some of the unspoken material in relation to a specific story will be unique to that story and some will be in the realm of what we could assume to be general knowledge (such as the generic structures of story). So the unspoken consists of:

- unspoken functions within the teller (e.g. internal experience brought to the story);
- unspoken functions within the listener (e.g. internal experience brought to the story);
- unspoken elements that are probably shared as common knowledge by both teller and listener (e.g. understandings of narrative structure – Chapter 4), non-verbal cues used to develop the atmosphere of the story, etc.

To explore the unspoken further, I have found it useful to use the following general headings – they are not mutually exclusive.

- the unspoken in the external context of the story;
- the manner in which the story is told;
- the unspoken in non-explicit intentions of the teller;
- the unspoken in non-explicit meanings of the story generated by the listener;
- the unspoken in sensory imagery that is generated;
- the unspoken in unconscious elements of story;
- the unspoken in the form and genre of stories.

There is much that is unspoken in the external context of a story. It includes what a teller and a listener bring to the story that is not explicit – the relevant prior knowledge or the current state of the cognitive structure or both. It contains, as McDrury and Alterio (2003: 31) put it, the conveying of the essence of 'the worlds, real or imagined, that we inhabit' and our orientations to those worlds (McAllister *et al.*, 2008). Alterio and McDrury (2003) describe the use of story in collaborative storytelling with healthworkers, where there are unspoken expectations about the sharing of insights that can influence subsequent professional practice. They employ the scriptwriting term 'backstory' – to refer to any implicit previous story that 'has shaped the main story being told at the time' (p. 40).

The external context also includes the influences of the physical environment of the telling, whether the story is told in a formal or informal setting – round a campfire with a ghostly breeze fluttering the branches of nearby trees or in a classroom, for example. There may be an effect from the relationship between teller and listener, whether, for example, the story is told in an atmosphere of wrapt attention within the context of bonding and love, or in a professional development formal learning situation. The manner in which a story is told can create further unspoken information beyond what is transmitted by the teller. For example, a woman tells a story of how she unexpectedly met Jim, a colleague of her husband's, when she tripped and fell in the street. Jim helped her up. They started talking, got on to talking of places they had both visited and decided to continue the conversation over a coffee. The woman can tell this story to her husband in a matter-of-fact manner – as news of a coincidence, or, by manipulating intonation and pacing, she could use the same story to encourage jealous disquiet. Stories are often told without the underlying intentions of the teller or her choice of that particular story being made explicit. This may or may not matter. Sometimes the telling of a story is cathartic for the teller (Plummer, 1995), and sometimes the teller wants to generate catharsis in the listener (Gersie, 1991; Thomas and Killick, 2007), or enjoys the generation of surprise in telling 'news', or wants the listener to tell her own stories (Gersie, 1991; Thomas and Killick, 2007; Fisher, n.d.; Fisher, 1996; Kenyon *et al.*, 2001). Sometimes stories are told in order to stimulate religious or moral thinking, as in parables (e.g. McFague TeSelle, 1975). Mostly such stories are simply told, with the teller's purpose implicit. There are times when I wonder why someone is telling me a particular story: what is going on? What is the intention? What am I meant to take from the story? Intentions may or may not become clear.

The unspoken arises also in the deployment of sensory imagery in the telling of a story. Stimulation of imagination can be central to the purpose of story; for example, Alvarez and Merchan (1992) use fiction to generate imagination to improve management behaviours. The use of words about imagery can vary in different tellings of the same story. The story of Cinderella or of a critical incident in a social worker's day may be told as a series of actions or with emphasis on the generation of images – the sights, the sounds and smells of a situation. The teller can stimulate imagination through sparse but evocative words or rich language that directs the imagination. Pacing can be an issue. Since I have been thinking about the unspoken in story, I have noticed stories in which there are many close-packed actions that leave little room for me, as reader/listener, to develop imagery.

As with other issues in story, the experience of imagery may differ for the teller and the listener. I might tell a story about an event at a historic garden which I visited. I enjoyed the visit and wish to generate similar pleasurable images in a listener. But the listener may have slipped and covered her dress in mud on a dank wet day at the same garden and the unspoken meaning made of a story might be very different, but these differences may remain unspoken and possibly unconscious.

The unspoken includes conscious and unconscious material for the teller and the listener. The unconscious elements of a story are present in the content of the internal experiences that I 'bring to bear' on listening to a story. I may think that I can list what I 'know' that seems related to the story, but less easily can I explore how I feel in relation to the story and whether the feelings are to do with the present or based on past experiences that are related directly or indirectly to the content of the story. There are different schools of interpretation with regard to the unconscious and how it relates to our functioning. I have been inspired by Jung's (1977) description of how, at a time of emotional and intellectual disturbance as he endeavoured to relate his ideas to those of Sigmund Freud, daily he would go to the side of a lake and follow a creative urge to build a model village from the stones he could find there. This story-building activity had the effect of clearing his mind and freeing his creativity for writing. I would call this an example of emotional insight (see p. 44). But we only have Jung's idea of what was going on for him in the process.

Sparkes (2002) discusses a different aspect of unconscious functioning in which the consciously told story differs from a parallel 'under'-story. He talks of the 'disembodied' power of autoethnographic stories, saying that 'well crafted' stories 'are not just about the body but they are told through the body of the author. They … are voiced in multiple ways that can connect people (ie listeners) in their shared vulnerabilities' whatever the actual subject matter (p. 100). Bayliss (1998) refers similarly to the involvement of the body in the 'pain narratives' that patients bring to medical practitioners. He recommends that the doctor needs to 'keep both ears and eyes open to receive [the] two important complimentary narratives' (p. 75) from the body as well as the voice. Lauritzen and Jaeger (1997) extend these notions of bodily involvement in story in the context of childhood education. They talk of the 'visceral bonding' that 'occurs between listeners and the characters of a story'. 'We share in their emotions: we triumph in success … and fear in anticipation. We take ownership of their story as our story. Through stories, learners can experience other lives vicariously' (p. 36). They argue that story in this way extends the experience of children (and I would extend this to any age group). The teller of a story can invite listeners to step into the shoes of another for a while.

Learning to view the world as others view it is an important aspect also of epistemological development (Chapter 4). Similar principles are applied in the work of many professional groups, particularly in health and social care and law and counselling. Greenhalgh and Collard (2003), in their description of the development of workshops to educate those who work with diabetes in the family, talk of how 'illness narratives' based on the patients' own words enable the support workers to 'join' the patients. Hunt (2000) applies these ideas in the context of therapeutic writing by, for example, working on the fictionalising of ourselves or significant other people in our lives in order to let go 'of the usual control we exert over … representation and [thus] allow … new versions to emerge' (p. 96).

Another area of work on the unconscious aspects of story concerns traditional story and myth. I have mentioned that Bettelheim (1976) sees fairy tale as playing an unconscious role in the development of children. He argues the particular suitability of these stories, orally transmitted because they have been shaped into fundamental psychological stereotypes over their centuries of reinterpretation (see Chapter 5). Others apply similar ideas of the symbolism in myth, folk and fairy tale to aspects of adult life. Estes (1992), a Jungian analyst, applies analytic theory through story to generate the strength and power of womanhood. Bly (1992) bases his celebration of manhood in all its expressions on the Grimms' tale of Iron Hans (Grimm and Grimm, n.d.; Zipes, 2000). Perhaps some of the mechanism at work here is not so much that of the influence of the symbols, but the way in which stories provide concrete descriptions of how events affect individuals – and they thereby invite reflection. It is relevant here to mention a research finding that information about mass horrors (e.g. war and genocide) is apparently less effective in evoking responses in an audience than stories about a few individuals (Slovic, 2007). Almost by definition fairy stories provide concrete and absolute descriptions of the reactions to difficult events of a small numbers of actors. This extends to creation myths from all over the world (e.g. McCaughrean, 1999)

The form and genre of a story are another aspect of the unspoken. The fact that a story is presented as a short story or a myth or fairy story encourages the building of expectations about the nature of the story itself. In a short story I will be looking for the rationale for the story to be provided quickly and I will know that every piece of information will be relevant to the storyline. If I am told that it is foggy in a short story, it will be important. In a novel, such information may be general scene setting. There is a body of literature that suggests that, as humans, we hold common knowledge of what we expect of the structure of stories ('narrative grammar'). I consider this in Chapter 4.

Insights from considering the unspoken in story

I have said that from my general reading of the literature and involvement with story, I see the volume and usual significance of the unspoken content of story as one of the key attributes of story in comparison with other forms of communication. In a lecture, an account or a lesson, or in simple conversation (there are exceptions here), the speaker intends to make meaning as clear as possible within the constraints of vocabulary, time limits and attention capacities – and the focus of communication is language. It seems that a story is likely to carry more than the sum of its spoken language meanings in unspoken elements, and the language and unspoken work together to form the unit that is the story. I am led to consider that this could be a reason for the enormous use of story in communication. It is a carrier of more than the sum of its language parts.

Thinkpoint

... narrative is a cognitively efficient compromise between uniqueness and universality.

(Robinson and Hawpe, 1986: 18)

Chapter 4

The deployment of meaning in story

Introduction

Chapter 3 considered story in the way it relates to learning. It was the first of the three sections on theoretical aspects of story. This chapter covers the second section of theoretical material, focusing on the deployment of meaning in story. The chapter consists of three sections. The first (and largest) (p. 54) examines the ways in which meaning is constructed for tellers and listeners of stories by reviewing various ways in which stories and features of story are distinctively 'framed'. The idea of a frame seems to provide a useful structure for the discussion of deployment of meaning. Factors that frame story include the most obvious ways in which a person knows that a story is being told, the notion that there is a distinctive 'grammatical structure' of stories and the way in which story can remove the listener from what we understand as reality. I look also the quality of engagement, and at reality and fiction and listener responses to story such as the 'suspension of disbelief'. The last part of the discussion about the framing of meaning in story relates to the way in which a story, acting as a unit, is often used to stimulate the listener into particular kinds of thinking and reflection. This is the manner in which story is often used in therapy and in organisational change.

The other shorter two sections of the chapter have more general reference to the interpretation of meaning in story. I address the idea that story can be seen as a form of knowledge and therefore its interpretation varies with the under-standing that the listener and teller have of the nature of knowledge (epistemo-logical beliefs) (p. 69). In the last section I consider the ways in which the processes of memory influence the manner in which stories are told, heard and retransmitted (p. 73).

The many frames of story

In this section I have used a number of headings. I start with some introductory ideas about frame and story. I go on to look at the obvious frames that tell us a story is being told. I then look at the suggestions that humans are 'pre-wired' to work with story, or come to expect story to have a 'narrative grammar'. Stories, almost by definition, have a quality of engagement. This distinguishes them from their context (hence the change of attention of listeners when someone says, 'I will tell you a story'). I then come to the 'reality frame'. When we hear a story, we are usually shifted from the current time and place. The last frame is the way in which story can work as a framed stimulus for change. This lies behind its use, for example, in therapy and organisational management.

Some introductory ideas about frame and story

A story needs to be distinct from its context for a range of reasons – to start with, if it were not distinctive then this book would have no subject. I begin this large section with a general illustration of the notion of frame as I have used it here, and the manner in which it relates to meaning:

> The writer [of a story] invites the reader to enter, Alicelike, through the looking glass and into the imagined story world. This is like entering a particular kind of social interaction, as Goffman (1961), has proposed, through a semipermeable membrane within which is a world with its own history and its own conventions from which meanings are constructed.
>
> Oatley (1999: 106)

The quotation above relates to fiction, but I suggest that it applies to story in general. Stories are framed distinctively from their context, which might, for example, be general conversation. I am using the term 'frame' here descriptively and not as a means of applying a particular theory, though I acknowledge general inspiration in my thinking by Hertog and McLeod (2001), who apply framing analysis to sociology, politics and media as a research tool. In terms of meaning, I note that a frame is a way of separating an object from its context, but it is also a way of focusing attention on the object (as in a 'frame of reference'). Both of these ideas are used in my notion of frames. I also note that in framing a story we are distinguishing figure from ground (see Chapter 3), and, of course, in understanding the story there are many other figure/ground systems operating simultaneously in the processes of learning and making meaning. In terms of the whole story, I will manage my figure/ground and variation processes in relation to the story, knowing where they begin and end. I will expect the story to have internal coherence and other features of story, and I will expect in some ways to judge its meaning as a whole. I may suspend disbelief in the story and I am likely, as a result of cues from the story frame, to be able to predict how to manage the meaning of the elements within the story in relation to each other, to my internal experience, and in relation to its broader context (for example the purpose for its telling). If a story is introduced as fiction, then I may be entertained. If it is presented to illustrate a theoretical construct in politics, then I will know that I should interpret the meaning of the framed story in relation to the given theory. The frame tells us that the story is a unit, and it helps us in dealing with its meaning.

So if, on television, I am told a story about a how a couple of policemen managed a drunken man who had been (privately) deprived of his credit card by his concerned and pregnant wife (*Night Cops*, Sky2, 9 p.m., 9 February 2009), I can take the point of the story itself and the issues that it raises and the idea that police can be subtle in their dealings with difficult marital situations, and relate them to the theme of the programme as well (the range of nighttime police activities).

The obvious frames

Some frames are overt and conscious (e.g. 'Are you all sitting comfortably? Then we'll begin' – BBC Radio Home Service series *Listen with Mother*). Others are unspoken and more likely to be unconscious. We might be in a place where stories are told (theatre, cinema, storytelling performance, childhood bedtime, etc.). Sometimes the teller (or another) indicates an imminent story. She might, for example, introduce the purpose of the story (e.g. 'I am going to tell you a story about the case of Mungster versus Pertuna – dated 1989. This will help you to understand the concern we have about this area of legal practice'). Or the teller might say, 'OK, here's what happened' or 'Well, the amazing story goes like this ... ' A story may begin with 'Once upon a time' or other traditional beginnings and finish with 'and they all lived happily ever after'. Such traditional beginnings and endings vary in different countries. Sometimes there are cues to the beginning of a story because it fulfils a particular purpose (e.g. 'news' is brought or an explanation for an event, or the story is a response to a question). A further cue might be a change in the quality of voice or a shuffling of posture ('Well [pause], it's like this ... '). Or there may be a series of stories being told, one after another, among a group of friends. These stories will often be personal experiences of those present, initially around some experience like 'things that have happened to me at airports', though the theme may shift. In social situations like these, each story may be tenuously linked to the previous story, giving an impression of people listening to each other, but the links may be superficial if the participants' real purposes are to be in the limelight for few moments.

Narrative structure/grammar as a frame

The frames mentioned so far have been external to the story but stories are also framed by their internal characteristics. These define story for what it is itself rather than what it is in relation to its context. There are many references in the literature to the idea that stories have narrative or story structures (or grammars) which are consistent internal structures that are familiar to listeners (e.g. Sarbin, 1986; Robinson and Hawpe, 1986; Bruner, 1986, 1990; Polkinghorne, 1988; McEwan and Egan, 1995; McLeod, 1997). Some see these structures as an innate and specific linguistic capacity, and some see them as structures that characterise what we recognise as story, suggesting that early on we learn to recognise them to aid story comprehension. Bruner (2002), as an example of the former, says that humans have a 'precocity' for narrative structure or 'some core knowledge about narratives' (pp. 32, 33). As 'core' knowledge, I would see this as an unspoken element of story. Bruner (1990) considers the tasks involved in comprehending the narrative structure to be a dual process: 'the interpreter has to grasp the narrative's configuring plot in order to make sense of its constituents, which he must relate to that plot. But the plot configuration must itself be extracted from the succession of events' (pp. 43–44). These processes involve complex distinctions of figures from grounds within the story structure (Chapter 3).

Narrative structure, as it is described in the literature, acts as a pattern of expectations that facilitate the telling of or listening to a story through a number of processes. It starts with the use of cues that signal that a story is being told (see the last section). This sets up an expectation in internal experience of the narrative structure, and it enables the listener to bring to bear this element of internal experience to manage the comprehension of the story (accommodation). What I talk of here is not the subject matter of the story (for which also these accommodation processes occur), but the 'deep' knowledge of the ordering of the information flow in this kind of story.

Expectation, described in the paragraph above, enables prediction. The ability to predict economises on our listening effort as we do not need to hear everything anew, but only to note when something differs from what is predicted. If I am listening to a short story on the radio and become distracted for a moment, my sense of story structure will probably enable me to pick up and make sense of the story again by reference to my general expectations. Of course, I may have missed important content information and now have a distorted understanding of the story. In attending to the predicted structure of the storyline, we can recognise how the unexpected – the plot or surprise – structures the story. In these processes, we are taking account of variation between internal and external experience in our management of meaning (Bruner, 1986).

In considering story structure as a set of expectations, my thinking coincides with that of Schank (1995). He calls the sets of expectations 'scripts' (p. 6) and sees these as memory devices that summarise how others behave, thereby enabling economy for the listener. In the language of cognitive functioning, a 'memory device' might accord with a stereotyped element in internal experience as I have described it (Ryan, 2008). A simple example of narrative structure and the manner in which it allows the listener to predict meaning is the introduction into a story of a character with an unfulfilled need (e.g. to overcome loneliness). The chances are that the story will concern the overcoming of barriers and fulfilment of the need as the conclusion. A listener can usually distinguish between a story that is coming to completion or when there is a pause but more will follow. This awareness is disturbingly obvious when a story is noticeably incomplete or is left 'hanging in the air' – though disturbance may be the effect that the teller wants.

Particular narrative structures can be associated with particular genres of story and the culture of origin (Holbeck, 1989). For example, in Western fairy tales events tend to come in threes. The heroine is offered three wishes or given three tasks, and it is on the third that the listener knows that her life is likely to change for ever ... etc. (Zipes 2006). A good storyteller paces and emphasises the events in a story to relate to the inherent structure. McLeod (1997) reviews story structures in different cultures and suggests that they could originate in the intention of the storytelling, the sequence, genre (Japanese children's stories were like haiku) or the preferences for particular subject matter. What is evident, however, is that stories that are commonly told in different cultures are 'highly dependent on cultural context and tradition' (p. 49) and what is recognised as good story in one culture is not the same in another.

In terms of research on narrative structure, awareness of such structure seems to be present early in a child's life. This may relate to the seemingly 'instinctive' manner in which story is employed with young children. Bruner (2002) audiotaped a child (Emmy, aged three) telling stories to herself. He observes that 'Emmy seemed to know what a story required for its telling before she had the grammar to tell it right' (p. 32). In several studies, Mancuso (1986) shows that children of four use what he calls narrative structure in telling stories.

Other research on narrative structures has involved listeners in judging whether material heard or read can be classified as a story. There are also studies of quality of recall of story material in relation to its conventional, unconventional or absent story structure. Such research has led to the identification of fairly detailed descriptions of generic story structures, such as the presence of an 'animate protagonist' and a form of 'story sequence' (Stein and Policastro, 1984: 147). Mandler (1984) mentions a setting and the kind of events to which a protagonist reacts. What is found in such studies, of course, depends on the material for story used, its cultural origin and the story definition on which the study is based. Chapter 2 indicates the broad range of material that is designated as 'story' and much of this kind of research does not question the identity of story. Schank considers the role of story structure in the interactions between people. I have said that Schank links the management of story to intelligence. He says that it takes intelligence in conversational contexts to comprehend the gist (essential meaning) of a story that has been told – and to respond using an appropriate story to match that gist. In this case, it would seem that the structure is set by the conversational context of the story-sharing.

These various interpretations of structure suggest that the notion of script overlaps into genre and the character of a story, its actions, subjects and events, and the intentions for telling (explicit or unspoken) by the group or individual. A recent radio programme illustrated how a multiplicity of structures can operate at the same time. A paramedic described how he and his colleagues would cope with the stress from incidents by telling the stories back at their base. One might talk about an incident in which a man lost an arm. Another would counter with a story in which a man lost two arms and a third would counter with a story about a man losing two arms and a leg. He commented that the countering of the story about the current incident with others that were worse in their consequences served to reduce the horror and stress of the current incident (BBC Radio 4,

Midweek, 11 February 2009). Presumably these stories had their own structures, but individuals used individual story 'intelligences' (Schank, 1995) to create a generalised and predictable storytelling structure that met their current needs (which would further influence structure).

As a storyteller, needing to learn the gist of stories for retelling, I find that stories with familiar structures are much easier to recall than others in which the structure is unusual. Indeed, the structure of a story has a lot to do with the stories that I feel are suitable for retelling in performance. I reject many on the basis that their structure is not distinctive – or the ending is not sufficiently powerful as a resolution for entertainment purposes. Whole collections of stories may 'work' or 'not work' in this sense because of the way they are told. McCaughrean's (1999) collection, for example, mostly 'works' for me in terms of structure. This may represent something about mutual personal preferences or rewriting styles (probably both).

I conclude this section with a more general point. The notion of narrative structure has implications for more than just our comprehension of stories. While Bruner (2002) argues that there is a story structure that we acquire, he also says that narrative 'gives shape to things in the real world' (p. 8), suggesting that we impose narrative shape on our internal experience of the world in which we live. This brings us back to the quotation at the start of this book – 'We see shapes in the clouds and a man in the moon' (Goldacre, 2008: 226). We have an urge to make sense of the world and to account for things we see. How is this related to the structure that Bruner and the others cited suggest that we impose on story? I muse on this and on Mancuso's (extreme?) statement that 'persons fit textual input into a narrative grammar whose basic categories can be explicated' (Mancuso, 1986: 98).

The quality of engagement of story as a frame

Gabriel starts the introduction to his book on story in organisations with an invitation to explore engagement in story:

> 'Once upon a time a cat drank a bottle of green ink. At once the cat turned green ... ' Thus is a story announced. Thus does it command attention no less firmly than the opening bars of a Beethoven piano sonata ... Thus does each story hold promise.
>
> (Gabriel, 2000: 1)

The idea that story is engaging seems to float out of most texts about story but is rarely explored as a matter of significance (Packer, 1991). I see engagement, not as a by-product of story, but as an important characteristic that may often be justification for telling a story. Engagement acts as a frame for story because it distinguishes story material from the context (Gargiulo, 2006). Like narrative structure engagement is an internal quality of the story.

The capacity to use story to engage is powerful. McKee talks of 'a good story well told as " ... a world driven by (the teller's) passion, courage and creative gifts ..."' (McKee, 1999: 21). Engagement applies to both the teller and listener. If, as Nwobani (2008) says, 'Great leaders are storytellers' they could be said to pull us into the frame that is the story to 'make' us listen. The capacity to engage is a reason why story is a powerful tool in the hands of a teacher. A geography lecturer is teaching about the gradation of small stones and pebbles along Chesil Beach in the south of England. She has talked of the tidal forces and the effect of storm surges, and she stops and says, 'I will tell you a story about that ...' She tells a personal story of the delight she experienced one day when walking in a Devon bay. There had been a storm and there was sand where normally it was a shingle beach. The sand was there just for three days and during that time children made sandcastles and swimming was much more enjoyable – and then it was gone again. The attentions of students that may just have been wandering in the talk of tidal forces are engaged by the story. Engagement not only aids learners but is satisfying to the teller. The scant literature on engagement as a quality of story tends to focus on oral storytelling, where of course engagement is generated by the presentation as well as the story itself (e.g. Claxton, 1999; Thomas and Killick, 2007; Gersie, 1992, Crimmens, 1998). It is important to the writer too. When writing a short story is going well, it is like having a different life to which to escape.

So what is implied by engagement? Broadly I mean that the listener's attention is drawn in towards the events of the story and its structure, and that listeners contemplate and anticipate the actions of the story in an ongoing manner, becoming involved with the meaning of the story. It seems as if the story 'takes over' the structuring of the listener's internal experience and external experience (accommodation processes). When I have seen a good film and walk out through the foyer of a cinema, it is as if I am surrounded by the emotion and story of the film, like being in a bubble of a different life. A good story seems to facilitate listeners and the teller in moving around in the psychological space of the story, guided by the unfolding actions of the story. For the listener to allow herself vicariously to experience the 'story world' involves her in 'suspending her disbelief' and thereby suspending some current connections with the here and now. She allows herself to be transported 'aboard' the story and may encounter different reality.

In connection with the suspension of disbelief, Wheeler et al. (1999) confirmed the findings of earlier work by Prentice et al. (1997), that the beliefs of subjects are influenced by fiction. They tended to accept false assertions after reading fiction in which these assertions were made. This occurred 'even when they were explicitly told that the story was fictional'. Marsh et al. (2003) found that correct information and misinformation in previously read fiction was often repeated in response to test questions and that the subjects, in both cases, thought that they knew the ideas before they had read the stories. In another experiment, Marsh and Fazio (2006) demonstrated that subjects seem to have difficulty in noting factual errors in the content of fictitious stories. They could detect the errors if reminded, but it took them more time to read the text. This empirical work seems to suggest that engagement with story tends to 'turn off' readers' critical faculties and therefore supports the notion that disbelief is suspended. I return to this area of work at the end of this chapter.

Engagement may characterise stories, but stories are also deliberately designed to engage. Devices are used by tellers, consciously or unconsciously, to draw in listeners. A sequence of events may be altered to create suspense or amidst a comfortable scenario there are hints that the state will soon change. The voice of the teller is lowered, or the pace of telling slowed or speeded up, or the look of the teller becomes more intense, or in written text the sentences become clipped. The structure of a story will often play a part in engagement by implying a lead-up to excitement, a resolution of tensions or answers to be produced to questions posed. Emotions are variously stirred, soothed or stimulated – feelings of fear, romance or mystery are generated to encourage the listener to engage. A good storyteller is an unashamed manipulator!

Another factor in story that may aid the processes of engagement is the content of unspoken ambiguity or uncertainty in story, which draws in the listener because she is actively constructing the story, using imagination and working hard in assimilation and accommodation as she hears it (Bruner 1990). The listener is not only aboard the story, but is involved in its creation. These are far from the passive actions usually associated with the act of listening.

Stories also engage through their social function. A story told to a group draws listeners in common along the storyline within the context of the story. I am tempted to say that they are drawn towards a common internal experience, but that cannot be since internal experience is a product of the individual. The social function of stories is particularly important for pedagogical situations and I explore it further in Chapter 5.

I gained an additional perspective on the issue of engagement in my role as an oral storyteller recently. It is initially to practise telling a story out loud to no one, but once I can 'get inside the story' and focus on the images I can engage with it sufficiently to tell it as if in public. Recently, however, I was asked to do a 'run-through' of a story in a village hall before a concert the next day. There were people around, but no one was listening. I could not tell the story. I was too distracted by people being around from 'getting inside' the story on my own, and could not tell it to them either. I gave up. Interestingly the performance the next day was difficult for another reason. The stage lights blinded me so that I couldn't see the audience and respond to their engagement.

The last point I will make about engagement may be one of the important reasons why humans tell stories as much as they do. I have mentioned Slovic's (2007) reseach that suggests that humans tend to identify with or respond in a greater way to information about the activities of individuals rather than information about mass events. From his research on decision-making and with regard to responses to mass events, Slovic says that statistics on mass killings (he mentions Rwanda and Cambodia under Pol Pot) 'fail to spark emotion or feeling and thus fail to motivate action ... ' Statistics seem to 'dissipate any emotion we might feel towards a victim'. We are more likely to respond to the plight of an individual. Slovic cites research in which one group was asked to contribute towards a costly lifesaving treatment needed by eight children and another group was asked to contribute the same amount to the same treatment needed by one of the eight. People contributed far more to the single child. This response to individuals is exploited in fund-raising by charities. Charity appeals on the UK BBC Radio 4 are usually introduced with the story of how the life of a named individual has been transformed because of the charitable work. For example, the Send a Cow appeal (2009) for money to purchase cows in Uganda was introduced by a story of how the lives of named family members were transformed through ownership of a cow. This discrepancy between our responses to a mass or individual plight could be explained either because our inability to identify with the mass or because of our greater engagement with stories of individuals. It is interesting to note how the folk traditions and religions treat their theories about formative events in the human universe. Most creation myths involve individuals (e.g. Adam and Eve in the Bible).

From the mix of evidence, observation and experience on engagement, I suggest that the engaging quality of a story and the act of engagement between teller and audience are very significant in the human propensity to tell stories.

The reality frame: introduction

I have split this long section on the different realities in stories into two. The first part of it deals with a wide range of different meanings of 'reality'; the second part deals specifically with research on vicarious experiencing and simulation through story. I start this section with a quotation that illustrates how reality is a frame for story. Scheibe (1998) takes us back to the cinema. His example illustrates engagement and reality as frames:

> Attention shifts as we enter the movie house and once again as we leave it. Reality is convincing as long as attention lasts and, as we continue attending to the movies, their reality becomes pervasive. For some of us the movie continues to seem more real than ordinary Main Street as we come out of the theatre blinking in the sunlight after a Saturday movie.
>
> (Scheibe, 1998: 54)

The reality frame: different meanings of 'reality'

For convenience I will start by identifying reality with the current perception of experience of the 'here and now' (Vinden, 1998) so that I can consider how story takes us away from this state. In one sense, I could say that all stories are shifts from reality – or else they would be little more than descriptions (Ryan, 2008). They are all constructs too. They are 'relative and provisional'. They are 'but temporary way points in the ongoing construction of meaning' (Mitchell and Charmaz,

1996; also Martin, 1981). A story of 'fiction' or 'imagination' cannot completely be separated from real lives (reality) because it is developed out of the real-life experience content of a human brain in its interactions between internal and external experiences. A story 'embodies the actual experience and ideas' (Winter et al., 1999: 21). It is understood, too, in relation to the listener's internal experience, which is itself a unique interpretation of the world. So in the same story many 'overlapping' realities may be represented.

When a person suspends her disbelief, she holds back from critique or dismissal of a different reality either completely or until the story has been heard (Gabriel, 2000). Gabriel suggests that the story is distinguished from the chronicle by its focus on effect rather than accuracy. He asks, 'would a listener respond (to a story) by challenging the factual accuracy of the text … ? The suspension of disbelief and poetic licence are acknowledged privileges of the teller of story but not the chronicler' (Gabriel, 2000: 28). We must here primarily be referring to strong story, for a story told in a court of law, of course, would be subject to challenge if necessary (Bruner, 2002). Bruner adds to this idea, saying that 'Great fiction proceeds by making the familiar ordinary and the ordinary strange again' (p. 9).

There are simpler and more complex ways in which stories shift from 'here and now' reality. One of the simpler shifts is that in space and time. Stories are set in places never visited by the listener, and in historical and future times that cannot be visited (Plummer, 1995; Mar and Oatley, 2008). A story may be written about two completely different events in the same place – about people in a room and the family of mice in the skirting board of that room. The reality frame focuses in or out – either into the mind or out into the big wide world anywhere. Story has the capacity to link past, present and future (Pinar, 1975; McLeod, 1997; Parkin, 1998), to show examples of how events in the past might influence the present or future or perhaps (maybe in *Dr Who*) how the future influences the past – or at least our view of the past. This linking of ideas is crucial to the uses of story in therapies and the interpretation that is involved in working with past stories (historiography) (Scheibe, 1998).

A more complex shift from reality is that between non-fiction and fiction and what we mean by 'real', and other words like 'true', 'imagined' and 'factual' material (White, 1981; Gough, 1993; Phillips, 1995. Richardson (2000) demonstrates that there is no stability in the historical and current conceptions of the nature of fiction and non-fiction, except perhaps that 'unreality' is definitely signalled at the start of the story with something like 'Once upon a time … ' (McLeod, 1997). Richardson (2000) recounts the history of writing styles and demonstrates how they have been dominated by different paradigms over the years. Over the twentieth century, with the growing complexity of relationships between different styles of writing, the 'presumed solid demarcations between "fact" and "fiction" and between "true" and "imagined" were blurred' (p. 925). While she accepts that the notions of fact and fiction may be technically indistinguishable, she suggests that we should take into account the story writer's intentions in her writing. Mostly listeners are conscious of the fiction/non-fiction intentions but they may deliberately be mystified as an element of entertainment or sometimes in order that a point shall be made (e.g. Castaneda, 1970, 1971; Hines, 1988; Ayalon, 1991; Phillips, 1995; Fowles, 1997).

It is not just the content of stories that may swim around in the non-fiction/ fiction divide. The use of the word 'story' itself may imply that the truth has been stretched. However, as Plummer (1995) points out, the labelling of material as (only a) story often serves to diminish those with genuine points to make – 'Rape victims know only too well the frequent charge that they are simply making up stories' (p. 167). Plummer's point is that the sexual stories that he studies are 'grounded in the social processes that … are "beyond the stories"' (p. 167). So at the same time that the word 'story' is castigated for not being 'real life', its value is recognised as giving a more 'real' picture of life. Claxton (1999) says 'stories may be attempting to say something that is true *to* life, but not true *of* life', but they have 'enormous power to teach about life, albeit indirectly' (p. 137). In his study of 'tales in sport and physical activity', Sparkes (2002) illustrates the manner in which tales that represent an array of different dimensions of reality labelled fiction, non-fiction, poetry, etc. integrate to provide a richer picture of the subject matter. These are important developments, associated with postmodernist thinking, which recognise the multiple influences that shape and direct the written and spoken word and that situate it within a particular context (Alvarez and Merchan, 1992; Gough, 1993; Phillips, 1995, Richardson, 2000).

Another form of reality that frames a story and separates it from its context is the involvement of imagination and fantasy. I link these with dreaming and 'altered states' of consciousness because they are also products of the non-rational mind. Vinden (1998) talks of imaginings as mental events that do not have 'real world correlates' (p. 74). We do, though, still interpret them in relation to current (here-and-now-based) internal experience. An interesting issue here is how we relate to these imagined stories and how we distinguish 'non-believed-in imaginings' from 'believed-in imaginings' (de Rivera and Sarbin, 1998). The distinction is not always clear and reality as a frame can become somewhat blurred. We can, of course, combine real and non-real events in imagining. For example, on a real journey an imagined wrong turning leads to fictitious events. We may assume that we are aware of the pretence when imagining, but it is not always clear. Those imaginings that occur under hypnosis, or particularly in so-called 'past-life regression' can appear very real (Kirsch, 1998). Though in this state people are telling a story, their emotions are as real as in the here and now – they cry or laugh at events and feel that they are in the clothes that they describe, though they may also know that they are not in that reality. There is evidence from social psychology research that that people may knowingly respond to ideas that they know are imaginary. Vinden reports on a study by Rozin et al. (1986) in which subjects watched two bottles being filled with sugar. They were then asked to label the bottles 'sugar' and 'cyanide'. Despite the fact that the subjects had done the labelling, they were reluctant to taste the sugar from the cyanide-labelled bottle. Where is 'reality' in this situation?

The material of dreams might sometimes be counted as story. It tends to have some reference to aspects of the real world but dream events tend to have stronger relationships to each other (one thing happens, and then another ...) than to their broader context. Perhaps they are coherent in terms of emotion and other unspoken content than the imagery. Spence (1998) associates believed-in imaginings of dreams and altered states of consciousness with, for example, the attribution of efficacy to fashionable medical treatments and the belief in 'tall stories' and urban myths as well as the more fantastic believed-in tales of kidnappings by space travellers. He suggests that such 'mythic explanations' characteristically 'suppress complicating variations (of explanation) and replace them with a kind of uniform simplicity' (Spence, 1998: 221). In his comments, Spence is close to the literature of 'bad science' (Goldacre, 2008).

There are also differences in reality when the same story is represented in different media. The medium in itself may distinguish the story from its context (e.g. it is on television), but for the same story told through different media, other different realities are evident. A fairy story such as 'Sleeping Beauty' may be told, read or acted, animated or depicted in cartoon on paper or screen. The different representations provide different areas of information about the story and consequently require different responses from the listener/reader/viewer. A written story tells us about the evil stepmother who thought she was the most beautiful woman in the world – and we work to imagine the person, but an animated presentation gives us a vision of her 'ready made'. Perhaps because of this, there is less personal involvement with the character, but colour and movement might be compensation and there might be more ability to focus on other aspects of the story. In an academic context, Sparkes (2002) describes the different aspects of meaning that are captured when the outcomes of social research are depicted in ethnographic drama rather than written media. He gives as an example the dramatisation of abortion stories narrated by those involved (citing Ellis and Bochner, 1992). The aim was to enable viewers to 'come away with a sense of what the experience must have felt like' (Sparkes, 2002: 129).

Reflection on the self forms another frame of reality which can also be story. I have dealt with this in Chapter 8.

The reality frame: the values of seeing through others' eyes

Another manner in which reality issues frame story is where a story takes us into the ways in which others see, experience and interpret life. The most obvious case is in biographical material in which an author will demonstrate how she sees the other seeing the world. An important role has been argued for fiction in management and organisational situations on the basis that it helps to develop understanding of how others view the world. As Alvarez and Merchan (1992) put it, 'in the process of writing and reading, both the author and reader become others, able to see through different eyes. This makes possible a communication in which the interlocutors occupy a position different from the ordinary one'. They link this aspect of fiction with the development of ethical sensitivity – of being able to take another's point of view. Phillips (1995) makes a similar point for organisational development. He suggests that 'successful narrative fiction creates a world in which what happens is not simply plausible but so realistic that readers can learn from the fact that these things happened Thus complexity and ambiguity of the resulting representation is one of the strengths of narrative fiction'. Phillips goes on to say that narrative fiction can enable readers to 'enter the story and vicariously experience the events portrayed'. A similar point is made by Lauritzen and Jaeger (1997) in the context of working with children. They discuss how story can confront children with situations of cognitive dissonance and it is in wrestling with this that learning occurs because it stimulates change.

Mar and Oatley (2008) and others at the University of Toronto suggest that 'literary fiction allows us to experience social situations vicariously'. This notion is central to their argument that story (specifically, in this case, fiction) is special because it involves readers in simulations of psychological events in life as they read. Oatley (2008b) suggests that there are two kinds of simulation in operation. The first stimulates our self-understanding to enable us to comprehend the psychological processing of characters. The ability to infer the psychological views of others is called the 'theory of mind' (Astington, 1990, cited in Mar et al., 2006), and it is essential for social interaction. The second kind of simulation involves the reader in following the protagonists in the story in their dealings with complex situations of life. This 'gives us practice in navigating in the social domain. Such practice should then [they argue], promote transfer of these skills to the real world'. They call this the Social Improvement Hypothesis (Mar et al., 2008). Completely independently I came to a similar suggestion through consideration of epistemological development (see next section).

The University of Toronto group explore the implication that humans learn social processes in the context of reading fiction in reports on several experiments. They found that readers of non-fiction were less socially adept than readers of fiction (Mar *et al.*, 2006). Rather surprisingly, they observed that there were immediate social/personality effects in a group of students who were asked to read a short story by Chekhov. A control group read a text with similar content, but in documentary format, and they underwent significantly less change in a similar set of characteristics. The writers stress that the subjects did not demonstrate a specific change in a particular direction, but they changed from their pre-experiment state (Djikic et al., 2009). The team considered that the changes were mediated by the emotional involvement of the subjects with the text. The findings might lead to speculation as to whether reading fiction could be used to improve social skills in formal situations.

Story as a framed stimulus for reflection and change

Because story as change agent is the topic of Chapter 10, I will only sketch out some of the dimensions of this issue here, without detail.

Stories are used as a framed stimulus to prompt reflection and change even when the anticipated changes are not directly related to the overt subject matter of the story. A story used for change seems to be like an object 'that we hold dear' – it has a 'power to move us (or) to forge new ideas' (Turkle, 2007). In overt terms, a story that is about how a plain fawn cat came to change her coat to the pattern of an elegant tabby might be used to encourage a person to think about how to change her image; however, the influence may be unconscious (Jung, 1977).

I start by describing an experiment that was designed to demonstrate how story material is effective in eliciting personal memories. Oatley (1999) and Larsen and Seilman (1988) gave 3,000-word texts to readers. One text was fiction and one was expository. The readers were asked to mark the texts when a memory arose during their reading. The memories were to be classified as personally experienced or observed. The fiction text elicited twice as many personal memories as the expository text. This was seen to demonstrate the 'resonance between themes of a story and personal life'. While this experiment seems to illustrate the potential role of story in eliciting material for reflection, it also relates to the phenomenon of engagement. Oatley (1999) conducted a further experiment in which readers reported experiences of emotion. This led him to view emotion as central to fiction (see Chapter 3) and to develop a hypothesis that when reading fiction insights 'of a personal kind are more likely to occur when the reader is moved emotionally by what he or she is reading and when the accompanying context helps the understanding of the resulting emotions'. Given the complexity of emotion (Chapter 3) and that it is interpreted as an experience by the reader, I am not sure how one should distinguish the emotion that might be stimulated by the story from that arising as a result of moments of insight.

Story can also provide a 'space for contemplation' (Dawson, 2003), though the story material means that it is a 'guided' space (Phillips, 1995). Denning's use of story exemplifies this principle well. Denning (2001) promotes the use of 'springboard' story in the context of organisations. These stories are designed to prompt the listener to construct her personal story, which in turn can bring about personal and organisational change. There are issues of what sort of story stimulates what sort of thinking, and thence what sort of change. Winter et al. (1999) discuss the way in which a writer can learn how readers of her story interpret the meaning of it, suggesting that 'the fictional form allows the unconscious meanings to surface both in what the writer has included and in how the reader responds' (p. 23).

If it is to be used to stimulate thinking, a story should first provide a 'semblance of a stable and secure background' for the development of further meaning from the story. This is achieved through processes of 'distancing and involvement' (Ayalon, 1991: 16). Ayalon says that the notion of 'distance' of a story in a therapeutic situation means 'not too close' to real life in the storyline but 'close enough' to enable some identification and projection ('ie the … listeners attribute their own motives and emotions to one or more of the characters featured in the story' (p. 16), leading to insight – sometimes through catharsis). More simply put, stories provide 'food for thought and salve for troubled minds' (M. Warner, *In Our Time*, BBC Radio 4, 5 February 2009).

Stories may also work to change through structures such as metaphor. Metaphor encourages the imagination to work either in the construction of a story or in the manner that meaning is taken from it (Gabriel, 2000). It is powerful perhaps because it is partially unspoken and can invite broad interpretation (Lakoff and Johnson 1980). In the context of business training, Parkin comments:

> many stories can be seen in some way as metaphors for life. At a surface level, they provide. ... enjoyment and a chance to exercise our imagination ... but at a deeper level, they can help us to deal with the most difficult and complex aspects of our own lives by offering a simpler and more positive parallel ... giving us more choices as to how to deal with our own problems. What is 'The Ugly Duckling' but a lesson in time management and planning.
>
> (Parkin 1998: 7)

Parkin goes on to suggest other well-known stories that can act as metaphors for issues in organisations. She discusses the merit of revealing or not revealing the underlying 'meaning' for particular circumstances, though meaning is in the eye or ear of the beholder.

Parable (which may coincide with metaphor) also stimulates thought about change. A parable is usually a simple story told with the intention of illustrating a moral or religious principle or event. For some, the concept of parable should also allude to mystery or the qualities of godly love (McFague TeSelle, 1975).

Another group of stories engender reflection and the exploration of philosophies or value systems through fiction. This kind of writing spans the centuries from ancient Greece. Claxton says they 'give life to philosophies and value systems against which one can measure oneself' (Claxton, 1999: 137). Plato's allegories about the Cave (Cornford, 1945) is an early example and I have mentioned *Sophie's World* (Gaardner, 1996) and *The Green Child*, the only novel by Herbert Read (1935), the art critic, which explores aesthetics and politics.

Case studies, critical incidents and scenarios are often stories (Chapter 9). They are used to explore and learn from events or the responses to events which typify 'real life' (Dawson, 2003). The story form in this case provides rich and holistic information that is closer to reality than a clinical description (Greenhalgh and Hurwitz, 1998). The use of story in professional development or education enables learners to share their experiences and thus to shape their own and others' understanding of new situations (McDrury and Alterio, 2003; Whelan et al., 2001). While case studies tend to be based on real situations, there are advantages in using fiction as material as it can exercise minds in more challenging ways. It can look at the 'what ifs' of situations (Moon and Fowler, 2008).

Then there is also the telling of our own stories as a means of facilitating reflection. Personal story is the subject of Chapter 8. I split personal storytelling in relation to personal change into two parts. There is the initial act of telling (or writing) a personal story, which involves the recasting of it as thought is represented in writing or speech (etc.) and we learn from the process of representation.

However, we can look back on stories that have been generated in reflection as a means of stimulating more thought (and potentially change) in the process of secondary reflection. I have come to see the initial writing in journals or 'reflective pieces' as like writing lecture notes – simply making the initial recordings. I see the real value for learning as occurring when the material is read through and mulled over later, with ideas related to each other and maybe to further material (Moon, 2004, 2006). It seems to me that unless the reflective writing situations in formal education are engineered so that learners engage in secondary reflection, the potential value of the activity is lost. McLeod (1997) sums up both aspects of reflective learning and the telling of one's own story as stimulation for further thought. He says:

> Everyone has experiences that are perplexing and somehow 'unfinished' until they can be told to someone else, written in a diary or in some other way 'narrativised'. Putting them in story form is an effective method of sorting out and making sense of them. Retelling stories is also a means of problem solving. Each time the story is told the teller gains the opportunity to revisit that set of experiences that have hitherto remained unnamed or have not fitted into the sequence (or made sense).
>
> (McLeod, 1997: 37–38)

Such ideas lie behind many therapeutic processes and professional development processes that are mentioned in later chapters (e.g. Rollnick et al., 1993; Bolton, 1999; Winter et al., 1999; Hunt, 2000; McDrury and Alterio, 2003; Alterio and McDrury, 2003; Chan and Chung, 2004).

Here I conclude the first part of this chapter. I have reviewed various ways in which stories generate and convey their meaning, and to do this I have suggested that they are separated from their general context by various conceptual frames – such as obvious beginnings, reality, engagement and so on. I move on to the last two sections in this chapter, in which I will explore more general issues around the understanding of the meaning of stories, epistemological beliefs and memory.

Story, meaning and the development of epistemological beliefs

In this section, I consider the development of a learner's understanding of the nature of knowledge (epistemological development/epistemological beliefs) and its relation to story material. In particular, I focus on how story material might help learners in their development towards the sophisticated thinking that we expect of graduates or postgraduates. I first provide an overview of some key work in this area and then consider the roles of story in relation to the findings (Moon 2004, 2008a). Lucas (2008) has said that 'each way of knowing provides a lens through which the learning environment is viewed'. These stages of understanding or 'ways of knowing' are states of internal experience that are brought to bear on external experience. They affect our capacity for critical thinking, our understanding of the provisional nature of knowledge, our management of uncertainty and therefore of our understanding of processes of scientific endeavour, our conception of the role of theory and its relationship to evidence (Moon, 2008a). In my view, progression in the sophistication of understanding of knowledge is central to higher education progression.

Epistemological development has been the subject of a number of studies over the last half-century. The research implies that at any point in higher education learners who are learning the same material and attending the same lectures may understand the material in different ways. Perry (1985) captured this idea in a chapter called 'Different worlds in the same classroom'. I suggest that many teachers forget that their own understanding of knowledge is different from that of their students, even though they came through the same stages. The introduction of concepts such as 'deep critical thinking' and 'theory' – the jargon of higher education – can be beyond the comprehension of learners in the early undergraduate stages.

The findings of four substantial projects on epistemological development broadly coincide in their conclusions that there is a sequence of qualitative changes that occurs in learners' conceptions of knowledge during higher education (Perry, 1970; Belenky et al., 1986; King and Kitchener, 1994; Baxter Magolda, 1992, 1994, 1996). These (American) studies differ in their terminology, in the populations studied, in research methods and in the number of stages that they identify, but broadly suggest the same continuum of development. In recent research, Lucas and Meyer (2005; Lucas 2008) have observed similar epistemological development in UK accountancy students.

To describe this continuum of epistemological development, I use Baxter Magolda's four-stage terminology, though I consider the identification of actual stages mainly as a linguistically convenient means of describing a continuum. In higher education, learners tend to start as absolute knowers: they are likely to see knowledge as 'right or wrong', black or white – as a series of facts that they will 'absorb' from a teacher who is the expert. They see teaching as the process of the 'passing over of knowledge' (as the 'brick wall view' – Chapter 3) and knowledge as a commodity. In progressing, learners in stimulating educational situations shift towards the sophisticated thinking that is characterized ultimately by constructivist conceptions of knowledge. At this most advanced stage, learners are able to take a relativist view, recognizing that there may be a range of perspectives on an idea. They then can understand and judge the relationships between the different perspectives – which might be called theories or paradigms – and the issue in question. They can work in uncertain situations, taking appropriate measures to manage the knowledge in relation to their current purposes. They see their 'teachers' as partners in the development of knowledge. Very few undergraduates in Baxter Magolda's original study (1992) reached this latter stage in fully developed form. I see it as epitomising the functioning that we should expect of learners on a Master's programme.

Baxter Magolda's more recent work has suggested that learners progress on the continuum particularly when they are challenged in educational environments or in situations where they need to exercise independent judgement such as in professional or work experience situations. Their progression is probably a matter of shifting forwards and backwards as they confront different areas of knowledge and challenges to their thinking. It is to be assumed that most of the general population functions largely with absolutist conceptions of knowledge.

As I have indicated, there are important implications of this work on epistemological development for higher education learning. The ability to think critically might be said to be central to higher education learning, but fully developed critical thinking involves the making of a judgement with appropriate use of evidence, and involves an inherent recognition that knowledge is contestable. It follows from this that fully developed critical thinking is not possible until the learner can function with sophisticated epistemological beliefs for at least some of the time (Kuhn, 1999; Kember, 2001). Writing at a time when Perry's work was the main source for epistemological development, Meyers (1986) says 'the real value of Perry's work is the insight it offers into the reasons why most students do not think critically' (p. 97) – they are just simply not yet able to conceive of knowledge in a manner that allows them to engage fully with the process of critical thinking.

To link epistemological development to story, it is useful to consider what kinds of thinking educators might be aiming to facilitate in learners in order to support their development. Some are:

- the ability to manage situations of uncertainty;
- an understanding that the same thing can be viewed from different perspectives;
- an understanding of what it means to say than a term is constructed and that many word meanings, treated as absolute, are constructed;
- the ability to comprehend knowledge as constructed and provisional;
- an understanding that the word 'theory' does not necessarily mean that one theory is right and the others are wrong; around a discipline there is generic 'theory' (in contrast to practice) and there are specific theories – these word uses have different meanings;
- the understanding that teaching is not a process of experts 'passing over' knowledge;
- understanding that learning is change of conceptions, not accumulation of facts;
- the ability to manage evidence appropriately to make good-quality independent judgements.

We should expect postgraduates to be able to think in this way and undergraduates to be 'on the way' to such thinking.

So what role could story have in epistemological development? Before I explore this more generally, I review the 'knowledge material' that carries meaning in stories:

- a story contains new ideas for learners;
- story is told in the first/second person; in the past, present or future tense; is fiction or 'real life' and so on – this has connotations for the listener's comprehension processes;

- stories may be based on a particular belief perspective (e.g. religious stories and ghost stories);
- different genres can view the same knowledge in different ways – a poem about a nursing incident carries different perspectives from a description (Holmes and Gregory, 1998);
- stories may show how characters process ideas, problems and decisions or differ in viewpoints from one another, and how they apply their knowledge in different ways, with different consequences;
- the listener can experience seeing the world through the 'eyes' of different people, particularly in the case of first-person stories (e.g. Oatley, 2008a);
- story can be a stimulus for reflection and possibly change;
- stories may be used by tellers to explore and stretch ideas (e.g. science fiction);
- some stories manipulate the comprehension of listeners, introducing uncertainty, for example about the nature of reality;
- the knowledge in story may actually or potentially challenge or confront listeners' epistemological beliefs.

In any of these cases, the learner can react to a story by saying, 'Oh it is only a story', and allow herself to be entertained. She can suspend her disbelief as a holding device or a way of containing discomfort. Alternatively she can allow the story to challenge her. The confrontation may concern the story itself or it may relate to the bigger picture of the nature of knowledge or knowing. Secure internal experience (which could be a belief system) may be contradicted by persuasive or apparently valid external experience and cognitive dissonance is produced. Such an experience can lead to valuable learning. There are different words for such situations of challenge: Mezirow (1991) calls them 'perspective transformation'; Carey and Smith (1999) talk of 'epistemological crises'; and Lucas (2008) talks of 'moments of surprise' or 'being pulled up short', 'viewing ... the world, differently from before'. She applies the term to the processes of learners, and recognizes them in her own experiences as a teacher. These are the more dramatic moments of change in epistemological development, but there are likely to be many strands of ongoing development. For example, Mar and Oatley (2008) discuss a continuum of development in the ability of readers to discuss the 'theory of mind' of characters in a story (Zunshine, 2006). They suggest that this grows from a stage in which the theory of mind is related only to the context of the story, towards a situation in which there is generalization beyond the context of the story into the theorizing of cultural studies. They cite McKeough and Genereux (2003), who found a trend in this development in children that seems to continue well beyond the teenage years.

However, there may be more to this link between epistemological development and story. Thus far, I have not distinguished between the listener and the teller. It seems obvious to say that, at a given stage of epistemological development, for a learner to follow the ideas material that is challenging to her epistemological beliefs is likely to be easier than for her to construct or argue ideas of a similar challenge or complexity for herself. She might be able to understand that colour is a constructed concept (Lehrer, 2007) but she might not be able to explain and consider the implications of the idea. Thus epistemological development could be said to be functioning at different rates in the ability to follow the argument of another and in the ability to argue for oneself. A town planning student may be able to understand the reasoning behind the decision to build a road in one place rather than another but unable to represent a similar depth of reasoning in a report or in oral discussion or where judgements need to be made. It would be interesting to reconsider the methodology of epistemological development research on this basis.

Bringing this back to story, I suggest that story material, with all the means by which it can challenge the listener epistemologically, can be a valuable way of facilitating comprehension of the nature of knowledge in advance of the learner's current stage of development. It is possible then that asking learners to practise representing argument and ways of working with knowledge within the context of story (e.g. fiction – Chapter 12) could be a good way of aiding their development. The exercises on graduated scenarios and other exercises in Chapter 7 exploit these ideas and the following references are generally relevant (e.g. Hines, 1988; Kloss, 1994; Lauritzen and Jaeger, 1997; Fisher, 1999; Richardson, 2000; Gold and Holman, 2001; Laming, 2004; Lucas and Meyer, 2005).

I now turn to the third section of this chapter to consider how memory and story might interrelate.

Story and memory

I have at times wondered why the topic of memory is mentioned so little in books about learning at advanced levels. Memory might seem to be important, but with the model of learning that I have described in Chapter 4 there is relatively little need to see the process of commitment to memory as distinct from learning itself. The processes of assimilation and accommodation model the manner in which new material of learning in external experience is – or is not – incorporated into the cognitive structure, which may in turn change in response to the new material. As a result of that process, these new ideas – now as internal experience – become part of the guiding system for the brain in its dealing with further new ideas. So, to some extent, to have knowledge is to have memory of that knowledge and to be able to represent it in one way or another because otherwise there is no means of knowing that a person has that knowledge. In many ways, what is more important is to focus on forgetting (Schank, 1995), considering what is lost or modified in the representation of the material, other than what the subject deliberately chooses to neglect.

Bruner captures a spectrum of relationships of story and memory in this inspired paragraph:

> Through narrative we construct, reconstruct, in some ways reinvent yesterday and tomorrow. Memory and imagination fuse in the process. Even when we create the possible worlds of fiction, we do not desert the familiar but

subjunctivise it into what might have been and what might be. The human mind, however cultivated its memory or refined its recording systems, can never fully and faithfully recapture the past, but neither can it escape from it. Memory and imagination supply and consume each other's wares.

(Bruner, 2002: 93)

The teller of a known story endeavours to remember and reconstructs the story from her memory and her imagination, while the listener reconstructs the story using her own memory and imagination (internal experience). It is interesting to recall that memories are evoked in the mind of the listener to or reader of story more than are evoked by expository material (Larsen and Seilman, 1988; Mar and Oatley, 2008). It is a matter not just of the memorising of story, but of the construction and reconstruction of story from memory.

Memory for telling stories

When I run a workshop on learning to tell oral stories, the primary concern of participants is how they will remember the story. Despite recognising that storytellers do not learn stories word by word, they still find it difficult to conceive of how 'so much' can be learned. The method commonly used by storytellers is to visualise each story scene so that it can be described (detail in Chapter 13). The storyline and the images then 'wheel' the story along together.

Various bases for the recall of story have been suggested elsewhere that appear to differ from this method that I describe and they are usually based mainly on language. In a series of experiments, Mandler and her associates suggested that the story grammar or structure is important in the support of recall – and it is more important to children than to adults, who can become more flexible in their retrieval strategy (Mandler and DeForest, 1979). Schank (1995), in his quest to link story with 'artificial intelligence', suggests that it is the 'gist' of a story that we remember – 'We take the gist of a story as it exists in memory and then transform that gist into a verbal expression of the story that perhaps leaves out one point or embellishes another' (p. 25). Schank also argues that we have to tell stories in order to fix them in memory and that as we tell them and modify them for the current context the version of story that is recalled most easily is that most recently told. In this way, he suggests, stories become shorter and simpler. This is not my experience of learning and retelling the same story to different groups at different times. I – and I suspect other storytellers – adapt the story length and its content to the present context and time available for telling.

Memory is constructed: the implications for story

If memory is constructed, then story is reconstructed when told from memory. Middleton and Edwards (1990) say that 'Memory of individuals does not just act as a passive "storehouse" of past experience, but changes what is remembered in ways that transform it according to present circumstances' (p. 6). Bartlett (1932) did much to demonstrate what occurs when we remember and the implications for the restructuring process in the transmission of information – in this case, of story. Much has been written on this, but of particular relevance is research on the transmission of folklore. This has come to include work on so called 'modern' folklore that includes rumour and urban legend. In considering 'why fairy stories stick', Zipes (2007) suggests that they persist because they carry basic messages about how to survive and these important elements of information tend to be retained in their original form because it is in the interest of listeners (and possibly parents) that they are retained. Perhaps adding to this, Heath et al. (2001) suggest that one of the remembered features of urban legends that encourages their retelling is a sense of emotional disgust that is enhanced within them. For example, they give an example of an urban legend in which at Halloween children return home with more in their stomachs than sweets. The story goes that glass shards have 'found their way' into sweet packets as a deterrent against future knocking at doors. Guerin and Miyazaki (2006) may be saying something similar in suggesting that the features of stories that are memorised for retelling are those that enhance conversation or the esteem of the teller.

Distinguishing between the needs of the teller and those of the listener is important here. It would seem that stories are memorised for retelling when they meet the needs of one or the other. Schank (1995) adds that it is the nature of story to have many indices linking to other thoughts, feelings and memories so they are effective in activating prior knowledge. The same story can link into many areas of cognitive structure, some of which are unspoken. Schank suggests that a recalled memory of any one of the indices will enable us to recall the gist of the story and then the story itself. Popular myth concurs with this, indicating that if one wants to convey an idea that will be retained, one should tell it in a story (Lesser and Prusak, 2004; Swap et al., 2004). However, the same reasoning could be applied on the basis of the engagement qualities of story (see earlier).

Memory for ideas within a story

So far, most of what I have said is related to memory for stories themselves. However, what may often be more important in education is the memorisation for ideas within stories. If a listener is interested in learning about something within the story she will need to distinguish it from its context in the story (separate figure from ground) and focus attention. I mentioned earlier that Marsh et al. (2003) were interested in how subjects were able to learn and remember factual material from stories and whether they recognised the source of the learning in the process of recall. They gave adult subjects story material to read. In some of the material all of the information was 'true' and in some there was true and untrue information. At least some of the information was new to subjects. In a test subsequent to the reading, there was evidence of some learning from the stories and subjects said that they could distinguish what they had learned from the recent story and what they knew already. However, they tended to attribute more of the material to prior knowledge than was the case. The researchers concluded that there was integration of the story knowledge with prior knowledge, but not always awareness of the source. They suggest that where subjects had known of the answers in prior knowledge, this probably 'increased the ease with which it came to mind at test' (Marsh et al., 2003). Where material in the stories was untrue, even though subjects knew that there was misinformation within the stories, they were influenced by the stories and often gave the untrue responses in the test, saying that they had known this before. The researchers suggest that we may tend to approach stories less critically than other material. In other experiments, Prentice et al. (1997) and Wheeler et al. (1999) showed that learners were apt to believe and reassert ideas after reading stories, when the idea was inaccurate and when the fictitious nature of the story was emphasised. In the earlier section, I suggest that these findings relate to processes of engagement and the suspension of disbelief. Clearly they relate also to the nature of memory for ideas in story.

Social memory

Much of what I have said above about the reconstructive processes of memory relates also to the social aspects of memory, but the significance of this in terms of memory is the social influence of stories passed through communities and cultures. Individuals remember and learn from ideas that have been produced in the milieu of a culture. Middleton and Edwards indicate that this is more than saying that people reminisce together about their family experiences, for example at a wedding:

> what is recalled ... extends beyond the sum of the participants' individual perspectives: it becomes the basis of future reminiscence ... People reinterpret and discover features of the past that become the context and content of what they will jointly recall on future occasions. [Groups] collectively reconstruct what the culture already 'knows' as part of its socio-historical evolution.
>
> (Middleton and Edwards, 1990: 7, 8)

Within a culture we learn what to remember or/and what it is acceptable to represent from memory. I use this to lead into Chapter 5 on social and cultural influences and story.

Thinkpoint

... humanity might be enchanted into a less destructive, more meditative mode by reading stories.

(From an article about Gregory Bateson in the *Guardian* by Tim Parks (2008))

Social, cultural and communication functions of story

Introduction

Stories create many social and cultural links with people and places perhaps far away in distance, time or life experience. This chapter addresses these communications function of story, though I am choosing not to separate them. If a story is communicated by one person to another, there is inevitably a social element, and if there is a social element, there is inevitably a cultural context within the story, affecting the storytelling and its teller and listeners. If I talk of story as a repository of cultural information there are associated social and communication issues. The meaning of 'culture' has required a little more consideration. I can apply the term to the culture of a nation or race, or I can apply it to an organisation or small community or group. Much of what I will be saying in this chapter applies at all levels – and I will comment where distinction needs to be made.

As with the previous two theory chapters, there are many aspects of this chapter to which I will return in later areas of the book, but here, in particular, I focus on story at the interpersonal level and education as a site of significant interpersonal interactions. Where I return to a topic later, I deal with it here in less detail.

Within this chapter, I have considered various social uses of story and have covered each under a separate heading. I list them here in order to provide an overview of the chapter, though the first heading is a review in itself. I have tried to sequence the sections so that they most logically feed into each other. The sections are as follows:

- a review of the social role of story;
- story as satisfying human interaction needs and entertainment;
- story as a means of conveying information, knowledge and unspoken understandings in a social group;
- story as a representation of expectations and norms of behaviour;
- story as a means of transmitting culture and as a repository for culture; ·
- story as a conveyor of morality and subversion and as an initiator of social change;
- story and its role in education and the sharing of views of the world.

In the text, to avoid the cumbersome wording 'social/cultural/communication', I will tend to refer to the social function of story unless I need to be more specific.

A review of the social role of story

I start this section by drawing together ideas that have been discussed in previous chapters and I then cover some general issues.

In Chapter 4, I suggested that the quality of engagement is important in stories. It is central to many of the social functions of story as it provides the incentive for people to listen to story. People also seem to have a drive to tell stories, to think in stories (Goldacre, 2008) and to remember story material as a package (Crace, 2008) – communicating in the unspoken areas as well as in language. The unspoken element may be enhanced by the manner in which stories can be made vivid through visual or other imagery, and the range of information carried in a story increases the likelihood of remembering (Schank, 1995). Something that is memorable has a greater chance of becoming embedded in cultural 'memory' and thence part of what we call tradition or heritage. There is also a greater chance that the story will move into circulation in a community, where it may undergo transformative processes. Something that is memorable is also more likely to be influential. I have talked about how story can influence people, by shaping the manner in which they think and behave, and sometimes it will lead them to change (Chapters 4 and 10). In the context of this chapter, I see change not only as personal, but also as potentially political (Grumet, 1987). Stories may deal with power in their subject matter – and they can be powerful (Campbell with Moyers, 1988; Plummer, 1995; Hertog and McLeod, 2001). Through their power, they can subvert even on a world scale (Zipes, 2006). Leman (2007), for example, talks of the role of stories in the 'sewing of mistrust between east and west' during the cold war. Stories can educate or manipulate and there may sometimes be little to distinguish between these intentions. Influential stories can become infused with meaning that is not that intended by the teller, but equally stories can encourage the rethinking of issues – perhaps about the societal group or the organisation of which listeners are a part (Snowden, 2004). Story as a form of communication is centrally involved in the manner in which human societies function.

In this chapter, it is also important to bear in mind some of the rhetoric of story and human lives. We can be said to live our lives through layers of story. We construct and create our selves by seeing ourselves as part of the stories that 'we continually spin for ourselves, inside or outside ourselves. We "story" our lives' (Kenyon and Randall, 2001: 4). We are also part of 'larger stories' that are 'intersecting social systems ... each with their own plot lines, characters, genres ... and implicit master narratives in terms of which we interpret the wider world' – the master narratives being 'friends, family, institutions, community ... in concentric layers' (Randall, 2001: 39–40). So there is story within individual identity and within the social and cultural aspects of the life of that individual. Around and about that individual are the stories of others touching the individual through hearsay or the media. While stories are mainly social (McCloskey, 1990) it is important not to forget the exceptions to this. There can sometimes be comfort in making sense of something by telling a story to oneself, in one's mind, or in writing in a journal (Moon, 2006) or in the construction of a satisfying piece of fiction in written or spoken form.

Story as satisfying human interaction needs and entertainment

If, as it seems, each person has to make sense of the world though her unique internal experience (Chapter 3), it could be said that as individuals we have a lonely existence as no one else sees the world in the same way. However, because they engage, because they draw from human experiences of emotion and knowledge and because they draw context along with them, stories potentially build on listeners' internal experiences. This implies that people listening to the same story can become involved in a kind of community experience (Gersie, 1992; Thomas and Killick, 2007). As Lauritzen and Jaeger say:

> Story provides a sense of community with its common points of reference ... With each story that we share, we feel a closer relationship with each other. If we know the same stories, we share much more than just the information contained in the pages.
>
> (Lauritzen and Jaeger, 1997: 43)

Maslin-Ostrowski and Ackerman (1998), talking of learning from 'case stories', emphasise the importance of the sharing process in working in this way. They say: 'story works ... as a communal activity. The power of sharing stories lies. ... in the communal act of sharing stories. Meaning for participants doesn't only lie in their stories. The collective grasping of experiences reflectively also leads to meaning' (Maslin-Ostrowski and Ackerman, 1998: 315).

These ideas of communality of story may be implied in Bruner's words – that story works 'by making the familiar more familiar' (Bruner 1990: 41). Stories confirm our state within a culture or a group of people both because we have common understandings and experiences and also because other groups have different implicit understandings of what counts as a story (Claxton, 1999; McLeod, 1997). We identify with one group or we determine our difference from another. Both contribute towards the development of the sense of belonging – of being bound socially with others (Donald, 1998).

The sense of belonging through story is often enacted at informal social gatherings. After the sharing of news, conversation will often turn into the exchange of stories. Schank (1995) talks of the process of exchange as 'story trading' (p. 20). He says: 'Participating in a conversation means reminding oneself of a good story to tell, either by telling one you have already told or by the far more difficult process of creating a new one' (p. 26).

There are various social motivations at work in these story exchanges. It is interesting, for example, to consider for whose benefit any story is told. Is it the teller or the listener who benefits – or are both engaged in 'having a good social time' through the agency of stories? I have mentioned the people who do not tell stories in social (or work) situations, and their conversation can seem drab; and there are others who trade on the same stories over and again. Schank (1995) observed that people are skilled and less skilled in telling appropriate stories that sufficiently relate to the previously told story to keep a sense of coherence to the conversation. There is also capability in sensing the appropriate length of the story and general 'tone' for a social setting. We might think of awkward times when we have told stories that have come to seem inappropriate halfway through. We detect this by 'reading' the response of others! I will return to Wilson's (2006) argument that higher education graduates need 'story literacy' and Schank's point that the ability to manage story in conversation is a form of intelligence.

The trading of stories can have an important place in work/organisational situations (McNaughton, 1998). Gabriel (2000) talks at length about his study of the role of story in organisations. While often they might seem to be simply social communication, he suggests that they can be a means of humanising 'the impersonal spaces of bureaucratic organisations, to mark them as human territory, as does a vase of flowers or the family picture on the executive desk' (Gabriel, 2000: 57). He found that many of the stories that were told to him could be seen 'as attempts to conquer human suffering' (p. 93), attempts to feel cared for and respected as a person in 'impersonal spaces'. They were not told simply for social purposes.

Whether we would classify the role of story in general conversation as 'entertainment' or as a way of seeking comfort depends on the perception of 'entertainment'. The same story could be entertaining to one listener in a conversation and not entertaining to another. Gabriel gives an example of a story that could be either entertainment or relief from suffering depending on interpretation. The story goes thus: a man hurried into work each day, past the same guards on the gate. He would shout good morning and wave his ID card at them. But one day he did not have his card with him. He was sent home. For the subject telling the story about his experience, telling might have been a relief from suffering. However, later the story might have been told to raise humour at the absurdity of strict rules. There is little point in trying to make firm distinctions between the 'entertainment' and general social interaction roles of story – unless the situation is clearly one with the named purpose of entertainment.

The entertainment role of story has an important social application. Stories feature in the novels that we read, the stories of creative writing sessions, on the news, in poetry, film and in drama, 'soap' and in the strip cartoon (etc.). They are entertainment in the sense that storytelling traditions have existed throughout histories across the world. Oral storytelling has never gone away, though its role may change. It is 'a fixture of both the past and the present' (Lauritzen and Jaeger, 1997: 35). Oral storytelling is the subject of Chapter 13.

Story as a means of conveying information, knowledge and unspoken understandings in a social group

I begin this section by thinking of story and communication in a personal context in order to illustrate some of the issues to be covered. Supposing I listen to a radio play which is set in a country that I plan to visit. I might be keen to learn from the story. But what do I mean by 'learn'? If I assume that to 'learn' means to change my internal experience and to have a better conception of what it is to be in that country, how do I judge what is relevant in the story for this learning – and how do I learn it? How do I retain the information and to what structures of knowledge can I link it in my cognitive structure? I might be better able to retain the information if I retain the context of the story – though it could take effort/time to abstract the generalised learning from the story. How would I then judge the credibility of the story separately from the story? I would probably find the knowledge patchy (McCloskey, 1990). However, some of what I would have learned is likely to have been in the nature of the unspoken – the atmosphere portrayed of the country, the imagery and scenes that I might encounter, the moods and feelings that I might experience. The unspoken, of course, is just as likely to be designed to make a 'good story' as to be 'accurate' portrayal – do I need to put it into words to retain it?

Oral storytelling in the past did not just entertain. Storytellers carried news between isolated communities, and the exchange of news represents a power to exchange experiences that lies at the heart of storytelling (Benjamin, 1968). In this section I consider the role of story in conveying ideas, the nature of information that can be conveyed well by story and where story does not work so well. This is an important issue in this book on educational situations.

I start with a couple of observations. The first relates to the historical context of story. In the relative absence of literacy or print, the main spread of information in communities was through oral story in person to person interaction. In this age of information technology, it is easy to get factual information and it may be that the role of stories in the spread of information and knowledge has changed. Second, it seems that when something surprising or significant happens, many enjoy the anticipation of conveying the story of it to others. 'Being first with the news' can bring a sense of importance.

There are some factors in story that can distort the conveying of information. I have said that stories tend to be designed to engage the listener (Chapter 4). The need to engage may affect the manner in which information is carried in a story. It may be held back in order to engage through suspense, and then it becomes subservient to the storyline. In a similar way, there is an issue about reality and the passage of information if it is the case that listeners tend to forgo some critical judgements in listening to story. It is relevant to cite again Gabriel's question: 'would a listener respond [to a story] by challenging the factual accuracy of the text?' (2000: 28). A state of suspended judgement is not most suited to the reception of reliable information! So the making of a good story may supersede the importance of conveying information. In this context I have mentioned already the distortion of scientific or health information, particularly by the media, that has come to be known as 'bad science' (Goldacre, 2008).

However, I have also said also that sometimes stories convey information in a way that does help learning. The chance of learning from story may be increased if there is knowledge to build on – if the internal experience is such that it is ready for the assimilation of the information in the story, and possible accommodation to it. This relates to the suggestion by Swap et al. (2004) that stories help the memory for information when they elaborate on existing ideas.

Story is also valuable where the required learning focuses on the whole unit of the story, with its context. An example of this use of a story is case study or critical incident or in the sharing of professional (or other) experience for mutual development of understanding (Chapters 8 and 9). Perhaps the overriding value of story in its conveying of information is through its unspoken elements. I give an example. A new student – a fresher – wants to find her way around the college but feels alienated from those who pass her, walking confidently around, knowing their destinations. Finally it is the library assistant who really listens to her and helps her. The story conveys little real information, but much unspoken material. If the story about the student was a case study for academics working on improving the induction processes for new students, it would be the link between the unspoken elements of story and the elements of information that would be important. It is for this mix of story elements – information and unspoken – that story is valued and utilised in many contexts. It is seen as a holder of the 'soft knowledge' of how to operate in a particular context.

Stories may not work well for the conveyance of straight facts or 'fact-as-information' Gabriel (2000: 27). In the context of organisations, Swap et al. (2004) say, 'Stories do not lend themselves … to transferring (some) different kinds of knowledge. As a *strategy* for building core capabilities within an organisation, an indiscriminate use of stories … would probably be misguided … Deep knowledge of a content domain would be very difficult to transmit via stories' (Swap et al., 2004: 189). Reasons for this can be drawn from areas of Chapter 4 that suggests that stories are framed as units separated from their outside contexts but the information in a story is usually enmeshed within the storyline or the context of the story. It takes effort to extract it (Marsh et al., 2003). The information has a role in the story. In a story of how the survivor of a shipwreck fared on a desert island there might be much information about survival, but the information is there to make the story work. It is likely to be patchy and unsystematic. However, there have been stories written deliberately to convey information – and *Swiss Family Robinson* is one. It was written to promote good family values and good husbandry. The unabridged version contains more detail than is directly required for the storyline (Seelye, 2007). The UK's BBC Radio 4 story of farming life, *The Archers*, was initiated in order to pass on information about farming life, and again information may sometimes go beyond that required to drive the story.

However, now I must question what I have just written and, indeed, place the proverbial spanner into the whole of the works of this section. Maybe I cannot learn effectively from the story above because of the manner in which I have learned to learn and process information in this western culture. Donaldson (1992) suggests that there are differences in the manner in which people process information in different cultures and in different periods of history. I give an example. Lauritzen and Jaeger (1997) illustrate this. They say that Australian aboriginal peoples traditionally do not use maps in order to know their whereabouts but tell and learn special stories that include place names and their relative locations and positions and thus they find their way – 'The story provides a verbal map of the relationship of each place to other places' (Lauritzen and Jaeger, 1997: 36). This use of story for the transmission of information would be unfamiliar to many who have the formal and abstracted styles of education in what is termed 'the western world'.

Story as a representation of expectations and norms of behaviour

This heading can cover the specific expectations of behaviour of individuals or the more generalised expectation of groups in the population. I want to focus on the ways in which story might help people to learn to behave in accordance with the general norms of a social group. Early research on this related to early childhood education. Bettelheim's book (1976) is a classic. Bettelheim worked as a teacher with disturbed children and he wanted to find a way of restoring meaning to the lives of the children. He felt that children required literature that stimulated the imagination and helped them to clarify their emotions. He says:

> the child needs to be given the chance to understand himself in this complex world with which he must learn to cope ... [He must] be helped to make some coherent sense out of the turmoil of his feelings. He needs ideas on how to bring his inner house into order and on that basis to be able to create order in his life ... [He also needs] a moral education which subtly, and by implication only, conveys to him the advantages of moral behaviour ... The child finds this kind of meaning though fairy tales.
>
> (Bettelheim, 1976: 5)

Bettelheim (1976) says that fairy stories are attuned to the child's 'anxieties and expectations and give full recognition to his difficulties, while at the same time suggesting solutions to the problems which disturb[ed] him' (p. 5). They deal with the tragedies too, such as death, remarriage, aggression, love (and so on). They provide examples of solutions to the problems through working with stereotypes that are simplified versions of the real-world experiences. They work subconsciously and consciously and because the parent gives the stories to the child in such a way that the stories acquire a sense of acceptability. Bettelheim seems to suggest that fairy stories have been honed to relate to the stage of epistemological development of the young child. They might draw on some authority or 'wisdom of the past' (Wood and Richardson, 1992) – we could assume that they become shaped towards effectiveness over the many retellings, forgettings and reconstructions. Zipes (2007) adds that fairy stories have helpful outcomes for young people and he justifies his argument in relation to theoretical material from genetics, memetics (the evolutionary study of the cultural transmission of information), linguistics and evolutionary theory (Dowling, 2007). Zipes (1997) sees the 'modernised' and 'Disneyfied' versions of fairy stories as a profit-motivated distortion of the real stories.

Drama (Neelands, 1992), novels and television are all ways in which culture, with its associated expectations and norms, is transmitted. In some cases this can be more deliberate than in others. In recent years, there have been many books for teenagers that incorporate ideas about what it is to be a modern adolescent and how to deal with some of the problems that arise during those years (e.g. *Clean Break* by Jackie Wilson (2005)). Plummer's (1995) book on the telling of sexual stories demonstrates how people learn patterns of sexual expectations and behavioural norms from stories. He talks of 'puberty stories, marriage-bed stories, perversion stories, coming out stories, abuse survivor stories, women's fantasy stories, men's tribal fairy stories, stories of living – and dying – from Aids' (p. 4). Such real-life stories have become infinitely more common in media 'reality' since he wrote his book.

Empirical work on this topic of expectation, focusing on adults, has been published by the University of Toronto group. They argue, in a series of papers, that the brain is triggered by fiction stories to simulate the actions of the story – both those within the story itself and others triggered by the story (Oatley, 1999; Mar and Oatley, 2008; Oatley, 2008a). They suggest that the simulation supports the behaviour of the reader in social situations in real life. 'Thus imagined settings and characters evoked by fiction literature likely engage the same areas of the brain as those used during the performance of parallel actions and perceptions' (Mar and Oatley, 2008). The writers go on to cite a number of papers that indicate that 'four out of five of the brain areas commonly associated with narrative processing ... are also commonly implicated in studies of social processing' (e.g. Lieberman, 2007; Saxe and Wexler, 2005). They also suggest that those who read more fiction tend to be more socially adept than readers of non-fiction. Though it might follow logically from their findings, to me this generalisation is a little surprising in relation to personal observations.

There are occasions, of course, where stories misguide expectations. I mentioned the example of bad science above, and a recent BBC Radio 4 programme told of how Asian people who were expelled from Uganda in the 1970s came to the UK expecting it to be like the culture and country that are the setting for the stories of Enid Blyton that they had read (Collingridge, 2009).

Story as a means of transmitting culture and as a repository for culture

This section draws on what I have said of culture in earlier sections of this chapter. Culture determines the form of interaction between people, defines what is 'entertaining', affects styles of communication and the role of the unspoken, and it affects the expectations that people have. Bruner (1990) describes culture as a set of stories that we enter. He says that it is as if humans 'walk on stage into a play whose enactment is already in progress – a play whose somewhat open plot determines what part we may play' (p. 216). This is not very different from Campbell's suggestion that mythology (story) is like 'an interior road map of experience, drawn by people who have travelled it' (Campbell with Moyers, 1988: xiv). The notion that stories are a repository for culture relates to both of these quotations, even though the word 'repository' has somewhat static connotations. Stories reflect the current experiences of the teller and the listener, who interprets them in the context of her own present culture, even she is relying on a view of the past at the same time (Lieblich and Josselson, 1997). In this sense, culture is renewed and reformed all of the time by its constant reinterpretation and its content of story matter. Campbell makes this point very elegantly when he talks of a woman who held that 'all those Greek gods and stuff are irrelevant to the human condition today'. He comments:

> What she did not know – what most of us do not know – is that the remnants of all that 'stuff' line the walls of our interior system of belief like shards of broken pottery in an archaeological site. But as we are organic beings, there is energy in all that 'stuff'. Rituals evoke it.
>
> (Campbell with Moyers, 1988: xiv)

Stories are one of the important rituals that evoke those shards that line the substance of our lives. The sense of the past in the minds of most people is as a series of stories that have captured the imagination and lie in the memory with the associated unspoken material. The material is not systematic – it is distorted and stereotyped and it is only a sampling of realities, and we, as listeners, have filled in the 'gaps' (McCloskey, 1990: 19). Because stories incorporate our own cultural identities, there have been times when the carriage of traditional stories has been of great importance – such as when people have migrated. Then the telling and retelling of their own stories have been both comforting and an important manner in which their identity could be maintained. Judging by the manner in which the same story can appear in various versions all over the world, this 'weightless' possession has long been in the baggage of travellers, whether through entertainment of the local population or through eventual intermarriage. Cinderella is one such story (Carter, 1991).

Understanding the relationship between story and culture and identity, the Brothers Grimm reiterated and reinterpreted traditional stories in order to stabilise German society in the early to mid-1800s and to encourage a return to the Germanic traditions – as well as furthering their wish that the old tales should be preserved (Grimm and Grimm, n.d.; Carter, 1991). They were relying on the reciprocal manner in which culture and tradition influence story and stories told influence the culture and tradition and ensure that it maintains its vibrancy (Polkinghorne, 1988).

Culture is a word that is applied also to the culture of organisations – and similar relationships with story pertain. For Boje (1991) the telling of a diverse range of stories acts as the 'institutional memory of the organisation' (p. 106). Anyone in the organisation can construct the memory by adding and transmitting stories. They can tap into the culture in order to explain or construct another story, and they reconstruct the cultural memory continuously as they apply the stories to current experience. Gabriel (2000) is somewhat sceptical as to whether Boje's 'stories' would come into his definition of story, but he manages in his own research to provide evidence for the manner in which stories carry memory that supports workers in their working practices. He says that the support that knowing the common stories and traditions provides to the workers develops a sense of belonging. Telling a story or joke or sharing a rumour can confirm that belonging (Heath et al., 2001; Guerin and Miyazaki, 2006; Thomas and Killick, 2007). In turn that culture shapes the way people behave, and signals to them what they might find significant in that the subject matter in the stories and anecdotes often concerns what is considered to be exceptional in day-to-day living, pointing out the boundaries of 'usual' experience (McNaughton, 1998).

The knowledge in the repository may be the shards that line the walls of our life, but there are times when we need to dip back into more specific knowledge that they hold. The Transition Town movement (http://www.transitiontowns.org/) encourages communities across the world to develop an understanding of and ways of managing the threats of climate change. It is suggested that there is valuable learning from looking to the old skills, and stories of the way people managed on fewer resources (e.g. during wars) are becoming important in demonstrating resourcefulness and resilience (Hopkins, 2008).

Story as a conveyor of morality and subversion and as an initiator of social change

Morality includes knowing how others think or act and about making considered judgements about one's own actions. Knowledge of what is seen as moral and of moral behaviour and its consequences is displayed by characters in stories. There is also a moral stance implied in the telling (Tappan 1991). On the basis of his research, Day (1991) says that when participants in his studies 'give accounts of their moral conduct, they do it through the medium of stories. These stories are more than parallels to or corollaries of the information with which they are associated. They are central features of the meaning that participants have made, crucial elements in the behaviour that has been observed and reported' (p. 27, 28). They determine how the morality is interpreted.

The content of previous sections in this chapter is clearly relevant to this section. Morality is inevitably carried and revealed when story is a medium of human interaction, whether told as entertainment or in fulfilling any other purpose. Bettelheim's (1976) suggestion that children learn from the morality in fairy tales is paralleled by the concerns about the moralities portrayed in some current forms of story such as gaming. Stories in the media keep morality 'updated', or concern might be voiced that they seem to drive change in morality and to push the boundaries of acceptability at a given time.

Many of the issues of morality in story are not overt, but are conveyed though unspoken elements of the story – such as the way in which the story is told, its context, the words used or the manner in which people react to each other's behaviour. Some moral stories are explicit in their direct meaning, but many are in the form of allegory, fables and parables, and these rely on communication through metaphor (McFague TeSelle, 1975), with a message that is not usually explicit, though it may be obvious ('slow and steady won the race'). Another means by which a story can carry moral messages is, as Bruner (1990: 47) says, by 'explicating deviations from the normal in a comprehensible way' – by providing the logic and providing it in a manner that is designed to steer the beliefs of listeners in the direction desired by the teller. Hastie and Davies (2001) say in their research on courtroom stories that 'good trial attorneys know that good stories win cases' (p. 135). A more open manner of teaching moral thinking is that suggested by Fisher (1999) and Thomas and Killick (2007), where stories are designed to encourage thinking and discussion about particular issues – in these cases, with young children.

While stories can carry messages about how people do tend to act under normal circumstances, they can also subvert what is normal by demonstrating the successful breaking of established codes of morality or expected behaviour or by making the 'code' questionable. In this way they may initiate social change. Going back to Bruner's metaphor of culture being the ongoing play that we enter, story carries the message of the play but it can also carry a changing of the storyline. Rumour can be spread and stories planted in order to subvert the thinking of social groups, often against others. As I write this a media saga of this kind plays itself out. A close advisor to the current UK prime minister, Gordon Brown, sent e-mails to a colleague suggesting that fictitious stories, designed to smear the reputations of political opponents, should be put onto a website. Of course there is denial all round!

Various attempts are made to exert control over the content of formally produced stories (film and publication or speech) in the form of censorship or the banning of free speech. Carter (1991), for example, talks of the 'cleaning up' of traditional and fairy stories that occurred during the nineteenth century. This involved the removal of references to 'sexual and excremental functions' and modifications of the stories towards the standards of the 'refined pastime of the middle classes especially of the middle class nursery' (Carter, 1991: xvii). Fairy stories became then the material for childhood. Censorship may, of course, draw attention to the messages that it attempts to curtail and to the fact that one group is making judgements for another. The widespread availability of the relatively uncontrollable internet, changes the practices and issues of censorship considerably.

The subversive influences in story also may be focused on changing prevailing attitudes or allegiances towards action or behaviour. Zipes (2006) has called the story 'the cunning thief' in this connection (cited by Wilson, 2006). Subversive stories are cunning and undercover. Some advertising copy aims to subvert – where, for example, an effective story is generated that encourages the development of belief in one product in contrast to another, but which also survives the listener's critical considerations. Stories with unspoken elements that support the provision of selected information, and which, at the same time engage listeners, can be agents of change of attitude and subsequently of behaviour. This effectiveness might be explained again by the notion that stories encourage the suspension of disbelief. With criticality suspended and with the listener engaged, sense-making processes in accommodation may be seen as reduced and there is a chance that the persuasion to accept or change ideas is more acceptable. If the elements of the story itself are fairly consistent with elements of internal experience, and if they touch other aspects of experience, then it becomes more difficult for the listener to avoid persuasion.

Leman (2007) looked at the structure of persuasive conspiracy stories following the 9/11 attacks in New York, and the deaths of President Kennedy and Princess Diana. For a long time there was wide belief in a story that Diana's death was a deliberate and planned action, and not an accident. Conspiracy stories like this subvert the given story. Leman acknowledges that while 'we need people to "think outside the box", even if there is usually more sense to be found inside the box', we do need those who will question the 'official line'. He acknowledges too that 'for canny politicians or campaigners, conspiracy theories can be a good way of exploiting people's fears by promulgating rumours that are difficult … to disprove'. He goes on to look at the qualities of a conspiracy theory about a real event that would tend to attract followers. Important components include the creation of a sense of uncertainty about the first interpretations of the event and the construction of new information that 'weaves together into a compelling story' and that utilises material 'that fits with [people's] existing beliefs' (Leman, 2007). Movements for change need to work to utilise the same qualities of stories – that are compelling and that relate to people's existing beliefs. Health education and environmental change initiatives draw on these ideas.

Story and its role in education and the sharing of views of the world

Clearly story has many roles in education and education is about change and the developing knowledge of the world. Everything I have said in this chapter about the ways in which story impinges on social functioning is relevant to its roles in education. The roles interact and intersect. Some might seem to be surprising; for example, teaching and its content have often been seen to be subversive in delivering hidden curricula (Postman and Weingartner, 1969) but we can also say that the stories told by teachers can subvert the hidden agendas of poverty. It is through story that views of the world are shared and expectations of others are developed – and through stories too that such expectations can be crushed. An important element of work that needs to be done in education at all levels is to enable students to recognise when a persuasive or subversive story is being told, and to be able to step outside that story and question it (Wilson, 2006).

Clearly there is much more to be said about the role of story in education in the following parts of the book, and both to summarise this section in this chapter and to introduce the way into the rest of the book I provide a general summary of the roles of story in education:

- associated with teaching or presenting material;
- associated with learning;
- associated with the construction of story;
- associated with the representation of thought processes to others (communication);
- associated with research;
- associated with the building of community and team;
- associated with entertainment in the processes of learning and teaching.

Thinkpoint

In my view, stories ... consist of three parts: narration, which moves the story from point A to point B and finally to point Z; description, which creates a sensory reality for the reader; and dialogue, which brings characters to life through their speech. You may wonder where plot is in all this. This answer – my answer, anyway, is nowhere ... I want you to understand that my basic belief is that stories make themselves.

(King 2001: 187, 188)

king stock

Reflecting on insights and the educational roles of story

Introduction

This book is in the spirit of enquiry – an exploration as much as an exposition. I have set out to learn about story and that was particularly the project of these first few chapters on theory. This chapter is a pause to reflect and to gather ideas and insights before I turn towards the educational applications in Part III. This chapter does not contain much new material and I have not repeated references.

In the first section of this chapter (p. 90) I aim to:

- reflect on what I have written and learned in the first five chapters;
- identify what I would call my 'insights' that arose in the writing – insights are marked with an asterisk (*);
- conclude this theory section of the book, having prepared the ground for the more practical chapters.

Reference to material of the earlier chapters is not necessarily in the sequence of those chapters.

The second section of this chapter turns to story in education, specifically higher education and professional development (p. 95). I gather educational issues and insights from the previous five chapters. These issues tend to be general – but important. Some are related to the insights described in the first section.

Taking stock: some reflection

I said in the Preface that in this project *I have been struck by the way in which humans seem to be driven to tell stories. They seem to be characteristic of our humanity, though I question some of the rather glib ways of saying this (that man is a 'storied' being). Another insight also arouse early on. *I had thought that story was one entity and that I would be able to construct a framework for it and relate all of story's uses in higher education to it. However, not only is story many different things, but there is also a vast number of purposes for telling and some purposes are beneficial for the teller and some for the listener. *The range of purposes for story was a surprise to me. So rapidly I found that story is very diverse and that creating one theory, one framework, one way of deriving the story activities of higher education is far from possible. Most others who write on story circumvent this problem by defining the area of story that is their concern and ignoring other meanings of story.

*Purposes that I found for story fell under the following headings:

- it acts as communication;
- it is a means of learning from experience;
- it can encompass the 'the bigger picture' about something, including unspoken material;
- it is a medium for the development of skills (storytelling);
- stories carry knowledge for learning;
- the construction of a story can be an aid to learning communication skills;
- a story can make a topic distinctive, assigning meanings, connotations, etc.
- stories are told in order to affect listeners – to act as entertainment, *aide-mémoires*, aid learning, engineer attitudes, aid identity formation, support thinking/change;
- stories have a role in shaping social behaviour, creating commonality/or influencing;
- stories have an effect on the teller;
- story is a way of stimulating thought in the listener;
- it is a means of research in academic or professional learning;
- it is a means of clarifying a complex or difficult situation;
- story is a means of constructing new knowledge;
- it is a form of transmission of traditional culture;
- it has a role in shaping belief systems.

Looking at the purposes for story was a way of 'reining in' the topic, in order to define it. *However, in the end it was convenient to think not of definition, but of boundaries inside which story sits. I used a large general boundary that enclosed all types of story, and two inner groupings – one that enclosed what I called the strong form of story (e.g. with structure, beginning, middle and end) and another that enclosed stories that do not have the tight structure (broad form story). In the course of this work on definition I had to think about the idea of plot. Plot provides surprise – it 'plays with' our cognitive dissonance (see Chapter 3). Stories with plot tend to fit into the strong story group. However, *I also began to see that new information that will surprise the listener also provides an experience of cognitive dissonance. In this case, however, the dissonance does not happen within the story but occurs between what is known already and the new information. So 'news' that surprises is a form of plot, and the contrast is not just inside the story, but between the story and its context.

In a book about the role of story in education, I needed to think about how humans might learn from story. As in other writing about pedagogy, I have taken a constructivist approach because it makes best sense to me. Chapter 3 aided my understanding of how humans learn from story and provided concepts to which I referred in subsequent chapters. *I find helpful the concepts of learning from story through the interplay of external and internal experiences and processes of elaboration from the flow of meaning in the story. *Stories may play with our processes of establishing internal experience by the deliberate creation of dissonance, where external experience is put into conflict with current internal experience. This is the stuff of plots and twists in story – and the idea of 'news'. I found that ideas such as figure/ground discrimination and variation have fitted in well with what I wanted to say about story.

After I had written the chapter on learning from story (Chapter 3), I came across the work of Keith Oatley and the team at the University of Toronto who work on the function of fiction. Though the team reasoned from a very different direction and they work with a narrower definition of story than me (fiction only) and draw on empirical studies, their material ties in with my own reasoning about learning from story. They use constructivist interpretations, though I feel that in the work that I have seen they do not express the full implications of this for human learning from story and they do not mention the role of the unspoken (see p. 46). Their view is that reading fiction is satisfying for humans as a learning experience because engaging in fiction is like engaging in a simulation of the events of the story.

There were a number of further insights about learning and story. *The first is that all story is fiction. It is all constructed. If I tell a story about a personal experience, I construct my perception of the experience and then I reconstruct the event in telling the story, and I probably tell the version of the story that is most appropriate for my audience and what I want to achieve from the telling.

*The second insight concerns the importance of the unspoken elements of story. In tuning the story that I tell to another, I manage the unspoken elements of the story as much as I manage the language of it. The association of what I have called the unspoken with story has been with me for some time, and the notion that story might be distinguished from what is not story partly on the basis of its unspoken content has developed as I have written and pondered further. There are two ways of looking at this and both may be correct. Either expository material may tend to favour explicit expression in language to a greater degree than story or story may be made engaging and more worthy of the effort to listen because of its unspoken content. Of course, stories differ in the amount of unspoken content present, and I suspect that stories that are strong form may contain more unspoken material than those that are broad form. *I think that it is the incorporation of unspoken material that makes story a powerful transmitter of information where holistic material is the main concern.

Emotion is significant as part of the unspoken content in story, although it may also be explicit. *I found that I could apply to story the ideas I developed in earlier books on emotion and learning. Emotion is related to story in many different ways. It can be the subject matter of story, generated in the story, in the atmosphere of the story, a consequence for the listener to story, catharsis for teller or listener. Many writers on story make scant reference to emotional content, but I suspect that emotion in its various forms, and explicit or unspoken, is a central feature of story.

*A third insight concerns the manner in which, as well as sitting in an external context, a story carries its own context with it. The metaphor of a snail in its environment, carrying its shell, comes to me. A story tends to be a unit unlike other forms of exposition. It has a flow of meaning of the unfolding storyline. The explicit and implicit content is likely to have stimulated the imagination of the listener, who is also likely to have some idea of the expected structure of the story (narrative/story structure). I have said that we are guided in learning by what we know already (internal experience) and that learning comprises the interplay between internal and new external experience. I suggest that the comprehensive nature of the internal context of story means that as the story progresses the context could be seen increasingly to 'take over' the content of the internal experience, which further guides understanding of the story as it unfolds through the continuing flow of the storyline as new external experience. I find it useful to imagine that the context of story aligns the new external experience with what we know already within the story. The further implication of this is that different people hearing the story are guided by the context to interpret story material similarly. This would suggest another reason why story is a powerful means of transmitting an idea.

*The thinking in the paragraph above suggests again the power of the unspoken and the process of engagement in story. The teller of a story manages the flow of potential external experience for the listener as best she can in order to manipulate the processes of assimilation and accommodation of the material for the listener. The teller cannot make the listener follow the direction; she can only entice the listener by making the storyline compelling (engaging).

I moved on in the theory chapters from thinking about the cognitive aspects of learning and story to thinking about the way in which we manage meaning. I use the word 'frame' as a tool for exploring what makes the meaning of story distinctive in itself or distinctive from its external context. Other than the obvious messages that a story is about to be told, the frames of meaning that I explored are:

- the 'narrative/story grammar or structure': an innate understanding of how a story is structured;
- the quality of engagement of a story: the many ways in which a story draws listeners in;
- issues of reality and unreality;
- the manner in which a story as a unit can stimulate reflection and possibly change.

At different times there were other features in this list, but they seemed to dissolve into one of these four.

I briefly review the meaning frames for story. In terms of narrative grammar, I do not feel a need to propose that we are 'programmed' for story. *I came to see the understanding of it as something more general, such as a set of expectations based on experience of stories and a tendency to endeavour to make sense and to explain – to round off meaning in some way. The sense-making, resolution and the teller's telling of story are factors among others that engage listeners. Why else tell a story to another but in order to engage? Engagement is also related to the way in which a story is a construction of a reality, whether purporting to be 'real life' or fiction or fantasy. Engagement is also related to the fourth of these frames of meaning – the way in which story can stimulate reflection and possibly change. There are sometimes elements in a story or in the broader context of the telling of a story that stimulate the listener to listen, and stimulate her to construct her own related stories. This may result from the pace of the telling (giving the listener time to think) or the existence of topics that link with her experiences. Such a mechanism for the encouragement of change is used in therapy and in situations in which change is desired.

Epistemological development and its relationship to story was another topic that I explored in order to reach new understandings. Epistemological development concerns the suggestion that there are qualitative differences in the manner in which people understand the nature of knowledge and that these can be described as a continuum of development. Epistemological development, in my view, is central to educational progress. *An insight that arose in this writing was the idea that a person's stage of epistemological development may differ according to whether she is following someone else's argument or constructing her own. I suggest that we may be able to function at an apparently higher stage of development if we are following ideas within a story, with the context built in, than if we are endeavouring to espouse our own ideas. *A means of supporting epistemological development might be to comprehend more sophisticated reasoning within fictitious content before we express material personally, and, indeed, *these ideas do lie behind some materials that are described in Chapter 7 – which I call 'graduated scenarios'.

At the end of the chapter on the deployment of meaning (Chapter 4) I consider the issue of memory. Memory issues include the unspoken as well as explicit story. *Some of the significance of memory disappears when one takes a constructivist view of learning because memory comprises the prior experience – the internal experience. Taking a constructivist view of learning also accounts for the constructed nature of memory. *In thinking about this it became evident just how much reconstruction occurs when a story is told from memory. It is reconstructed in the process of learning and telling, and finally it is reconstructed by the listener as she listens to it and interprets its meaning in relation to her prior experiences. *This demonstrates to me the significance of 'fixing' stories in the written word.

The topic of memory runs over into the chapter on social, cultural and communication functions of story (Chapter 5) because the memory of story, with its reconstructive processes, is at the heart of the communication of tradition and culture. Beyond the more general review of the social role of story, other roles for story are:

- satisfying needs for human interaction and entertainment;
- as a means of conveying information, knowledge and unspoken understandings in a social group;
- teaching us what to expect and the norms of behaviour;
- as a means of transmitting culture and as a repository for culture;
- as a conveyor of morality and subversion and an initiator of social change;
- many roles in education.

During the writing of this chapter I was thinking more of how all of this material relates to the activities of education and higher education in particular. *A growing insight related to the importance of being able to manage story in conversation, whether at the professional level or in everyday interactions. At first Schank's (1995) association of the personal management of story with intelligence seemed nonsensical, but I have come to agree with his case.

All of the social aspects of story have relevance to different areas of education because the process of educating – teaching and encouraging learning – is a social activity. The last heading is the start of the rest of the book!

Taking stock: some general issues for story in higher education

This section gathers issues and insights from earlier chapters that concern story in education. I repeat some of the insights above and much of the material will be elaborated later in later chapters.

I start by considering *where story finds a place in education*. Quite separately, it is associated with:

- teaching or presenting material;
- learning (subject of study or of learning from experience in professional development);
- the construction process (e.g. in creative writing, drama, etc.);
- the representation of thought to others (as a communication ability);
- research (in different ways);
- the building of community (among and between groups who work in an educational institution, organisation, research community, etc.);
- entertainment within disciplines (e.g. drama) or as a component of pedagogy techniques.

While story is beneficial in many areas of education, though, also *education is about counteracting our drives to tell stories too easily*. This is derived from the thinking around the suggestion that humans seem to be driven to make sense of their environment in stories – and perhaps to 'jump to conclusions' in the form of a good story. It often seems that we need story more than we need 'truth' – especially when 'truth' is not entertaining to us. Education – especially higher education – is partly about the development of the ability to make good independent judgements using good critical thinking. Higher education could be said to be about countering our human tendency to be lured by the satisfying story. Students need to learn to recognise story and to work with it in a critical manner, particularly where it is presented as explanation (across all disciplines). In science this idea is represented in the notion of 'bad science'. Alongside that we have movements towards raising public awareness of science and often this involves conveying scientific ideas to the public in attractive story forms.

I have suggested in the first section that story seems to be an efficient carrier of information and that this is likely to be because of the volume of unspoken information carried in a story. Perhaps it is because of this that the University of Toronto group's empirical research indicates that *fictitious story simulates reality* and from that, *it facilitates the learning of social capacities*. This might also be taken to mean that *from story we can learn from experience in a vicarious manner*. Much of the content of formal education is about vicarious experiencing.

Beyond the communication and knowledge construction aspects of story to the individual, one could say that *it is a graduate and professional skill to be able to use, respond to and work with story effectively*. Being sensitive to story and knowing how to manage it (whether fiction or non-fiction) is an important capacity in communication. Being able to get the gist of a story and to respond appropriately is a form of social intelligence and a component of 'being professional'. In many teamwork situations, the basis of the team's functioning and operation is the telling of and listening to stories, both formally and informally.

Following from the last paragraph, *the sharing stories is part of the way in which community works*. Higher education for teaching staff and students is a set of communities to which people belong within the greater community of the institution. People probably learn what their colleagues are doing often more through stories told socially than through formal information sessions.

Story has many features that make it *attractive as an educational resource or tool*. We need to attract students, to engage their attention and enable them to enjoy learning. Story engages in the following ways:

- it can capture the holistic and lived experience of the subject being taught;
- it can tap into the imagination and emotions and form new and meaningful connections between existing areas of knowledge that can be neglected in conventional practices;
- it can work in the mind of students in the way that lectures do not – because it is not a traditional teaching method it represents a 'change';
- it is a tool for the enhancement of reflective learning;
- it seems possible to enhance memory by embedding ideas in story: there seems to be a 'holistic' memory which is more effective than that of isolated facts; some evidence for this is in the manner in which stories are learned in the processes of oral storytelling by storytellers – however, extracting ideas from story can be difficult.

Story is the stuff of examples and illustrations. Sometimes too it is the way of *trying out or exploring ideas.* It is often the representation of the real world that enables us to relate the abstractions of theory to the range of human everyday or professional experiences. Case studies, case histories or critical incidents exploit this. Sometimes the material that is explored in story is personal. *Story relates to learning about the self,* for example in learning journals in the context of discipline learning or in student success programmes in the USA or personal development planning in the UK.

The ability to tell stories orally is strongly related to the process of teaching and presentation. Telling a story involves engaging listeners and other capabilities of presentation. Teachers learning to teach and students learning to present and communicate with others need these capabilities. Oral storytelling practice can have a valuable role in teacher education and in teaching students to give presentations.

Story is, of course, a formal part of some disciplines – it is the subject matter in media and journalism, drama, culture and language subjects, anthropology, history and creative writing, law and more. It plays a part in sociology and medicine, and then I could add social work and nursing and other professional subjects. The list grows as I shift from strong to broad story form.

There are many different ways in which *we, as humans, learn from story – whether it is fiction or labeled 'fact'.* The priority might first be to recognise where story is being used, and then to think about how it is being used.

Thinkpoint

The missing nail caused the horse to go lame, caused the message to arrive late, caused the army to be unprepared, caused the invader's victory, caused the nation to lose the war, caused the monarch to lose the throne ... Human beings, perhaps uniquely among animals, create mental models of situations they are in, and those situation models often take the form of stories.

(Hastie and Davies, 2001: 130)

Story in higher education and professional development

A treasury of ideas

Part III of the book is written with a practical slant, and in a variety of styles and depth of detail – sometimes as flowing text and sometimes as collections of ideas and reports on what others have done. There are reports on what others have done with references, and bullet points. There are examples and illustrations. However, all focus on the teaching and learning processes of advanced education.

This part of the book, therefore, is not very systematic. Some readers may pick chapters of apparent relevance to their needs, though I believe that in every chapter there will be references to ideas that should interest anyone working in higher education, professional development or other areas of education. The chapter titles more or less indicate their own subject matter and they cover the enhancement of thinking (Chapter 7); the role of story in personal and professional development (Chapter 8); story as case study, scenario and critical incident (Chapter 9); the manner in which story can stimulate change, particularly in therapy and organisations (Chapter 10); the roles of story in research (Chapter 11). Then there are three chapters (Chapters 11, 12 and 13) on special factors: the use of fiction in education; oral storytelling; and what I have called 'new ways' with story, which mainly concerns technological developments that affect the manner in which stories are told, or sometimes constructed.

Chapter 7

Enhancing thinking and learning processes with story

Introduction

This chapter is a collection of story techniques that are designed to help to improve processes of thinking, learning and the representation of learning. They are arranged in four sections. The first, on graduated scenarios (p. 101), presents a method of helping learners to understand difficult-to-describe learning practices – such as reflective learning and critical thinking. I include a sample activity on reflective learning. It is a basic method waiting to be adapted to other contexts. The second section concerns the use of patchwork texts that allow learners to approach a topic from different perspectives (p. 108). The third section describes some story-based materials designed to prompt thinking and discussion about working in groups (p. 110).

The fourth section consists of activities to enhance the epistemological development and critical thinking of learners (p. 111). A number of references cited in theory chapters are repeated in this practical context.

Graduated scenarios: facilitating learning of difficult-to-describe practices (e.g. reflective learning, critical thinking)

Introduction

Learners in higher education not only have to learn to manage knowledge that is epistemologically complex but they also have to learn to process knowledge using challenging methods. Examples of the methods are reflective writing, critical thinking, clinical reasoning, processes of evaluation and professional practice (e.g. teaching itself). These methods are often unfamiliar to learners and difficult to convey. They are the sort of activities about which teachers themselves might say, 'I cannot explain it but I know good practice when I see it.' In addition, the ideas behind the practices are constructed and therefore definitions vary, which complicates matters further, and the ideas involved are often unspoken and not accessible in language – the communication of the classroom.

I first encountered such difficulties in working with learners on reflective writing. Some could write reflectively straightaway, but many would struggle and then write superficially or descriptively in ways that are less conducive to learning. Graduated scenario exercises deal with both introducing and improving these difficult-to-describe practices (Moon, 2004, 2006, 2008a, 2009b). In this section, I illustrate graduated scenarios with an example for reflective writing (the actual exercise at the end of the section, p. 103).

I use the graduated scenario exercise on reflective learning for both teachers and learners. The handouts consist of:

- three or four accounts of the same incident or story written, in the case of reflective writing, to demonstrate a progression from superficial and descriptive writing to deep reflective writing ('depth' being well researched – Moon, 2004);
- a list of changes in the quality of reflective writing from the first to final account;
- the Generic Framework for Reflective Writing.

Learners work in groups of around six. They are asked to read the first account, starting at the same time. When most have finished reading, groups are asked to discuss how reflective the account is. After a few minutes, they are asked to read the next account, and again, when it is read, discuss it – and so on. When groups have discussed the last account, participants are asked to identify the 'strands' that change between the accounts that make the final account more deeply reflective than the first. For example, one strand concerns the emotional content and management of it. These strands may not be represented in all of the accounts (e.g. in this example, it is only in the last two that there is any metacognition). Groups are then given flipchart paper and markers and are asked to depict the ways in which the strands relate to the accounts and where the changes occur. The focus is on the identification of what makes deep reflective writing different from description (i.e. the strands). I do not mind how they represent the changes on paper. The paper exercise aids their efforts to focus on the task. The exercise is rounded up by groups in turn identifying one strand. They are then shown the list of strands on a PowerPoint slide (or on handouts) and attention is drawn to the Generic Framework for Reflective Writing to provide long-term guidance in their own reflective writing.

A development that can follow the exercise is to ask learners to write their own version of a first account similar to those in the exercise (fiction or non-fiction). I then ask them either directly to write a second account at a deeper level of reflection using the Generic Framework as guidance or to pass their first account to another and to write the deeper reflection on someone else's account. This latter version unties them from 'truths' and allows them to think better on the techniques of reflection.

Graduated scenarios for other learning practices

The format of the graduated scenario exercise can be used to support understanding of critical thinking and how to improve its depth (Moon, 2008a) and other difficult-to-learn concepts. For formulation of a graduated scenario exercise, there has to be some conception of a continuum from poor/superficial practice to deeper/more sophisticated practice, which can be described in a framework. This may be done from literature or from discussions by an expert group (an excellent educational development exercise). I list some practices below for which graduated scenario exercises could be developed:

- clinical reasoning processes in health and medical subjects;
- diagnosis of problems/error in medicine, engineering, etc.;
- decision-making;
- the making of professional judgements, consultancy processes;
- the management of personal interactions in professional situations (counselling, mentoring: human resource management);
- leadership;
- practices of telling bad news;
- sport coaching or other such activity;
- evaluation;
- critique in the arts;

Further information/resources

The exercises and background theory for graduates scenarios are described in Moon 2004, 2006, 2008a, 2009b. They can also be found at http://www.CEMP.ac.uk/people/jennymoon.php under Reflective Learning, Critical Thinking and Learning Journals. There are no copying restrictions.

A graduated scenario method to support reflective learning/writing

The park I

I went through the park the other day. The sun shone sometimes but large clouds floated across the sky in a breeze. It reminded me of a time that I was walking on St David's Head in Wales – when there was a hard and bright light and anything I looked at was bright. It was really quite hot – so much nicer than the day before, which was rainy. I went over to the children's playing field. I had not been there for a while and wanted to see the improvements. There were several children there and one, in particular, I noticed, was in too many clothes for the heat. The children were running about and this child became red in the face and began to slow down and then he sat. He must have been about 10. Some of the others called him up again and he got to his feet. He stumbled into the game for a few moments, tripping once or twice. It seemed to me that he had just not got the energy to lift his feet. Eventually he stumbled down and did not get up, but he was still moving and he shuffled into a half-sitting and half-lying position watching the other children, and I think he was calling out to them. I don't know.

Anyway, I had to get on to get to the shop to buy some meat for the chilli that my children had asked for for their party. The twins had invited many friends round for an end-of-term celebration of the beginning of the summer holidays. They might think that they have cause to celebrate but it makes a lot more work for me when they are home. I find that their holiday time makes a lot more work.

It was the next day when the paper came through the door – in it there was a report of a child who had been taken seriously ill in the park the previous day. He was fighting for his life in hospital and they said that the seriousness of the situation was due to the delay before he was brought to hospital. The report commented on the fact that he had been lying unattended for half an hour before someone saw him. By then the other children had gone. It said that several passers-by might have seen him looking ill and even on the ground, and the report went on to ask why passers-by do not take action when they see that something is wrong. The article was headed 'Why do they "Walk on by"?' I have been terribly upset since then. James says I should not worry – it is just a headline.

The park (2)

I went to the park the other day. I was going to the supermarket to get some meat to make the chilli that I had promised the children. They were having one of their end-of-term celebrations with friends. I wonder what drew me to the playground and why I ended up standing and watching those children playing with a rough old football? I am not sure as I don't usually look at other people's children – I just did. Anyway there were a number of kids there. I noticed, in particular, one child who seemed to be overdressed for the weather. I try now to recall what he looked like – his face was red. He was a boy of around 10 – not unlike Charlie was at that age – maybe that is why I noticed him to start with when he was running around with the others. But then he was beginning to look distressed. I felt uneasy about him – sort of maternal – but I did not do anything. What could I have done? I remember thinking I had little time and the supermarket would get crowded. What a strange way of thinking, in the circumstances!

In retrospect I wish I had acted. I ask myself what stopped me – but I don't know what I might have done at that point. Anyway, he sat down, looking absolutely exhausted and as if he had no energy to do anything. A few moments later, the other children called him up to run about again. I felt more uneasy and watched as he got up and tried to run, then fell, ran again and fell and half sat and half lay. Still I did nothing more than look – what was going on with me?

Eventually I went on I tell myself now that it was really important to get to the shops. It was the next day when the paper came through the door that I had a real shock. In the paper there was a report of a child who had been taken seriously ill in the park the previous day. He was fighting for his life in the hospital and the situation was much more serious because there had been such a delay in getting help. The report commented on the fact that he had been lying, unattended, for half an hour or more. At first, I wondered why the other children had not been more responsible. The article went on to say that several passers-by might have seen him playing and looking ill, and the report questioned why passers-by do not take action when they see that something is wrong.

The event has affected me for some days but I do not know where to go or whom to tell. I do want to own up to my part in it to someone, though.

The park (3)

The incident happened in Ingle Park and it is very much still on my mind. There was a child playing with others. He looked hot and unfit and kept sitting down but the other children kept on getting him back up and making him play with them. I was on my way to the shop and only watched the children for a while before I walked on. Next day it was reported in the paper that the child had been taken to hospital seriously ill – very seriously ill. The report said that there were several passers-by in the park who had seen the child looking ill and who had done nothing. It was a scathing report about those who do not take action in such situations.

Reading the report, I felt dreadful and it has been very difficult to shift the feelings. I did not stop to see to the child because I told myself that I was on my way to the shops to buy food for a meal that I had to cook for the children's party – what do I mean that *I had to* cook it? Though I saw that the child was ill, I didn't do anything. It is hard to say what I was really thinking at the time – to what degree I was determined to go on with my day in the way I had planned it (the party really was not that important, was it?). Or did I genuinely not think that the boy was ill – but just overdressed and a bit tired? To what extent did I try to make convenient excuses and to what extent was my action based on an attempt to really understand the situation? Looking back, I could have cut through my excuses at the time – rather than now.

I did not go over to the child and ask what was wrong, but I should have done. I could have talked to the other children – and even got one of the other children to call for help. I am not sure if the help would have been ambulance or doctor at that stage – but it does not matter now. If he had been given help then, he might not be fighting for his life.

It would be helpful to me if I could work out what I was really thinking and why I acted as I did. This event has really shaken me to my roots – more than I would have expected. It made me feel really guilty. I do not usually do wrong; in fact I think of myself as a good person. This event is also making me think about actions in all sorts of areas of my life. It reminds me of some things in the past, as when my uncle died; but then again, I don't really think that that is relevant – he was going to die anyway. My bad feelings then were due to sheer sadness and some irrational regrets that I did not visit him on the day before. Strangely it also reminds me of how bad I felt when Charlie was ill while we went on that anniversary weekend away. As I think more about Charlie being ill, I recognise that there are commonalities in the situations. I also keep wondering if I knew that boy …

The park (4)

It happened in Ingle Park and this event is very much still on my mind. It feels significant. There was a child playing with others. He looked hot and unfit and kept sitting down, but the other children kept on getting him back up and making him play with them. I was on my way to the shop and only watched the children for a while before I walked on. Next day it was reported in the paper that the child had been taken to hospital seriously ill – very seriously ill. The report said that there were several passers-by in the park who had seen the child looking ill and who had done nothing. It was a scathing report about those who do not take action in such situations.

It was the report initially that made me think more deeply. It kept coming back in my mind and over the next few days – I began to think of the situation in lots of different ways. Initially I considered my urge to get to the shop – regardless of the state of the boy. That was an easy way of excusing myself – to say that I had to get to the shop. Then I began to go through all of the agonising as to whether I could have mis-read the situation and really thought that the boy was simply overdressed or perhaps play-acting or trying to gain sympathy from me or the others. Could I have believed that the situation was all right? All of that thinking, I now notice, would also have let me off the hook – made it not my fault that I did not take action at the time.

I talked with Tom, about my reflections on the event – on the incident, on my thinking about it at the time and then immediately after. He observed that my sense of myself as a 'good person who always lends a helping hand when others need help' was put in some jeopardy by it all. At the time and immediately after, it might have been easier to avoid shaking my view of myself than to admit that I had avoided facing up to the situation and admitting that I had not acted as 'a good person'. With this hindsight, I notice that I can probably find it easier to admit that I am not always 'a good person' and that I made a mistake in retrospect than immediately after the event. I suspect that this may apply to other situations.

As I think about the situation now, I recall some more of the thoughts – or were they feelings mixed up with thoughts? I remember a sense at the time that this boy looked quite scruffy and reminded me of a child who used to play with Charlie. We did not feel happy during the brief period of their friendship because this boy was known as a bully and we were uneasy either that Charlie would end up being bullied or that Charlie would learn to bully. Funnily enough we were talking about this boy – I now remember – at the dinner table the night before. The conversation had reminded me of all of the agonising about the children's friends at the time. The fleeting thought/feeling was possibly something like this: if this boy is like one I did not feel comfortable with, then maybe he deserves to get left in this way. Maybe he was a brother of the original child. I remember social psychology research along the lines of attributing blame to victims to justify their plight. Then it might not have been anything to do with Charlie's friend.

So I can see how I looked at that event and perhaps interpreted it in a manner that was consistent with my emotional frame of mind at the time. Seeing the same events without that dinnertime conversation might have led me to see the whole thing in an entirely different manner and I might have acted differently. The significance of this whole event is chilling when I realise that my lack of action nearly resulted in his death – and it might have been because of an attitude that was formed years ago in relation to a different situation.

This has all made me thing about how we view things. The way I saw this event at the time was quite different to the way I see it now – even this few days later. Writing an account at the time would have been different to the account – or several accounts that I would write now. I cannot know what 'story' is 'true'. The bullying story may be one that I have constructed retrospectively – fabricated. Interestingly I can believe that story completely.

Changes in the quality of reflective writing in the four sections

The deepening of reflection entails change in the following ways:

- from description to reflective account;
- from no questions to questions to responding to questions;
- emotional influence is recognised, and then handled increasingly effectively;
- there is a 'standing back from the event';
- self-questioning challenge to one's own ideas;
- recognition of relevance of prior experience;
- the taking into account of others' views;
- metacognition – review of one's own reflective processes.

A Generic Framework for Reflective Writing

There are four 'levels' of depth of reflection described in the next subsections. They do not necessarily accord directly with the accounts in exercises such as 'The Park' but provide a general guide.

Descriptive writing

This account is descriptive and it contains little reflection. It may tell a story, but from one point of view at a time, and generally one point at a time is made. Ideas tend to be linked by the sequence of the account/story rather than by meaning. The account describes what happened, sometimes mentioning past experiences, sometimes anticipating the future – but all in the context of an account of the event.

There may be references to emotional reactions but they are not explored and not related to behaviour.

The account may relate to ideas or external information, but these are not considered or questioned and the possible impact on behaviour or the meaning of events is not mentioned.

There is little attempt to focus on particular issues. Most points are made with similar weight.

The writing could hardly be deemed to be reflective at all. It could be a reasonably written account of an event that would serve as a basis on which reflection might start, though a good description that precedes reflective accounts will tend to be more focused and to signal points and issues for further reflection.

Descriptive account with some reflection

This is a descriptive account that signals points for reflection while not actually showing much reflection.

The basic account is descriptive in the manner of description above. There is little addition of ideas from outside the event, reference to alternative viewpoints or attitudes to others, comment and so on. However, the account is more than just a story. It is focused on the event as if there is a big question or there are questions to be asked and answered. Points on which reflection could occur are signalled.

There is recognition of the worth of further exploring but it does not go very far. In other words, asking the questions makes it more than a descriptive account, but the lack of attempt to respond to the questions means that there is little actual analysis of the events.

The questioning does begin to suggest a 'standing back from the event' in (usually) isolated areas of the account.

The account may mention emotional reactions, or be influenced by emotion. Any influence may be noted, and possibly questioned.

There is a sense of recognition that this is an incident from which learning can be gained, but the reflection does not go sufficiently deep to enable the learning to begin to occur.

Reflective writing (1)

There is description but it is focused, with particular aspects accentuated for reflective comment. There may be a sense that the material is being mulled over. It is no longer a straightforward account of an event, but it is definitely reflective.

There is evidence of external ideas or information, and where this occurs, the material is subjected to reflection.

The account shows some analysis and there is recognition of the worth of exploring motives or reasons for behaviour.

Where relevant, there is willingness to be critical of the action of self or others. There is likely to be some self-questioning and willingness also to recognise the overall effect of the event on self. In other words, there is some 'standing back' from the event.

There is recognition of any emotional content, a questioning of its role and influence and an attempt to consider its significance in shaping the views presented.

There may be recognition that things might look different from other perspectives and that views can change with time or the emotional state. The existence of several alternative points of view may be acknowledged but not analysed.

In other words, in a relatively limited way the account may recognise that frames of reference affect the manner in which we reflect at a given time but it does not deal with this in a way that links it effectively to issues about the quality of personal judgement.

Reflective writing (2)

Description now only serves the process of reflection, covering the issues for reflection and noting their context. There is clear evidence of standing back from an event and there is mulling over and internal dialogue.

The account shows deep reflection, and it incorporates a recognition that the frame of reference with which an event is viewed can change.

A metacognitive stance is taken (i.e. critical awareness of one's own processes of mental functioning – including reflection).

The account probably recognises that events exist in a historical or social context that may be influential on a person's reaction to them. In other words, multiple perspectives are noted.

Self-questioning is evident (an 'internal dialogue' is set up at times), deliberating between different views of personal behaviour and that of others.

The views and motives of others are taken into account and considered against those of the writer.

There is recognition of the role of emotion in shaping the ideas and recognition of the manner in which different emotional influences can frame the account in different ways.

There is recognition that prior experience and thoughts (one's own and other's) interact with the production of current behaviour.

There is observation that there is learning to be gained from the experience and points for learning are noted.

There is recognition that the personal frame of reference can change according to the emotional state in which the account is written, the acquisition of new information, the review of ideas and the effect of time passing.

The effectiveness of these variables on personal judgement is taken into account in making judgements.

Patchwork texts

Introduction

Patchwork texts are coherent 'packages' of representations of student work (mostly written) around a topic (chosen or given). They may or may not include actual story, but the whole text is story-like in its attempt to create a broad view of a theme. Patchwork texts come to use writing as a method of inquiry (Richardson, 2000) rather than as for representation in assessment. They often seem to require learners to work in what Shotter (2001) describes as 'a pre-scholarly, pre-intellectual way ... rediscovering ... some of the rich, living, responsively related activities' from which our intellectual approaches have emerged.

There are usually around six elements ('patches'). Typically they differ in genre – and may include fiction, imagined dialogue, review, poetry and graphical material. Reflection is likely to be part of the work and a reflective piece summarises the whole. Often learners present their pieces for discussion in a group as an ongoing process. Such groups, which may be organised as action learning sets (Tibble 2008), can lend support in this often unfamiliar way of working.

The purpose of the patchwork text is to enable students to build their understanding about the theme by approaching it from different perspectives, which can include affect as well as reasoning. The texts can be seen as a way of letting the arts and philosophy into science and vice versa (Ovens, 2003), and of enabling students to find their own 'voice', as well as demonstrating the variety of perspectives that can make up a single story (Winter et al., 1999; Shotter, 2001). The idea of patchwork text is usually introduced early in a module (or programme, if it is to equate to a Master's dissertation) so that it is part of the learning process and not just a final assessment.

For assessment of the text, assessment criteria do need to be developed to meet the purpose for which this method has been chosen (which should be expressed in the learning outcomes – Moon, 2002). Criteria are unlikely to resemble those for an essay.

Further information on patchwork texts

Information can be obtained from Winter et al., 1999; Winter, 2000, 2003a, 2003b; Smith and Winter, 2003.

Examples of texts are in Winter et al., 1999; Scroggins and Winter, 1999; Brown, 2003.

Examples of use in disciplines – Health/Social Care (PGCert): Tibble, 2008; Family Therapy: Akister, 2005; Social Work: Scroggins and Winter, 1999; Maisch, 2003; Classics: Parker, 2003; Community Nursing: Brown, 2003; Smith and Winter, 2003; Business: Illes, 2003; Education Programme for Primary Science Specialists: Ovens, 2003.

Using story to encourage thought about potentially difficult situations

I present this description as an example of how stories can be linked to discussion or other activities in order to facilitate thinking about behaviours or skills.

In writing a book on academic assertiveness for a student audience, I made extensive use of stories/scenarios to illustrate behaviours and their outcomes.

The use of story in such a situation enables the writer to 'put over' important unspoken information. An example is the following. The text indicates that a consequence of being assertive is uncomfortable guilt which is not helpful to the subject.

> Jem has finished the essay that needs to be handed in tomorrow. Tod has not done his yet. He comes round to see Jem, chats for a while over a coffee and then asks Jem if he can have a look at his completed essay. 'Like – just so as I can get some ideas,' he says. Jem is not naïve. He knows that Tod wants to use his references and probably to copy some of the ideas or structure. He says 'No.'
>
> Tod says, 'I thought you were a friend. I've left this a bit late and am in trouble with it and you will not help. Thanks Mate!' He picks up his coat and walks out. Jem feels pangs of guilt and sad for not helping, but feels that he has made the right decision.
>
> (Moon, 2009a: 24–25)

This idea was subsequently developed and transformed into classroom materials to support the group-work activities of learners. Relevant text with ideas on academic assertiveness that relate to group work (illustrated with scenarios) (16 pages) is set for learners to read. In the next class session they are given new scenarios about difficult situations in student groups to discuss, using their prior experience as well as the new ideas from the reading. This provides them with enhanced language and ideas for dealing with difficult situations when they arise in their groups. (Moon, 2008b; Ireland and Moon, 2008 – for media students) (All the materials are free to use).

A similar pattern could be used to encourage thinking through discussion about other behaviours that we expect graduates to exhibit.

Supporting epistemological development and effective critical thinking

I described epistemological development in Chapter 4 and suggested that it is closely related to the development of critical thinking and that both, in different ways, can be supported by different uses of story. It may be useful to refer to that earlier section for the kinds of thinking that educators might aim to facilitate in learners when enhancing their epistemological development. The examples below work through these ideas.

Perhaps the most important factor in supporting learners to progress in their epistemological development is to work with a teacher who understands the need to challenge learners and to facilitate thinking (Meyers, 1986; Brookfield, 1987, 1990, 1998; Brookfield and Preskill, 1999; Kloss, 1994; Baxter Magolda, 1999; Lucas, 2008). It is also important to help learners to manage 'the insecurity of not knowing something securely' (Kloss, 1994). In addition, learners' discussion about the activity is a crucial forum for development of thinking and the recognition of alternative perspectives (Meyers, 1986; Kloss 1994, Fisher, 1996). In the following pages are some uses of story (fiction and non-fiction) that can support epistemological development. It is worth considering this in the choice of subject matter of the story. If it is related to the discipline, learners will tend to focus on disciplinary issues and 'miss' the idea of the exercise, but if you use other materials than the discipline, some students will ask why the activity is relevant. In the ideas below, learners might construct the story or be listeners. They will gain more, but be more challenged as constructors.

Showing multiple perspectives with stories

Perspectives on a topic may differ within a discipline (e.g. different views expressed) or they may be from different disciplines. In the use of multiple perspectives within a discipline, a story about a real or fictitious issue can show how different views are expressed. Or learners might construct a fictionalised debate – in a professional group, in a committee, in Parliament, among experts, among laymen and experts and so on. I have mentioned Greenhalgh and Collard's (2003) programme for service development in which real and diverse experiences of Bangladeshi patients with diabetes were collected. Mansfield and Bidwell (2005) suggest the rewriting of personal events from a third-person perspective. McLeod (1997) talks of the use of 'jigsawing' – in which people involved in an event combine their stories to provide a coherent picture of the whole event. Sparkes (2002) shows how many sport stories, written in different genres, combine to a broader and deeper conception. A different view of the same idea is provided in the University of Toronto group (e.g. Oatley, 2008a), who suggest that enabling learners to see the world through the 'eyes' of different people in fiction helps them to develop better social skills. Greenhalgh and Collard call this 'exploring otherness'.

Another way of working with multiple perspectives is to work with dialogues. Learners write a dialogue between two characters with different perspectives on an issue, or between themselves and one other. The other could be a mentor, an imaginary character, a theorist, a god figure, etc. (More detail is given in Moon, 2006: 145.)

Perspectives on a topic differ when expressed in different disciplines. A simple example is to take a topic like 'a disabled child' or 'potato' and look at it from biological, sociological, historical, legal (etc.) perspectives. Other examples involve humanities and arts subjects being used to support subject understanding in scientific studies. Gough (1993), for example, provides valuable discussion and examples of the use of story to enhance the learning of environmental science. Squier (1998), from a medical perspective, comments that 'Humanities education challenges the scientific certainty that underpins Western Medicine by valuing subjective knowledge alongside the objective, inductive reasoning alongside deductive and human experience and emotion alongside scientific data' (p. 137). (See also Dittrich, 2001.)

Stories that play with reality

I have previously mentioned that some stories manipulate the comprehension of listeners, introducing uncertainty about reality within the story. Such material can extend learners' thinking about reality and certainty. I have mentioned *Sophie's World* (Gaardner, 1996), the Carlos Castaneda books (e.g. 1970), *The Magus* (Fowles, 1997) in this context.

Fiction that explores the nature of knowledge and the history of ideas

Many stories explore the nature of knowledge, or aspects of knowledge. I have mentioned *The Green Child*, which explores aesthetics. It has become fashionable to write stories based on the development of scientific ideas, such as longitude (Sobel, 1995) and others. Such stories also challenge the distinction between reality and fiction (see Chapter 12).

Stories specifically designed to stimulate thinking

Fisher (1996), Thomas and Killick (2007), Gersie's books (e.g. 1992; Gersie and King, 1990) and Crimmens (1998) and Denning (2004) include stories that are designed to stimulate thought, usually expanding the learner's view by their introduction of alternative perspectives. Discussion, thought-provoking questions or the requirement for learners to respond with short answers (half a side of A4) to a short question on the stories will enhance the effect of this kind of material.

In a management context, Gold et al. (2002) describe how their use of (personal) 'storytelling' 'promoted aspects of critical thinking such as critique of knowledge and authority, and questioning of assumptions'.

Demonstrating another aspect of story use to stimulate thinking, Saunders et al. (2004) describe the development of a Bachelor's degree in Science and Science Fiction using the link with fiction as a means of stirring controversy and discussion. The programme was designed initially to attract non-traditional learners into higher education. There are other examples of the use of science fiction in the learning of science (e.g. Turner, 2008; Gough, 1993).

Stories and the making of judgements

Working towards a judgement requires learners to use their understanding of the nature of knowledge. Laming (2004) includes much story-like material in his book about judgement, which is derived from an undergraduate module. Hardie (2007) describes a role-play exercise based on court case design, to put 'on trial' aspects of creative design. Hastie and Davies (2001) show the power of story construction in juror decision-making in real court cases, and Lucas (2008) uses a 'crime' story with undergraduate accountants to stimulate thinking about assumptions in making a judgement.

Poetry

Poetry can demonstrate the affective perspective of a topic. Holmes and Gregory (1998) use poetry in nursing, and Lucas (2008) refers to the use of poetry and the writing of messages in Valentine cards(!) with accountancy students. On a personal note I add this: recently, on my own in a restaurant, I was reading a vivid short story by Michael Morpurgo (2006), about a child involved in the Balkan conflicts. I felt my way of life and the experience of being in a place of luxury challenged because of the experiences of the child in that story. I took up a pen to write of the dissonance I experienced in a poem.

The writing of stories

Story writing is a means of inquiry in itself (Winter, 1986; Bolton, 1999; Hunt, 1998, 2000; for other books about writing, see Squier, 1998). It can be used as a means of exploring personal or professional ideas (Richardson, 2000). Robinson and Hawpe (1986) usefully comment: 'Stories are the natural mediators between the particular and the general in human experience' (p. 124).

Further resources

There are relevant story-based exercises to support thinking/epistemological development (including graduated scenarios) in Moon (2008a). There are supporting materials on many websites under the heading 'Theory of Knowledge', a subject on International Baccalaureate programmes.

Thinkpoint

Stories are marvelous, magical things, they are also, paradoxically mundane and commonplace – because they are everywhere. We cannot avoid telling them and making them. You yourself are a story; a story of how you have been and hope to be, of how you are and how you might be.

(Parkinson, n.d.; see also Parkinson, 2009)

Chapter 8

Stories of experience in personal and professional development

Introduction

This chapter covers the use of story in personal and professional development. I have not distinguished clearly between personal and professional development because they overlap so much – professional development is a focused form of personal development. I have adopted headings that seem best to cover the material that I want to include and there are many links with other chapters. After reviewing some general issues that concern both title topics in an initial section, I give brief descriptions of some methods and ideas that are associated with professional development, mostly involving the group sharing of experience stories. I then provide some ideas about the use of story in reflective personal writing and learning journals (which may be a part of professional development).

Story in personal and professional development: some general issues

First, I want to return to and amplify an idea that was expressed earlier that I consider to underpin the ideas in this chapter in particular. That is the suggested need for 'story literacy' (Wilson, 2006) in order to manage the complex communications of education and professional work (Zeldin, 1998). Story literacy includes the social skills of managing stories in conversation – both in listening to the stories of others, in recognising the gist or the point that is being made – and the need to be able to respond, appropriately, sometimes with another story. Schank's assertion that ability with story relates to intelligence, in the light of this, does not seem unreasonable. Wilson (2006) would add the requirement of good concentration to the quality of story literacy and he argues that story literacy needs to be nurtured in a technological and globalised world. He says, 'We need as much humanity and civility as we can possibly muster' to cope with the 'dangerous times' in which we live. 'If we manage to teach our students only one thing, then it should be to be able to tell their own stories for themselves and so become engaged with history, culture and the real world beyond celebrity.' Some thought is needed as to how higher education students might acquire these abilities.

Story also helps in the processes of learning in personal and professional development. This learning is often uncertain and 'messy' (Schon, 1983, 1987), with no clear solutions to problems. Bailey (1998) demonstrates this in reflecting on her own story in the context of nursing. Practice in the effective use of judgement of the quality of evidence involved in decisions is often best taught with reference to real situations, and story provides a means of working with real or life-like situations in the classroom. Stories may be imported as case studies, scenarios and critical incidents (Chapter 9), or in the experience of those present. Such stories may be personal, personally experienced or fictitious (Moon and Fowler, 2008) – and we may not know which!

Learning from shared stories

Story in professional development: a helpful framework

McDrury and Alterio (2003) suggest that stories represent a means of deepening understanding in a professional development context. They develop the idea in a five-stage framework (based partly on Moon, 1999a). The story is likely to be one from relevant personal or professional experience, told in a group situation. In the first stage the story is noticed as significant for development – there is something about it, perhaps that is unresolved or disturbing. In the telling there is a tendency to order the content to suggest a meaning or solution through the manner of the telling. In a further processing, the story is expanded in discussion between the teller and the group. They might relate the story to other issues, or query why the characters acted in such ways. Then, in the next stage, the story is processed – there is deeper reflection on it, critique and a checking of assumptions within the telling and about the characters involved. In the last stage there is a reconstruction of the story to take into account the outcomes of the processing. Citing Jackson (1995: 12), McDrury and Alterio (2003: 49) say that here 'there is a potential for those involved "to be transformed, transfigured and transported by stories" leading to change of practice'. They suggest many techniques of working with story at each of the stages, which, overall, work towards transformation in personal and professional terms. In a later paper, Alterio and McDrury (2003) describe an application of the framework in more detail. Six to eight people from a similar work background are asked to think of a recent work situation. There are various ways of facilitating this. When a promising story has been 'found', it is told to the others, with note made of emotional content. In a subsequent stage, the listeners seek to clarify the story, bringing out further details. Links may be made, at this stage, with the listeners' personal stories. The emphasis is 'on *why* events occurred as they did and *why* those involved behaved in particular ways' (Alterio and McDrury, 2003: 48). In the next stage of critical reflection, 'assumptions and ideologies are challenged' by listeners in discussion, and the 'impact of the context is explored' (p. 48). This is a time when insights should emerge through the development of multiple perspectives and exploration of listeners' and tellers' emotions. In the last stage, the story is reconstructed from the points of view of the key players in the situation. The group members take on the role of one of the key players, and then role-play the story from all of the perspectives. There is then a debriefing and further reflection on the story that has been explored.

These ideas have been applied in a scheme of personal and professional education for undergraduates on return from placements (Tomkins, 2008). McDrury and Alterio's framework also underpins some of the other work with story described below. For example, it is interesting to note that the uses of story described above follow a similar sequence to story used in therapy though this situation may only involve the client and therapist (Chapter 10). At the heart of the process, a story first told is redeveloped to take account of other perspectives and meanings, and thus greater meaning and (hopefully) learning is derived from it.

'Structured critical conversation' (Brookfield, 1998)

In this group method, a professional experience story that 'puzzles by its layers and complexities' (Brookfield, 1998: 329) is selected and told by one of a group. Another is designated 'umpire'. The rest of the group are cast in the role of detectives and they listen in order to 'identify the explicit and implicit assumptions about the experience' (p. 330) made by the teller verbally and non-verbally. They may make notes of 'alternative interpretations' of the facts as given, by endeavouring to perceive the perspective of others within the story. Once the story is told, the detectives ask questions. They seek 'information that will help them to uncover the assumptions they think the storyteller holds' (p. 330). They report their perceptions to the teller but must not give the information as judgements. The teller may question the detectives too. Next, the detectives provide alternative interpretations and they describe how others involved might have perceived the events. Lastly there is a statement from all those involved as to what they have learned, and there is general discussion of the process.

Concentric storytelling

Drake and Elliot (2005) follow fairly similar processes to those described above, but they ask students to work in triads and they ask for groups of three stories from one person before the analysis of the stories begins. The two listeners analyse the stories using (provided) guidance notes for the interrogation. They might ask, for example, who is the hero of the story, and enquire into the nature of other roles. They ask about ethical issues and how the story aligns with formal standards of practice. Lastly there is discussion about what has been learned.

Story writing and telling in management education

Gold and Holman (2001) describe use of storytelling in a post-experience management education module. Students are asked to write about a current problem at work. They then respond to questions such as: 'Why has an issue arisen like this?' 'What were you arguing for in this story?'. The insights gained and issues remaining are gathered and discussed. The stories are retold to groups with a tutor present and other participants are encouraged to probe for deeper meanings. The intention of the process is not only to enable learning for the teller, but to demonstrate issues about, for example, expectations about the behaviour of managers. Gold et al. (2002) extend these ideas.

Life and professional stories and professional education in teaching

The telling of professional stories has been reported extensively in teacher education, though some of it is seen as 'study' of education rather than professional development. Witherell and Noddings provide a broad view of the uses of story in education and professional development. They say that 'the stories we hear and stories we tell shape the meaning and texture of our lives at every stage and juncture' (Witherell and Noddings, 1991: 1).

Much work on story in education has been published by Connelly and Clandinin (e.g. 1986, 1990). Their work espouses the view that a combination of interviewing, writing one's own stories and collaborative story work is 'a key to self understanding and, from there, change' (Huberman, 1995: 140). In interviewing, the facilitators 'try to capture generative themes in the life of the informant – the strands that give meaning to the many shifts that accompany the teaching career'. There are similarities to the framework of McDrury and Alterio (2003 – see pp. 000–00), though Connelly and Clandinin (1990) describe the eliciting of *written* story and further processing such as 'broadening' it to other situations or 'burrowing' in it for deeper meaning – the 'emotional, moral and aesthetic qualities' – and then a subsequent phase in which the material is related to present and future situations. A new story is then written that encompasses the essence of this work. Huberman (1995) and Carter (1993) are critical of these methods when used to teach new teachers. The latter suggests that confusion may be caused because novices expect to be told clearly how to operate as teachers. They are at the absolute knowing stage in epistemological development terms (Baxter Magolda, 1992; and Chapter 4) and are not able to cope with the 'messiness' of professional issues.

More recently, Whelan et al. (2001) reviewed these story approaches. They make the important distinction between stories told that perpetuate the status quo and stories that 'lead to restorying with growth and change'. This seems to distinguish, in the McDrury and Alterio (2003) framework, between the simple telling of stories and the further processing to a stage of reconstruction of the story and expected behaviour change.

Strong-Wilson (2006) and Pagano (1991) use fiction to enhance processes similar to the above (see Chapter 12).

The 'call of stories' in professional development in medicine

Many writers on the role of story in medicine (and other disciplines) mention the work of Robert Coles (1989). Coles describes how he transformed his view of the role of story in his practices in medicine and psychiatry through conversations with 'Dr Ludwig'. Coles says that initially he would expound theory, but came to understand that he was losing 'sight of human particularlity' (p. 21). '[We] doctors had become diggers trying hard to follow treasure maps in hope of discovering gold, then announcing to supervisors, to patients, and, not least, to one another – that we had found it' (p. 22). 'Dr Ludwig urged us to let the story itself be our discovery ... he urged me to be a good listener' (p. 22–23). Coleş talks of how the richness of story may used by first-year medical students, but by their fourth year they 'are apt to present cryptic, dryly condensed material ... And patients' health may be jeopardized' (p. 24) and their real concerns overlooked. In medical practice, McNaughton (1998: 205) talks of the importance of the role of anecdote not only between doctor and patient but in the ongoing development of doctors. She sees anecdotes as shared stories that note the exceptions to the 'commonplace'. They provide 'real examples and counter examples' that enable doctors 'to test their clinical judgements against that of their peers'. McNaughton sums up her chapter by saying that anecdotes are an 'inevitable and essential part of communication within medicine and are in constant use between doctors, doctors and patients and in the lay community ... By virtue of being short and therefore memorable, they have an impact upon the education of physicians [and] their understanding of patients' predicaments' (p. 210). I note again, in relation to McNaughton's comments, the increasingly recognised role of humanities in a packed medical curriculum (Squier, 1998; Dittrich, 2001).

The use of illness stories in professional education

I have mentioned the work of Greenhalgh and Collard (2003), who demonstrate a more structured use of patients' story in professional education. Health advocates collected stories from Bangladeshi families with a family member with diabetes. The stories formed the basis of professional education workshops for local health workers, which were in turn made into a workbook. The publication is the actual structured workbook. Collections of stories about other specific professional issues could be developed in this way.

Story-based material in nurse education

Fowler demonstrates a number of uses of story in his work with student nurses. In one example, he describes how he presents students with a story that gives a certain amount of information. They are asked to make decisions, based upon that information – but then, as might occur in real life, they are given further information, and are asked to make further decisions. A management game was developed using this technique (Fowler, 1985). The aim of the game is to enable appreciation of the issues involved in allocating patients to particular beds, on the basis of the patients' illness, age and cultural issues. Thus a real experience is encountered in a simulated manner, with the students experiencing the situation and making appropriate decisions. Fowler (2001: 188) provides further simulation exercises which help students to appreciate the interplay of reliability and validity in various research designs. The story is told of a research problem such as the 'evaluation of hand washing techniques following the use of the toilet'. Various research scenarios are presented to the students and they have to consider the reliability and validity of each approach. The benefits of the story approach in these situations are that it enables the student to interact with, reflect on and learn from real experiences. The value of the work is increased if the later analytical stages of the McDrury and Alterio framework are added.

'Footprints', a method of eliciting story material in professional development

This method relates to the stage of finding stories in the McDrury and Alterio (2003) framework. It is useful for eliciting almost forgotten early experiences (Moon, 2004; based on Progoff, 1975 – 'Steppingstones'). A general topic that is relevant to the current educational issues is selected. It might be 'learning situations' or 'experiences of teachers' or 'being ill' or 'being in trouble'. Participants, working alone, list personal memories of the experience in a strictly chronological order, starting with the earliest memory. They need to note only the gist of the experience – just sufficient to recall it later. When they have about seven memories between the distant and recent past, they start a second list, again in chronological order. This gives them a chance to include memories that were recalled out of sequence in the first list. This activity might continue for ten minutes, with each person able to construct at least two lists. Working in a group, the participants take turns sharing one memory and its associated story (e.g. for a time limit of two minutes each). The memory described can be anything from the lists. There can be a few moments for general comment. The effect of sharing of the stories will be to 'loosen' further memories of listeners and they will now recall more memories. These new memories are noted. Once everyone has shared at least one story, the participants go back to the list construction and now make a further chronological list that includes the new memories. The sharing activity can be run again, and stories selected for further work as described above and below in this chapter.

Personal story

Some general matters concerning personal story

I deal here with the use of story to stimulate reflection in personal development planning, student success programmes, personal appraisal, as well as in professional education and development – and there is inevitably overlap with the previous section. This section is not long because the work is available elsewhere (reflective learning, Moon, 2004; learning journals, Moon, 2006 and http://www.cemp.ac. uk/people/jennymoon.php). Learning journals can be seen as an ongoing story, with many subplots, each of which could be developed more fully. To see journal entries in this way can inspire new ways of working with the material. Other writers refer to the human tendency to construct stories about ourselves and our lives (Daniels, 2001; Crossley, 2002). Bruner says:

> our capacity to render experience in terms of narrative is ... an instrument for making meaning that dominates much of life in culture – from soliloquies at bedtime to the weighing of testimony in our legal system ... Our sense of the normative is nourished in the narrative, but so is our sense of breach and exception. Stories make 'reality' a mitigated reality.
>
> (Bruner, 1990: 97)

What is significant here is our ability 'to alter past stories to recast their light on our present experience and in the light of the present, to recast the past' (p. 109). In this process, we would often enrich our stories to make them better justifications for the present state (Polkinghorne, 1988). We might reformulate the past in relation to present interests (e.g. reinterpreting the past to justify a current identity of 'I have always been a jealous person') (Chapter 4 – memory). But our stories also 'press forward from the actual into the possible' (Packer, 1991) – the present into anticipations of the future – and stories even trial how the future may unfold.

We use story to create identities. They 'give concrete life to [our] philosophies and value systems' (Claxton, 1999: 137). Bruner draws on the collections of work by Ulric Neissler (e.g. with Winograd, 1988) to provide a list of ways in which we craft our stories (Bruner, 2002: 70), which, he concludes, match the qualities required for the writing of a good story (p. 72): our stories have plots, they talk of obstacles to goals; characters have moods and so on.

Some personal stories may be told to close associates only and some we make more public. Some are recounted many times and some once (e.g. an excuse). Some are stories that we live by and some we get 'stuck' in (Hastie and Davies, 2001). We may sometimes 'lose the thread' of the story (Fulford, 1999). Some stories appear within themes such as adventure (Scheibe, 1986) or sexual or coming out stories (Plummer, 1995) or as backstories to the others (Alterio and McDrury, 2003), and they may be fed by a background of fiction (Bettelheim, 1976; Sparkes, 1998). They may be written as life stories, as journals, in reflective pieces, and some are written to be read (Harrett, 2008). Some are told in reminiscence groups (Bluck, 2001; Gersie, 1991), or they may be played out in drama (Gersie, 1996; Boal, 1995; Neelands, 1992). Clandinin and Connelly (1994) list formats in which self story is recorded – oral history, chronicles, family stories, artefacts such as photographs, the outcomes of interviews, journals, autobiographical writing, letters and field stories. 'Whatever form a story takes', Plummer (1995) reminds us, 'it is not simply the lived life. It speaks all around the life: it provides routes into a life, lays down maps for lives to follow, suggests links between a life and a culture' (p. 186).

Examples of uses of personal stories relevant to education

I include a range of different uses of story.

The autobiography as a motivating activity

Redwine (1989) describes how non-traditional students, returning to education in their later years, were asked to write a substantial piece of autobiography as their first written assignment. Three days later, they shared the stories with each other. She sees this method as having three particular values. The activity is cathartic, allowing expression of disappointments and failures in previous attempts at education; it is a basis for experiential learning, reminding students of relevant prior learning experiences; and the sharing of the stories is valuable for group cohesion.

Stories with potentially therapeutic outcomes

Many people have written about the healing or positive growth effects of writing and there is much advice in publications such as Selling (1998), DeSalvo (2000) and, in particular, Bolton (1999) and Hunt (2000). Within these books are many ways of working with autobiographical material in order to achieve personal development benefits in the context of a group, a class or individually. Ira Progoff, a Jungian therapist, found himself regularly asking his clients to do writing activities between sessions. Over a period of time, he consolidated the activities and wrote about them (Progoff, 1975) and many have been modified and presented elsewhere (e.g. Rainer, 1978; Lukinsky, 1990; McLeod, 1997; Moon 2006).

Getting started on life story writing

Roorbach (1998) talks of writing life stories and he provides many activities that facilitate this. Some exercises described in his book follow:

- Imagine self story as it might be in film. Describe scenes and then consider what a voiceover might be saying as the scenes emerge and things happen.
- Get material down and then go back over it to 'crack open' (p. 45) the meaning of the words in order to get deeper into the ideas, atmospheres, images (unspoken) and meanings behind them.
- Juxtapose seemingly unrelated scenes from material already written. Roorbach suggests combining a skiing experience and the death of an aunt. What have the two events to tell one another (p. 137)?
- Conduct a notional interview (and write it) with a character from a personal story.
- Write about what makes you feel most happy, enraged, deeply sad – letting the emotional voice have free rein (p. 104).

Bolton (1999) suggests further ways of 'getting into the story' by writing what a character in a life story might be thinking at a point in the story; what might be a diary entry for a character; transcribing a (fictitious) phone conversation from one character to another at a particular point in the story and so on.

Deepening autobiographical stories

Autobiographical stories can be fictionalised, told from the viewpoint of others, transformed into dialogue between characters, shifted into another setting and written 'as if' and so on (Bolton, 1999; Hunt, 2000; Hunt and Sampson, 1998). They can be told and retold with different 'spins' to see how the story sounds. The process of moving beyond the simple description of life story and working on it matches the later stages of the framework for storytelling of McDrury and Alterio (2003 – see p. 116).

Rewriting of personal incidents as third-person stories

When stories are rewritten in this way they can be examined in ways that are less encumbered by context. It is as if the incident can be turned over in the hands, examined from different sides, looked at from underneath or looked at afresh. It can be passed over to others for examination.

Fictional journals

The writing of fictitious learning journal entries is an excellent means of exploring how people deal with particular situations, and the personal learning that comes from that. I used fictitious journals as a means of exploring and portraying the effects of students attending a course in academic assertiveness (Moon, 2009a).

Representing a personal story in sculpting

A story can be represented in words, pictures or cartoon, and other representations and different learning will emanate depending on the representation (Eisner, 1991). Fowler and Rigby (1994) describe the manner in which personal story (in this case with student nurses) is initially 'told' through sculpting. The technique involves participants being placed by the 'teller' in physical relation to each other to represent the story of the people and relationships between them (e.g. within a family) – the physical distance equating to the quality of emotional relationship. The poses are then changed according to new scenes or situations. At each change the participants are asked briefly to reflect upon their experience. The strength of the sculpting technique is in the physical and emotional involvement and in avoidance of actual language. Any life experience that involves two or more people can be retold using sculpting. An example could be the effect of sudden illness in a family or the death of a significant person.

Using objects to elicit stories

The notion of using an abstract object to construct meaning arises in therapeutic situations (e.g. work with clay, art therapy), but it is also a way of eliciting story.

Gauntlett describes the development of Lego structures as means of exploring ideas and identity – and maybe story too (Gauntlett, 2007). Story emerges from this kind of work. I have already referred to Jung's construction of a model village in order to explore his concerns (p. 51).

Freewriting

Many advocate free writing as a means of reaching what it is that we really want to say (e.g. Cameron, 1994; Hunt, 2000). Elbow (1981) sees writing like setting up the flow of water that you run until it runs clear (p. 28) and Grumet's (1987) words seem to fit here. She says that 'when we work with life history, the autobiographical act is not complete until the writer of the story becomes its reader'. The writer sees and feels the clear water.

Sharing autobiographical stories

This nearly takes us back to the previous section of this chapter. Alterio (2004) suggests ways in which stories from journals can be shared in order to foster personal and professional development. However, in this case there is anonymity and participants do not meet as a group. Cooper (1991) focuses on the issues in the sharing of journals, 'writing to educate ourselves', as she puts it (p. 96).

Stories retold

Cowling (2004) describes the use of unitary appreciative inquiry to explore the (self-reported) experiences of despair in groups of women. Following interviews with the women, during which he elicited their stories, the researcher wrote a story incorporating metaphor and endeavouring to get over the essence of the issues that he perceived. The story was offered to the women for revision if they wished. While technically this was a research approach, I have added it here as well because the method sits interestingly alongside the others outlined (Chapter 11).

Thinkpoint

[The] longing for 'one true story' has driven the construction of narrative strategies in which fact and fiction are mutually exclusive categories ... But fact and fiction are much closer ... The native American stories of salmon are fictions that are as epistemologically potent in their own way as those fictions of western science that we call 'scientific fact'.

(Gough, 1993)

Chapter 9

Story as case study, scenario and critical incident

Introduction

This short chapter considers one of the common forms of story in education, the uses of case studies, scenarios and critical incidents – though they are not always stories. The subject matter of the chapter overlaps that of several other chapters, particularly Chapters 8, 11 and 12 (professional development, research and fiction). I begin this chapter with some general comments on the use of scenarios (p. 125). Then I provide a variety of examples of the uses of scenarios that are suitable for application in a variety of educational contexts (p. 126). The last section describes a workshop process that illustrates an innovative means of developing of case study material for higher education and professional development (p. 129).

Scenarios: some general comments

I am not going to try to define case study, scenario and critical incident separately because the application of the terms varies. In general they represent relatively self-contained character descriptions in distinctive situations that are used to facilitate the thought or practices of others. Within a context, they 'record specifics, individualities, idiosyncrasies and lay out multiple meanings in a documentary style' (Goodson and Walker, 1995: 185). For convenience, I will use the term 'scenario' for general reference except where one term is clearly more appropriate. Often the three terms elide. It is often the disciplinary context that determines which term is employed. 'Case study', for example, is used in the medical and business contexts. With reference to the framework of Moon and Fowler (2008); and Chapter 2, scenarios may be personal stories or incidents, or those involving known others, or not known others, or they may be fiction, so the boundaries between these categories are 'soft'. Different people's view of the same story can seem like many different fictions (Whelan et al., 2001). However, scenarios are generally brief stories that describe a situation or an incident. They lift a selected situation out of the 'here and now' for special attention. In my terminology for story, they may be broad-form stories, or they may be strong story, with a beginning, middle, end and a surprise (Chapter 2). They may endeavour to characterise the normal or they may represent a unique event. Some are well known, for example the story of Phineas Gage and his amazing head injury (Hammond, 2008; and see other radio programmes in the series *Case Study*).

Scenarios may be used as a research method (Chapter 11) or in facilitating learning, particularly in professional education or development. The intention is to enable an audience to 'get below the surface' of something, acquiring, thereby, a deeper understanding (Ghaye and Lillyman, 1997; Tripp, 1993). The deeper understanding may be of the case described (e.g. Burke, 1991), or a generalisation, or it may be of the user's own learning processes – such as the assumptions that she may make (e.g. Brookfield, 1990). The scenario may be designed as a simulation, so vicarious learning is encouraged, or it may describe a unique event such as the murder of Victoria Climbie, which led to deep examination of UK social service practices. In the professional situations, scenarios will often provide the story of a real situation to which theoretical knowledge may be applied. They may be used in teaching to exemplify best practice or they might give practice in the development of hypotheses, or in detecting ideas that represent the focal point at issue in a situation (Launer, 2002). Sometimes the deeper understanding may simply be that enabled by the provision of scenario as an example. I have used scenarios in this manner in illustrating academic assertiveness (see pp. 000–00).

There will be different issues to consider in the selection of scenarios, depending on their purpose. Carter observes that they are not just raw data, but are selected (Carter, 1993). Where they illustrate best practice, it is politic to consider the philosophies and assumptions that underlie the selection of a scenario. In these situations, they may be seen to be 'enduring truths' and they then represent 'acts of theorising' in themselves (Winter, 1986) and they may sway the judgements of those learning from them (Strange and Leung, 1999). Sometimes, however, it is the study of the assumptions contained in a scenario that is of interest.

Another issue is how explicit the scenario is. Sometimes scenarios will be explicit because the detail relates to the interest of the listener – what actually happened, what was said and how. However, in many other cases, scenarios can encourage development of the sensitivity of the listener to the unspoken elements in the story – what is not said, the ways in which characters behave towards each other, the backstories and emotions.

Examples of the use of case study, scenario and critical incident

Working with scenarios to encourage critical thinking

Brookfield (1998: 325) provides learners with a written scenario which involves contemplating some action or a decision. First, learners are asked to list the assumptions they think are being made in the scenario. They then consider how the protagonist might check the 'accuracy and validity' of each assumption. Lastly they interpret the scenario in an alternative manner, 'that the protagonist would disagree with if confronted by it'. Brookfield provides an excellent example. This exercise could be used to introduce the next one, which involves personal incidents.

Critical incidents to encourage critical thinking

Brookfield (1990) describes the use of critical incidents as a means of developing the critical thinking of learners. In this, he asked teachers to write critical incidents from their experience. They should 'Think back over the past year. During that time [he asked], what event made you ... feel a real "high" of excitement, satisfaction and fulfillment? – a time when you said to yourself "This is what it's all about"'. He asked them to include details of the context and what it was that made the event special, but keeping it within one page. They were then to work in triads, each in turn reading the incident and listening to comments on inherent assumption as feedback from the two listeners. The assumptions were to be either those that contributed to the choice of this particular incident or those operating within the incident. There was then discussion. Brookfield says that he introduced the exercise by working through an incident of his own first.

Lucas (2008) describes the use of a very simple scenario – in which an apparent burglary takes place – as a means of helping her accountancy students to recognise how easy it is to make assumptions and to 'jump to conclusions'.

Critical incidents in the analysis of political assumptions

Brookfield (1990) also describes the use of critical incidents as portrayed by the media, where, for example, the behaviour of a politician is the focus. Learners are asked to write down the details and context of a broadcast media item that made them particularly angry, identifying the behaviours that provoked their anger. Working again in triads, they take turns (as above) in reading and listening to the analysis of the assumptions made by the two listening colleagues. The assumptions should relate, first, to the choice of the particular incident and values that determined the choice and, second, to the assumptions underlying the actions of the politician. Again this is followed up by more general discussion.

Structured writing of critical incidents

Griffin (2003) advocates the use of a detailed scenario in the context of teacher education. It is a group exercise, but he requires participants, individually and writing in the first person, to attend to the detail of the event, to the differences between fact and inference, to the emotions invoked and explanations of the event from each character involved. The learners are asked to consider the areas of learning from the incident, the general meaning, how issues relate to professional standards in teaching, and he asks for a summary of the beliefs of the writer and anticipation of any changes in practice in the light of the learning from the incident.

Scenarios to examine details of a situation or life

Scenarios may tell the story of one life over a long period or at a moment in time. In a discussion of 'Betty', for example, Fowler (1981) explores the way that a life was affected over a 20-year period by a chronic mental illness. The scenario tells of the effect that Betty's illness had upon her own life, the lives of her family, her friends and the impact upon the health and social services. In contrast the story of George happens over a very short time (Fowler, 1995). George, aged 80, was admitted to a hospice and the scenario details his last two weeks of life. It captures a holistic experience which is often difficult to convey through 'teaching'. Such material helps students to see the bigger picture involving the patient, the management system or institution and the impact of the situation on others.

Scenarios as simulation and vicarious experience

Slater (2002) describes the development of 'narrative simulations'. Originally developed for health and safety training, these are interactive scenarios in which a situation is introduced and developed. At each stage of its development, there are further discussions by the learners reflecting the current situation in the story. This way of working relates to Oatley's (2008a) view that stories act like simulations. Role-playing would be a development of such work.

Affect in scenarios

It is not easy to lecture to novice professionals about the emotional experiences of their future work. It is not even easy to tell them about it, but scenarios can portray the sense of emotion and the associated issues. Noddings (1996) describes the use of scenarios for this purpose with teaching students.

Learning about research from scenarios

I have mentioned how Fowler (2001: 188 – and see Chapter 8) uses scenarios to help learners with appreciation of the interplay between reliability and validity in research designs. The story is told of a research topic – the 'evaluation of hand washing techniques following the use of the toilet'. Various research scenarios are presented to the learners, who consider the issues of the reliability and validity of each approach. The benefits of the story approach in these situations is that learners are enabled to interact, reflect and learn from simulated experiences in a more interesting manner.

Working with simulated scenarios

In recent years, it has become possible to construct scenarios in simulated or virtual worlds such as Second Life (Savin-Baden et al., 2009). Savin-Baden describes her use of simulated scenarios as a basis for problem-based learning (Savin-Baden, 2008). Second Life may be used to produce single scenarios for learners, or it may be used by learners to create an environment for different kinds of exploration. Grove and Steventon (2008) describe its use with students in a module on community safety in a criminology programme. In this way they 'simulated "real-life" scenarios in a setting that mirrors a typical dysfunctional community without having to negotiate difficult practical and ethical issues'. (See also Chapter 14.)

A 'story development' workshop

This exercise involves learning from the development of typical case study material. The aim in the example below is to develop an understanding of the learning issues that confront non-traditional students. Participants are higher education teachers. The workshop is run entirely through groups (of about six, seated around tables). There can be any number of groups. The process generates information towards the development of a multi-dimensional picture of the learning of non-traditional students through a progressively developing case study approach. A by-product of the workshop is that teachers involved can learn about learning itself.

The workshop is supported by a two-part handout. In the first part there is a sequence of activities, including exercises on learning. In the second part there are materials to support the exercises. The workshop begins with the groups being asked to imagine a typical non-traditional student at the end of the first year of study. I might suggest that some groups choose a young student and others choose a mature student to ensure variety of outcome.

1 The groups are asked to discuss and record (on flipchart paper) details of the imaginary student, who is having some difficulties with study – name, age and discipline(s) studied, some social background details, work history, what the student wants to do on completion of her programme and her feelings about being in higher education.

2 There is a brief from the workshop facilitator on some research on orientations to study (based on Morgan (1995) and Beaty et al. (1997) in the second part of the handout). Then participants are asked to think about the study orientation of their imaginary student – and record it.

3 Working with all participants, the facilitator collects words that describe good learning and those that describe poor learning, and groups are asked to discuss the learning of their student and to record appropriate description.

4 Groups are referred to an extensive list of study issues in the second part of the handout and discuss which applies to their student.

5 Participants are then asked to think of the approaches to learning taken by the student. They are given a version of a questionnaire on approaches to learning and asked to fill it in for a 'good' or 'poor' other student (not the imagined student). There is some discussion of deep, surface and strategic

approaches to learning (Marton et al., 1997), and again the groups are asked to apply the ideas to the story of their imagined student and her life in higher education.

6 Later there is focus on a particular incident where the student hands in a poor piece of work and the participants are asked to think what the learner might say about her work and what her tutor says.

The workshop continues in this way. The imaginary student increasingly becomes 'known' as ideas about her life and learning are introduced and discussed. There are nine activities all together but I rarely have time for all nine. Around 20 minutes before the end of the workshop, the last activity is introduced.

7 Thinking now of the developed story about the imaginary non-traditional learner, the groups are asked to consider ideal and more practical ways to support this student in her studies.

The culmination of the workshop is the presentation of a short description of each imaginary student by each group and their decisions about learning support.

There is much discussion in this workshop. Teachers of different disciplines 'get together' and share ideas. The approach to the experiences of non-traditional learners is holistic and focuses on a practical outcome. A scenario results and ideas contained in the unspoken are made explicit in the conversations that take place. The same kind of workshop could be used to explore other student experiences (e.g. those of overseas or of dyslexic students). Further details of this workshop, including handouts, are freely available from the author (Jenny@cemp.ac.uk).

Thinkpoint

Narrative is: 'the primary form by which human experience is made meaningful. Narrative meaning is a cognitive process that organizes human experiences into temporally meaningful episodes'.

(Polkinghorne, 1988: 1)

Chapter 10

Story for promoting change

Introduction

This chapter focuses on the ways in which story can promote change in mind and behaviour. I have mentioned story and change in various places before, but now I focus on it. If a story can engage us, take us from current reality into story reality and return us to the here and now, then it is possible that it can promote change in the sense that learning is change (Chapter 3). This chapter covers situations in which the deliberate aim of story is change – in attitude or behaviour. Particular examples are in therapies and business, but the material is applicable elsewhere in education and is relevant to personal and professional development (Chapter 8).

In this chapter, I first look at where story as an agent of change is located in higher education and how it is relevant to learning (p. 131). I will then look generally at how story may be used for change (p. 132), and then I consider specific contexts of its use, providing practical ideas (p. 136). Mostly I have avoided reference to fiction and left this for Chapter 12.

Some general issues about story and change

In Chapter 3 I associated learning with change, and personal and professional development in particular imply change and the support of change. Many disciplines are focused on facilitating change too, such as counselling, social work, physiotherapy, as well as work with medical subjects or influencing or educating others (education, health education, religion, law, advertising and marketing, and environmental education), and other disciplines study change in their specific forms of story (e.g. history, sociology, politics, economics, folklore, etc.). The very act of research is about changing existing conceptions (Chapter 11). I have suggested elsewhere that it is a personal skill of graduates to be able to manage story – in telling and listening in personal and professional life (Schank, 1995). In business and management, story is seen to have a range of the roles, and universities and colleges are organisations in themselves, subject to change in the soft knowledge that can influence the manner in which they function.

Stories (fiction or non-fiction) are used to institute change in different ways. These ideas are drawn from the earlier theory chapters and I focus on individuals in this chapter since they are most relevant to higher education processes.

In stories that are heard:

- the actual content of the story plots or illustrates a way of change;
- the story acts as a springboard; it inspires thinking in the listener – who relates to herself her own story – that results in change.

Where people tell stories:

- a teller hears her story and makes greater sense of something – and changes;
- a story told becomes an object for reflection with others and further sense is made for change;
- telling a story is cathartic – resulting in change;
- the act of telling to a listener facilitates a positive change in level of self-esteem;
- the act of telling a story brings about emotional insight (p. 000) and change happens.

Stories for change in business, management and organisational studies

There is a great deal written about story and change in management in organisation and business contexts. In this section I intend to give the topic a brief overview to indicate some of the literature that informs it. Some of what I say may stretch the notion of story for change.

That story is a powerful tool for change in organisational contexts has been recognised widely in the literature (e.g. Hawes, 1991; Pollack, 2000; Nymark, 2000; Gargiulo, 2006). Boje (1991) describes stories as 'the "blood vessels" through which changes pulsate in the heart of organisational life'. Similarly Taylor et al. (2002) cite Cummings and Brocklesby (1997), who describe how the Greek philosopher Kleisthenes used story to develop unity in Athens. Through this they demonstrate how story is an influencing power of great speakers. Polkinghorne (1988: 122) suggests that the stories in organisations ('organisational myths, stories, sagas and legends') help to facilitate the interpretation and significance of 'the purpose of the organisation and the role of its individual members' and thereby understanding of the organisational culture. An interesting perspective is provided by Claxton (1999), who interprets the attention to story in organisations as a shift from bullet-point language towards concern for deeper meanings.

A perusal of the literature of story in organisational change indicates that there are different conceptions of story use. Some are more detailed than the simple categorisation that I introduce below (e.g. Seel, 2003; Denning, 2004).

Story as a stimulus for reflection

Mattingly (1990) describes how she used story to facilitate sense-making and learn-ing in action research projects with key professionals at the World Bank. She talks of story as 'this ordinary mode of talk' (p. 235). She sees stories as 'pointing to deep beliefs and assumptions that people cannot tell in propositional ... form', but she says that this unspoken material guides people's actions. She describes how she asked a World Bank employee how he learned about the projects in which he was involved. He responded that the formal reports did not help, but the local stories did. They focused on people who did things, their 'motives and intentions' (p. 244) and how their actions enabled change. Mattingly described stories as unwinding 'along a temporal axis' and yet displaying a wholeness in which each particular episode [takes] a meaning as part of the larger whole' (p. 243). Thus, in her research, they enabled a greater understanding of the projects undertaken. However, Mattingly points out that stories also play a part in obscuring experience – perhaps in the 'postmodern and chaotic soup of storytelling' that is described by Boje (2002).

Story for intervention

'Springboard' stories

One of the more powerful modern messages about story as intervention comes from Denning, who describes how he personally changed from a hard-hitting persuader to the use of story – 'Time after time, when faced with the task of persuading a group of managers ... in a large organisation to get enthusiastic about a major change, I found that storytelling was the only way' (Denning, 2004: xiii; Lesser and Prusak, 2004: 178). Denning suggests some characteristics of stories that best initiate change – they should be told orally and be true because more value is attributed to 'truth'. They should have positive endings that create warm feelings and, in particular, he suggests that stories should be minimalist so that the listener has time to put herself into the story, or she can use the story as a 'springboard' for development of her own story – to which she will subsequently respond (Denning, 2008). Taylor et al. (2002) add that change is more likely to be effected if the story is 'good and aesthetically pleasing'.

Training as intervention

In considering the role of story in training others for business situations, Parkin (1998) demonstrates the use of different kinds of story, chosen for the desired change in the training participants. Parkin uses myths, other fiction, metaphors and a range of other stories to achieve various purposes.

Using story in a strategy for change and improvement in an organisation

Linden (1999) describes a two-day workshop on the use of story ('narrative') for change in a university. Supervisors of PhD students were asked for true stories about situations in which there was some kind of complication as supervisors; 444 narratives were collected. It appears, she says, that 'people seem to understand the world by means of plots, a form of organisation integrating the ... circumstances of concrete persons with the typicality ... of certain prototypical stories'. The collected stories were categorised and used as the basis for discussions to increase the sensitivity of the supervisors on the second day of the workshop.

Story that arise in organisations/groups and that may require management

Stories are engendered in groups and abound in organisations in the form of rumour, myth, hearsay stories, etc., and higher education institutions are no exception. These stories are said to be shared 'around the water cooler' as a kind of collective organisational memory bank (Nymark, 2000: 57). Gabriel (2000) talks of how they 'slip furtively in and out of sight: they evade censors, they are easily camouflaged'. They can rapidly combine and are 'notoriously difficult to suppress' (pp. 127–128). He says that they thrive particularly in less managed situations. I suggest that stories such as these seem to be generated in greater volume when there is a sense of change or threat in the air (e.g. threatened redundancies – Jones, 1991). In them, information may become exaggerated, emphasised or satirised in a manner that suits the purposes of the group (Snowden, 2004). Sometimes the purpose would be entertainment, though the same story could be used to subvert, to warn others or to maintain the status quo – it depends on how it is told.

After an extensive study of story in five organisations, I have mentioned Gabriel's (2000) conclusion that story can be seen as an attempt to make work in organisations more tolerable and human. He says 'emotions, spontaneity and play' are 'systematically excluded' from many areas of organisations and story might represent 'attempts to gain readmission' (p. 57). Jones (1991) suggests something similar in that it is not unusual for such 'folklore' to oppose the culture of the organisation and thereby to challenge the management of organisational change. Both Jones and Gabriel recognise that while stories may often seem to be negative to the organisation, by providing a form of acceptable expression they also preserve the organisation.

Listening to the stories that emanate from within an organisation is an important way of learning about an organisation, and finding out what is going on in order to maintain good management. This is also true of student stories and the work of teachers or the stories of teachers and the greater management of their institutions. Gabriel (2000) and Jones (1991) provide strategies for research on story cultures of organisations. Snowden (2004) suggests ways of countering disruptive ('anti-') stories by means of 'story virus' methods. He says that direct contradiction is rarely effective. The methods he lists include reduction to the absurd, use of metaphor to encourage viewing the issue differently, the insertion of a 'killer' fact and exaggeration of the story until is it 'laughable'. He warns, however, that 'in playing with people's stories, you are playing with their souls and this requires a high level of responsibility' (p. 215).

Story as a means of illustration

Visualisation of new scenarios

In the process of change sometimes it is useful to attain an overview of a situation (Gargiulo, 2006). Story can be used to encapsulate or visualise the current state of an organisational situation, as well as ideas for the future. Claxton (1999) talks of story told at the company 3M – of how a scientist became irritated with book-marks falling out of his songbook as he sung in a choir and how this resulted in Post-it notes. Fowler (1987) illustrates the value of vision in a hospital. He talks of the vision of the ward generated by an imagined new ward sister, Sister Vision. Students consider how exploring her ideas though vision and discussion enabled her effectively to lead her staff into the change, and this provides a learning experience for students.

Story and change in therapeutic disciplines

Narrative therapy is a product of the mid- to late 1900s (e.g. McNamee and Gergen, 1992). It 'views people inside a story' (Osis and Stout, 2001: 275) and holds that people not only make sense of their lives in terms of unfolding stories, but believe these stories (de Rivera and Sarbin, 1998) and the stories influence them in choices that they make. The stories are constructed by the subject as well as those who influence her and cultural influences. Therapy consists of a co-authoring process of deconstruction of non-helpful stories and (re)construction of positive stories (Clark, 2001). In the process, the client should come to manage her own stories and there is work to be done to make future stories more achievable – what Osis and Stout call 'thicker'. This might also mean seeking out the stories that inhibit achievement. In all, it is a process of creating a balance, accepting the past story in all that it was and was not (Kenyon and Randall, 2001), and being better able to make good choices for the future. Work with narrative therapy may be on a self-help basis in groups (Rappaport, 1993; Jennings, 2008; Crimmens, 1998) or one to one with a therapist. As Schank (1995) notes, there are interesting issues as to which story is chosen for telling at a given time and how the choice relates to the therapist's apparent 'preferences'.

There are different ways of involving story in therapy (McLeod, 1997). What I have described above is generally seen as a constructivist approach. Psychody-namic therapists would be wishing to find the common patterns and motivations in life stories. Others, such as Bettelheim (1976), suggest that the subject – in this case a child – selects 'the fairy tale that makes best sense of his or her life situation' (McLeod, 1997: 59). In another form of therapy bothersome issues are externalised, and viewed, for example, as a character in a story. The story is then retold. There is also considerable literature on therapy through the provision of stories that support people, enable them to find more positive identities and to make meaning of difficult areas of their lives. Gersie and others have written about the use of story in therapeutic or 'growth' groups (Gersie, 1991; Gersie and King, 1990) and through drama (Gersie, 1996) (see also Playback Theatre, n.d.; Boal, 1995).

Story in the promotion of change

Story plays an important role in higher education disciplines that promote change in people's behaviour. I have listed relevant disciplines at the beginning of this chapter (p. 131). There are also social movements such as health and environmental education and marketing that promote change of behaviour. Two companies that have consciously used stories as part of their marketing strategies are Innocent Drinks and Lego (Kean, 2007). In health education, sequences similar to the deconstruction and reconstruction of personal stories in therapy may be used to facilitate change of habit – though the word 'story' may not be used (Moon, 1995). The stages of change model, generated in health education contexts (Prochaska and Velicer, 1997) and sometimes linked to motivational interviewing, is also a matter of eliciting personal stories that then shift from supporting the negative behaviour to those supporting the idea of change and then change itself. The same model has been applied to the required shifts in behaviour to embrace climate change and shortage of energy issues (Hopkins, 2008). In a book called *Earthtales*, Gersie (1992) provides story-based material for use with a group that is working on environmental issues, and the chapters then reflect the progression of issues that a group might face in the process of change.

At the beginning of change, there is often a need to stimulate thinking. A well-known example of a story that seems particularly inspiring in the environmental sense is *The Man Who Planted Trees* (Giono et al., 2005), which has been produced on DVD, made into film and has even reached Wikipedia!

Some ways of using story to initiate or support change

- Story can illustrate change: it might involve the whole story or one character.
- A discussion of 'what makes me think' can be generated from reading particular or chosen stories.
- Learners can write stories that illustrate processes of change.
- They can write fictitious journals that illustrate experiences of change from the point of view of one person (Moon, 2009a).
- The choice of two stories with contradictory messages can generate discussion.
- Guided imagery can generate a sense of imagined change.
- Imagined dialogues can be held about proposed change between two relevant characters (Moon, 2006).
- Case studies or critical incidents in which change has occurred can be studied.
- Parables and metaphors relating to change can be introduced.

- Folktales or myths may be chosen that that focus on the processes of, or on actual change.
- There can be a collection of a series of stories relevant to change and a learning what they collectively suggest.

Thinkpoint

The tendency towards reductionist thinking and discrete information flattens stories into component parts. But stories re-member parts into patterned wholes. Finding a story is finding or creating a pattern, a meaning. Once a pattern [story] is seen, it has a self-sufficiency within us ... we cannot undo the pattern, although we can revise and alter [it].

(Hart, 2001: 45)

Chapter 11

Story and research

Introduction

Story pervades research: it is the subject matter of research (we research material that is often a story); it is in the methodology of research (stories may be written in the collection of data or as a means of testing findings); and it is the method of writing up research since good research writing may often include the devices of good story writing such as engagement and the use of the twists, turns and resolution of the research question. Our tendency to construct story also has much to do with the distortion of research findings in their application. The ideas around story that I explore in these pages share the philosophical issues of research such as the incorporation of a multiplicity of perspectives and interpretations and the notions of reality and generalisability. And of course, ideas for research may arise from an unsolved mystery!

After I have made a few initial points, the large part of this chapter is a review of ways in which story can play a part in research (p. 140).

Some general points about the place of story in research

Story runs throughout research. Apart from the overt processes of research, story is in the minds of those who engage in research: in the imagination, anticipation and vision of what might be found; in the sense-making to account for phenomena; in the human processes of research, whether it goes according to plan or not, that might be recorded in a research journal. Sarbin (1986) describes the interview as 'an instrument for story making' (p. xiv). Then there is the story of the research process. Bartlett (1997) provides a good example of the role of the story that underlay some research that she conducted on a parasitic nematode. She discusses how the formal reporting of research involves anything story-like being squeezed out of the writing. The necessary style requires explicit prose that minimises the role of the unspoken elements of communication. Bartlett comments on the research paper that followed her nematode work – that 'the serendipitous and irrational elements, [the] dreaming and mystery were omitted ... when I communicated my discoveries to my scientific colleagues'. She goes on: 'Small wonder science has the reputation it does. Small wonder the connection between imagination and science is almost non-existent in the eyes of many people' (p. 37). Commenting similarly in the social sciences, Rappaport (1993) says that social change is 'simply not captured well by the sort of [scientifically described] data we have obtained'. He argues for story (Eisner, 1988).

However, some researchers do acknowledge story. Lindqvist tells his research students to write up their theses like a story, with a beginning, middle and end, and a 'twist'; and he suggests they need to engage the reader. He says that the first page should read like the beginning of a story, capturing interest. (Lindqvist, personal communication, 2009).

Research thinking is often story-like too. Many of the qualities of story mentioned earlier apply well to research. Stories are framed distinctively from their context, and, similarly, to generate a research question is to frame a query distinct from its context (Chapter 4). Story also involves working with realities that are not current, and research thinking requires this 'what if?' quality. Research thinking and story both make demands on the unspoken, the intuitive and the imagined. They involve sensitivity to assumptions and to the non-explicit; both require the willing suspension of disbelief; both involve surprises and twists in expectation; and both ultimately are about making a different sense of something.

This drive to make sense takes me into some thinking that I have come to see as particularly important as I have explored story. As I have said, I have noticed the tendency for the public to grasp at explanations that are 'good', or convenient stories, and the tendency of the media then to exploit this. I have come to think that the construction and perhaps partly the enjoyment of story by humans is driven by a constant urge to 'make sense', to find explanations for phenomena or observations. I suggest that his lies behind the cognitive development of children, and the social evolution of mankind. I see it linking with epistemological development (Chapter 4). A theme that runs through the stages of epistemological development, for example, is an increase in the ability to cope with uncertainty – in other words, to cope with things not making immediate sense and appropriately to be able to manage aspects of life without certainties. An aspect of good research is a 'holding back' from allowing distraction by the wish too hurriedly to make sense and to complete the story. I said earlier that human judgement can be influenced by a 'good story' (Hastie and Davies, 2001; Laming, 2004; Strange and Leung, 1999).

I conclude this introductory section with two points. The first is a response to the title of a paper: 'Storytelling: is it really research?' (Koch, 1998). I can hardly say that storytelling is research or that research is storytelling – but I can reiterate that story is entangled in every aspect of research, even the research of those who would say that story and research are opposite in meaning. The second point is made by Greenhalgh (1998) in discussion of the merits of evidence-based practice in health and how that relates to story. She concludes that it is not 'an either or or' but a matter of both having a valuable place. So I now look at the places for story in research.

The places for story in research

Research on the stories of lives

Goodson and Sikes (2001) describe a range of research across several disciplines that studies people's lives. Some of this research aims at practical outcomes, such as improvement of professional education through gaining understanding of professional practice, and some are theoretical. The word 'story' associated with the research seems to imply a concern to take a holistic approach (Denny, 1978; Zeller, 1995). Also it implies the operation of an interpretive process. In other words, the 'story' is a narrative construction of the teller and the researcher (if they are not the same person) (Goodson and Sikes, 2001: 2) but it is possible to distinguish different approaches.

Among the approaches to life story, first there are stories that are generated from within the community or the group of which the individual or group is a part. Such ethnographic studies aim 'to understand the world views and ways of life of actual people from the "inside" in the contexts of their everyday lived experiences' (Cook, 1997). There are issues that affect the kinds of stories collected that relate to the role of the researcher in the group – whether, for example the role is overt or covert, the purpose of the research, the recording methods and, in particular, the manner in which the observations are reconstructed as outcomes of the research. Jordan (1989) used ethnographic methods to research why it was proving difficult to upgrade the skills of village health workers in the Yucatan, Mexico. She worked with the midwives, and participated in the efforts to upgrade their work. Through her understanding of their stories, Jordan saw how problems arose from the clash between the traditional apprenticeship model of induction and the 'delivery' of training. She describes the important role of stories as a traditional means of transmitting knowledge and how these 'packages of situated knowledge' are not available in abstract form and are acquired over time. Having the store of stories is part of what it takes to become an indigenous midwife.

Case study research (see Chapter 9) may be conducted because the story of a particular case has rare elements that are of importance to others (e.g. a patient is afflicted with a rare disease), or because the study of one case can provide insights into a situation that requires elucidation. Case studies in research may be 'one off' or they may be collated with similar cases to provide more generalised information about a particular group of people. Linden's (1999) work on PhD supervision and Greenhalgh and Collard's (2003) work on diabetes cases exemplify the latter, so the sub-stories of individual cases are combined to a 'super'-story that may make reference to individuals in its telling. A case study can be a report-like record (and not story) or a narrative product of the research itself. In the latter case, unspoken elements of the account carry information about the case that is not explicit (Zeller 1995; Winter, 1986). 'Super-stories' may be presented in abstracted form, or they may contribute to a fictitious or more accessible form which relates closely to the lives described, but focuses on no one life (Phillips, 1995; Winter,

1986). In this manner, case study research comes close to lifespan research (Goodson and Sikes, 2001).

Another way in which life story relates to research is in the studies of the lives of those who have changed human thinking. Such work aims to develop understanding of the thinking or theorising that led to the outcomes. As I write this, there are many books about Darwin's life and how he came to his theoretical position on evolution. Such work may also contribute to the understanding of exceptional thought processes.

Then there are research studies that are based on elements of the researcher's own stories. Eisner (1997) comments that personal 'narrative', when it is 'well crafted', can provide a 'platform for seeing what might be called our "actual worlds" more clearly'; for example, I described how Milner (then Field, 1952) in the 1950s researched what made her happy. In the last ten or fifteen years, the importance of reflection on one's actions has brought the self into the research process in many different ways. It is not unusual to write a reflective commentary within a dissertation or thesis so that the story of the researcher's thinking and decision-making is more evident. This is a means of acknowledging a constructivist stance. There is a story that threads through this book about how I have made sense of story and a fat reflective journal is evidence of that reflective work! Clough (2002) points out the difficulties of this kind of research based on self-reflection since there are no rules and there is little guidance on it. Richardson (2000) argues for the wider acceptance of autoethnography, which she describes as the 'narratives about the contexts in which the writing is produced' (p. 931). These texts offer 'critical reflexivity about the writing-self in different contexts as a valuable creatively analytic practice'. She provides an example from her own work.

In other parts of the book, I have also mentioned collaborative work on story by teachers or other professionals whose aim is to increase their understanding of their work – sometimes for their own benefit or in order to improve professional education or development. Such work is sometimes described as research, sometimes as 'inquiry' (e.g. Connelly and Clandinin, 1990).

I have also mentioned, in different places in this book, the collection of multiple stories with a common element presented as a form of qualitative research, such as Sparkes' (2002) (sports studies). Sparkes presents this amalgam of fiction, non-fiction, drama, poetry and confessional literature as qualitative research and to support teaching. He argues that it is a representation of the richness of experience in the real world.

Research that involves the development of stories as part of the research method

Sometimes stories are generated within research to further that research by testing constructs against a form of reality. I give three examples. Wertner and Trudel (2006) used this method as a means of testing a model of how coaches learn to coach. They developed a story of how two coaches, Mark and Judy, attend a weekend course on dealing with athlete anxiety prior to competition and they apply their model of coach learning to them. Mark and Judy have different learning backgrounds (deliberate stereotypes) and Wertner and Trudel use the story to explore how these two might approach the learning on the course. Subsequently in their paper, the writers apply the outcomes of their research to a case study of a real coach.

In the second example, I use examples from the field of unitary appreciative inquiry. This is a method of researching concepts (in this case, despair) within the context of the unique lives of individuals (Cowling, 2001, 2004). Cowling describes how he listened to the stories of a number of women who saw themselves as 'in despair'. He, as researcher, reconceptualised the stories with associated music, which he then offered back to the women. The stories he calls 'pattern profiles', and the title of them suggests the theme that appears to be emerging (e.g. 'babies all over the place'). The stories, when shared, tended to generate further iterations from the women. This use of story works in the area of the unspoken. Repede (2008) says that 'Stories convey meaning and open us to the deep mystery of compassion. Stories are methodological tools in the aesthetic domain of nursing, paratelic ways of knowing that carry us beyond logic to a higher order of understanding'.

Another example of story in the research process is the use of the stories of the student trip to Beer and that of learning to change a tyre (p. 000). These stories originated in the context of my investigation of how reflective learning might relate to other aspects of the learning process (Moon, 2004). They tested ideas through simulation and inspired the development of new thinking. In this book I have used them differently – to suggest how the process of learning relates to story.

Research on stories already produced

In this category resides a range of research that includes story in literature and other representational arts, the formal study of folklore, the studies of stories in the print and electronic media and so on, and stories told in therapeutic contexts. I have also mentioned studies of the informal spread of rumour and urban myth, and that of Gabriel (2000) and others on the stories that circulate in workplaces. Gabriel approached his research on story in organisations though a detailed study of the nature of story (from which I have drawn), then he used this to review the use of stories in organisational research and the methodological issues that pervade such research. This is, in effect, the story of his own research.

Fiction and research

Many times in this book I have referred to the manner in which fiction and non-fiction elide and this is no less true for research than for other areas of academic pursuit. In this brief section I will review some of the issues around fiction and research which will inevitably overlap with Chapter 12 and with earlier material.

Fiction figures in research processes in several ways. It has a place at the beginning of research in indicating the gaps in our knowledge that are worthy of research. Phillips (1995) and Bolton (1994) point out how fiction can contain the data from many years of experience in a particular field. A similar idea is expressed by Winter (1986) – that telling a story is analogous to 'providing a theory'. It captures and organises a structure 'that lies behind ... the details and gives them a pattern and a significance in relation to some other situation'. Winter (1986), Rowland et al. (1990) and Bolton (1994) provide examples of using fiction in research on professional practice.

Fiction may play a part in the research method (e.g. the Beer story in Chapter 3 and Wertner and Trudel 2006), and Clough (2002) constructs a deeply considered argument for the role of 'narratives and fictions' within the process of educational research and in the writing up. He says that such writing 'offers the opportunity to import fragments of data from various real life events in order to speak to the heart of social consciousness – thus providing the protection of anonymity to the research participants without stripping away the rawness of real happenings' (p. 8). Adding to this, Phillips suggests that such writing supplies the 'ambiance' (an unspoken element of story) that underlies the situation that is being described. He suggests that this material is integrated into academic writing in the form of short anecdotes. Clough takes the argument for the role of fictional writing in educational inquiry and research into the philosophy of interpretation (hermeneutics). He sees fiction as another 'way of seeing' (p. 98) elements in the world that has its own validities and failings alongside other research forms. Its particular value lies in its close link to human experience. Perhaps the main difficulty lies in evaluation where evaluation is viewed traditionally.

Research based on piecing together a coherent story to explain observations

In this application of stories in research, I might be seen to be stretching the concept of research beyond its usual bounds – I refer to the work of archaeology, anthropology, aspects of history research and forensic investigation. Some, however, would say that what I cover here is the background to all research: the seeking of a coherent story that will satisfactorily explain observations. I use as example an anthropological/archaeological study of various structures on pebblebed heathland, including Bronze Age barrows and the possible site of an encampment that anticipated Napoleon's arrival on the English coast (www.pebblebeds.org.uk). The structures involved in the research appear to be unique in their pebble construction. There were stories at the beginning. Landowners in the past observed the barrows and then sought to make the heath more mysterious by building more barrows and planting pines. The genuine barrows stand in alignment to a high hill on the coast and are associated with the burial rites at other sites and the objects that might be found. Another story related to a meticulous investigator of these structures in the 1930s, his drawings, his interpretations and the stories of his own prior experiences that generated the conceptual tools that influenced his research and interpretation. There are also wider stories around in this investigation that concern the story of the research itself, how we all (from diverse backgrounds and disciplines) came to be involved – archaeologists, an artist, cultural anthropologists, an educationist.

For all of those on the project, the landscape is important as a context for the stories: the hills, the heather and gorse, the clouds that roll over the ridge, the winds sweeping down, the rain, the brown peat mud. And there are the pebbles, some too much for one hand, broken or whole, and their colours – browns, reds, whites, the colour of sunset and of those that are blue against the brown peat – and the clunking of their sounds when they are knocked. Did the people of the Bronze Age use specially chosen pebbles at the centre of the cairn? Were they chosen for their size and/or shape. Did they strike the quartzite pebbles against each other in order to create sparks (hence all the broken pebbles). Were these strange blue pebbles of significance to them? Which of these are part of our story, and which are part of their stories? We go on seeking the story or a story that gives us some meaning for these structures and for the totality of these experiences in the research process. It needs to be a story that feels satisfactory for the present.

But is this kind of human story not what applies to all research?

Story, research and the resisting of stories

I want to step back and to reiterate an important point which is background to this material on learning. I believe that it is part of effective human functioning to be driven to make sense of our experiences. For some that may mean local experience; others will have bigger questions. Stories arise in that sense-making. Most non-scientists tend to jump at the story as explanation if it is satisfying. The training of a scientist (and, I would argue, so it should be for any graduate) is to hold back and resist the good story.

Thinkpoint

Children enter school accomplished storytellers, veteran fantasy players only to discover quite abruptly that this great passion of theirs is not part of the curriculum. Their talents for imagery and illusion are sent outside to play where no teacher can make use of the stories they tell – or ever hear them.

(Paley, 1995: 95)

Chapter 12

Uses of fiction in education

Introduction

Gough (1993) says that he once saw in an English classroom a poster that said, 'The universe is not made of atoms – it is made of stories'. That seems a fitting start to this chapter. In the chapter, I draw together some ideas about the use of fiction in higher education. As with other topics in this part of the book, there will be over-laps with earlier references. Again like other chapters in this part, I start by gathering general ideas (p. 155) and there are two more sections in which I explore the use of fiction in higher education (p. 146) and professional development (p. 150). Most of the examples relate to broad areas of education.

Some general points about fiction

Sparkes (2002) says, 'the notion of stories and storytelling does not sit easily in many academic circles' (p. 180), often being seen as 'mere entertainment' (Mar and Oatley, 2008). If there is to be prejudice against the use of 'mere story' in education, it will be focused mostly on fiction – the 'made-up' story that might seem to oppose the quest for scientific evidence, although I have exceptions (e.g. Saunders et al., 2004). I have also argued that there is no clear boundary between fiction and non-fiction ('fact') (e.g. Chapters 2 and 4). Once the source of information is unknown to the recipient of the story, whether the story is authentic or based on authentic ideas in many educational situations may not matter.

All stories are constructed (Chapter 2). Bruner (1986) seems to link fiction and non-fiction in his suggestion that fiction develops the 'outer landscape of action and the inner one of thought' (p. 14) and this idea seems similar to Hardy's notion of the 'inner and outer storytelling that plays a major role in our sleeping and waking lives' (Hardy, 1977: 13). There is anecdotal evidence that stories are an intimate part of human development. Peter Pan did not hear stories and did not, as a con-sequence, grow up (Fulford 1999)! I have described the beginnings of work on how we learn from story in Chapter 4 (e.g. Wheeler et al., 1999; Marsh et al., 2003).

An important educational aspect of fiction is that it is 'free' and unbounded. In its different realities within the frames in which a story is set it can take people into new places, it can deal with difficult emotions, it can widen the experience of people away from their perceptions of their worlds and it is free of time constraints. It can give us that sense of 'otherness' described by Greenhalgh and Collard (2003) and is the place for imagination. Winter et al. (1999) wrote about 'The strange absence of the creative imagination in professional education' (p. 180). The 'absence' may largely be due to tensions between those who treat the 'made up' as 'only' imagination with no place in education and those who see it as valuable, who might argue that fiction is an untapped resource in education. This is nicely summarised by Gersie and King:

> The multi-dimensional quality of imagination makes it possible for us to echo the darkest corner of our being, to reveal our most hidden belongings and capacities ... The multi-functional aspect of imagination helps to resolve, reconcile, energise, stimulate and encourage. In itself, the imagination is neither good nor bad, it is the function which we give to it which determines its usefulness.
>
> (Gersie and King, 1990: 36)

The fictionalising of case material may be a deliberate process to meet ethical requirements; however, the focus of this section is not on 'fictionalising' for this kind of reason, but on the direct use of fiction.

Some uses of fiction in education

I start from more general ideas and move towards those more specific, though the intention is that the ideas can be applied across most disciplines and professional development. While most of the examples imply the use of fiction developed by others, there are many situations in which creative writing of fiction can be used similarly or to greater effect.

Fiction can serve to initiate dialogue or discussion

A story will first engage and draw in the listener. There may be no direct question asked, but a situation set up that begs resolution or stimulates thought. In that way the learner starts from inside a situation, rather than as an outsider to it. This can facilitate deeper and livelier discussion than that which might follow a direct question. This approach can be applied in any discipline; it may be introduced as problem-solving. Gersie (1992) demonstrates various uses of fiction in environmental groups (see also Seed et al., 1988; Alvarez and Merchan, 1992; Thomas and Killick, 2007).

Fiction gives practice in 'filling in the gaps'

McCloskey (1990) suggests that fictional stories in economics train the economist to recognise and address the gaps in accounts. He cites Niels Bohr's remark about physics that physics is 'not about the world, but about what we as human beings can say about the world' (McCloskey, 1990: 18). Stories in a discipline can invite consideration of what is not being said (the unspoken). Perhaps this is similar to saying that fiction can be used to 'probe our ignorances and create new conditions for knowledge' (Pagano, 1991: 210). Pagano suggests that 'ignorance' gives rise to a space for knowledge.

Some of the 'gaps' may be to do with experience of the situations to which reference is made in theory. Phillips (1995), in the context of organisational studies, suggests that fiction can act as a 'boot camp' for those with relatively little experience of organisations. The stories show up dysfunction or they challenge naïve attitudes.

Development of story literacy

I have referred to Wilson's (2006) comments on the development of story literacy previously. As well as learning to manage the gaps in knowledge, learners need to manage the telling of and listening to stories in professional and personal situations. They need to be able to learn from stories but also to learn to hold back from making judgements (Strange and Leung, 1999). There is also a need to come to understand that stories are constructed and that they 'mix truth and lies' (Lamarque, 1990, citing Llosa, 1986: 118). Learners need to learn how to be appropriately critical and to understand the uses that they do and can make of story. Plummer demonstrates this in the context of sexual stories analysed in the context of sociology (Plummer, 1995).

Another aspect of story literacy which involves fiction is the development of understanding of how the communication of events to others is ordered in order to engage the listening of others (Chapter 13). Fulford describes stories as the 'building blocks of human thought' (Fulford, 1999: 83). Similarly Wolf (2007) argues that students should be exposed to difficult texts in order to improve their expertise in reading and thinking processes.

Fiction as illustration

Far from shunning the relevance of fiction, some teaching embraces it. In a widely used textbook on the topic of organisational behaviour, at the end of each chapter there is a list of films or novels that illustrate the points made in the text (Huczynski and Buchanan, 2007). Examples of such recommended fiction is Kafka's novel *The Castle* (Kafka, 1997) and *Watership Down* (Adams, 1972). In a different way, fiction can 'give concrete life to philosophies' (Claxton, 1999) – I have mentioned several texts that set out to do just this (Gaardner, 1996; Read, 1935; Williams, 1995). A particular example of using fiction as illustration is Rosenstein, who uses the film version of *The Sorcerer's Apprentice* (Walt Disney, 1940) to illustrate Schon's (1983, 1987) concepts of reflection and professionalism.

Fiction to promote thinking and epistemological development

Gough (1993) describes the use of fiction in science. The aim is to explore and stimulate thinking on a topic. He argues that science fiction and postmodern texts model human interrelationships with the environment and understandings of 'nature' and 'reality' more effectively than much of the expository scientific writing. Along similar lines, Kloss (1994) and Phillips (1995) recommend various examples of fiction to facilitate epistemological development, and Hines (1988) is itself an example of such material (see Chapter 7).

A particular context for the encouragement of thought is in areas of ethics and moral development. Alvarez and Merchan (1992) connect fiction and ethics, saying that 'to act morally is to act in such a way that one is able to occupy the position of others, to have a feeling of belonging to a human community and to be a *we*, not an *I*' (see also Tappan, 1991; Zander, 2007).

Lucas (2008) describes how she tells her accountancy students a brief story – apparently about a theft. The story implies that there is a guilty party. She gives students a list of statements requiring 'true', 'false' or 'don't know' responses. Few will respond 'don't know', but of the eighteen statements there is actually no evidence for thirteen in the story. In groups students are asked to discuss their responses. Finally the story is told. The actions are actually innocent. Students are asked what they have learned – and they recognise that they have made assumptions and drawn conclusions too quickly. This exercise supports the suggestion that I have made several times that the human propensity for creating stories leads us to be insufficiently critical (Lucas, 2008; Glanz, 1995).

Fiction to relate theory to the real world in a holistic manner

Fiction can bring emotion and a sense of 'the "darker side of things" – different material from that of reports and essays' (Meek et al., 1977: 112). In Chapter 7 I have mentioned the use of patchwork texts. Students may be allowed or encouraged to include pieces of fiction (possibly their own writing) as a means of relating their material to real and holistically described situations. On a similar basis, Sparkes (2002) agues for the role of fiction in depicting the ways in which people identify themselves. In the context of work on organisations, Phillips (1995) talks of fiction as providing 'an additional point of contact in the everyday world of "real life" experiences and the theoretical models' (see also Wertner and Trudel 2006). It can 'mediate between the abstract wordless theories. ... and the subjective world in which the student lives' (Phillips, 1995). In addition, Phillips mentions the ability of fiction to reflect atmosphere and settings that 'add life and interest' to academic articles. In essence he is referring to the manner in which stories carry the unspoken.

Fiction has transformational potential (reflection and personal development)

Greene (1990) discusses the manner in which 'literature' raises awareness of issues towards transformational change and she says that 'certain aspects of the reader's lived biography will emerge as figures against a ground' (p. 257), such as examples of racism, superstition or powerlessness. Fiction can 'acquaint people with alternative ways of seeing, feeling and understanding' in 'emancipatory moments', with readers 'left with indignation aroused, with their lived worlds more problematic than before, with a praxis still to be devised' (pp. 262, 263, 265). In terms of recent developments, Murray (2001) talks of the development of computer game stories that are empowering and that develop social understanding (Chapter 14). Along similar lines, Baxter Magolda (1999) describes ways of using fiction to promote the 'self authorship' of a large group of students and Zander (2007) applies the ideas to art education, suggesting that the transformative role of story can encourage new approaches to art. Jackson (1995) discusses classroom management issues that can arise from such educational uses of story.

Several writers suggest that the material of learning journals can be explored further when it is made into fiction (Hunt, 2000) and fiction can provide protected space for exploration of journal ideas (Grainger, 1995). A first step can be shifting to third-person writing. Pagano (1991) asks her teacher education students to take elements of their journals and write a fictitious story based on the material. She suggests that this provides deep feedback to the students and their teachers about what they know and how they deploy their knowledge in the open space that fiction provides.

Fiction promotes imagination and flexibility of thinking

Greene (1990) points out that the suspension of disbelief that occurs in story 'entails a deliberate break with the habitual, the routine, the ordinary' (p. 254). This relates to a technique that I have used often in long workshops – to wake up minds, creativity and imagination. The method follows Allen (1997) and basically consists of writing a story in five minutes (I use seven minutes).

Alvarez and Merchan (1992) and Phillips (1995) describe the use of fiction for the development and deployment of imagination about future situations in organisational situations.

Fiction as a 'social facilitator' (book clubs)

An unusual example of the use of fiction in higher education is the setting up of book clubs as a means of encouraging reading but also for their social value. Book clubs may often be run by student unions, but could also be run in halls of residence, for example.

Fiction as engaging learners in introducing topics

Fiction has been used as a method for introducing topics and ideas. Turner (2008) suggests that *Dr Who* stories can lead to the investigation of many topics in science (e.g. robotics) and he also suggests that the special effects used to make the programme are also worthy of research. Bartlett (1997) talks of her use of the *Three Little Pigs* story and the functional strengths of the materials used to build the pigs' houses to introduce the 'concept in a living cell where the different functional abilities of biological molecules are related to the different chemical building blocks from which they are made' (p. 26). She provides a number of other examples, but she warns that while many students appreciate this approach, some do not (see Noddings, 1996).

I have mentioned Saunders et al. (2004), who have incorporated science fiction into the design of their whole curriculum.

Fiction as insight into or simulation of experiences and situations that may not be available

In this sense, fiction can act as a database. Phillips (1995) gives as an example for organisational studies *A Day in the Life of Ivan Denisovich* (Solzhenitsyn, 1963). Similarly, Gudmundsdottir (1995) talks of the use of stories to learn about different cultural perspectives. In either of these cases, a learning journal could be a useful adjunct to the 'sense-making' process.

I have mentioned the suggestion that story enables a simulation of life situations (e.g. Mar and Oatley, 2008a). Phillips (1995) says fiction (in all its forms) provides a space 'for the reader to enter the story and vicariously experience the events portrayed'. Fiction is an infinite source of 'events'. Greene (1990) adds to this, suggesting that the reader should endeavour to 'watch (herself) be involved in the story' (p. 257) in order to be aware of the issues prompted by the story. Murray (2001) suggests that technology can enable this shifting from one culture to another, from one viewpoint to another and the replaying of the same situation in a more flexible manner than can traditional stories.

Using fiction to elicit professional learning

Many of the general uses of fiction listed above can be applied valuably in professional education, particularly the use in simulation. However, I want to pick out a few more specific examples in this section.

Using fiction to elicit professional learning

Strong-Wilson (2006) used 'literature circles, interviews and the writing of literacy autobiography' as a means of exploring learners' constructions of the idea of 'difference' in relation to their prior knowledge. This involved the discussion of favourite literature to enrich the reflective process. Pagano (1991) recommends the use of fiction in professional story in education in order to create distance from the material. She contrasts this with the use of autobiographical writing because the later enables us to fictionalise ourselves as ego-ideals, which, she suggests, may often be unhelpful learning.

Richardson provides a book full of fiction and fables aimed at inspiring teachers (*Fortune and Fables*, 1996). I have mentioned Dittrich's (2001) book of medical story, poetry, pictures and thoughtful commentaries similarly to stimulate thought and Holmes and Gregory's (1998) use of poetry writing as a means of deeply knowing in nursing.

Fiction used to 'unlock' creativity

Mansfield and Bidwell (2005) suggest fiction as a means of 'illumination and increasing the understanding' of research processes. They work with a group of Master's level students on a Community Education programme and say that their students come onto the programme with a belief that they will be told to 'write themselves out' of their inquiries. Instead, they are asked to use story, creative writing techniques and 'reflexive journals' to enable them to 'regain trust in their own senses', to 'unlock their creativity' and thus to re-engage as autonomous learners with a range of ways of knowing.

Using fiction to explore portrayal of the professional

Gilbey (2008) stated that the portrayal of scientists in popular culture is 'mad, bad and dangerously keen on bubbling vials'. He questions whether this should be a concern. The image of professionals should be a concern in professional education, as stereotypes often lie in the background thinking of novices. Fiction is an ideal means of initiating discussion of this.

Fiction is a means of supporting learners' learning of difficult processes and concepts

In Chapter 7 I described graduated scenarios. I had been using the method for helping learners with reflective learning and critical thinking and was halfway into writing this book before I realised that graduated scenarios are examples of fiction being used for professional development.

Case studies can be fictitious

Chapter 9 concerns case studies. Case studies do not have to be authentic; they can be fictitious and, as such, they can be more useful for study because they are infinitely flexible.

Writing fiction in professional education

I have referred, a number of times, to the value of asking professionals to fictionalise aspects of their work both for the benefit of their own learning and also as a means of initiating discussion with colleagues or with novices. One method for this is the fictionalising and development of incidents noted in learning journals. In other situations it is more of a creative writing exercise, based on real-life experience (Winter, 1986, 1991; Rowland et al., 1990; Pagano, 1991; Bolton, 1994, 1999; Hunt, 2000).

Thinkpoint

At the end of the story, the nurse engaged in discussion about the context in which the event occurred. She suddenly remembered that there was a lot of crying going on in the ward at that time. She had not been conscious of it as part of the story, but now, thinking back, it was there in the background. It was then that she made the conscious connection that her own son had been to theatre that morning.

(McDrury and Alterio, 2003: 143–4)

Chapter 13

Oral storytelling in education

Introduction

This chapter differs from most of the rest of the book. It is about how stories are conveyed rather than the content or type of story. It is about what *I* call 'storytelling', the oral telling or retelling of a story by one person to others. As I said in Chapter 1, others use the word in a broader context. Storytelling is an old skill that still has a place in modern life, and in this chapter I will argue that there is a place for learning to tell oral stories in advanced education for learners and for teachers.

Oral storytelling has several characteristics. There is, first, the directness of voice (Rosen, 2009). Voice is used, of course, when stories are read out loud, so the second issue is the value of the oral telling – in Irish terms, the 'craic'. Harrett (2008) explores the difference between storytelling and story reading and seems to end up by describing in undefinable words the unspoken qualities of oral storytelling as opposed to reading. She talks of the 'magic – the indefinable spark that binds speaker and listeners in a shared journey through imagination'. I have suggested that we cannot define everything in words – which I think she demonstrates!

There are three sections to this chapter. In the first section I consider why storytelling is a capacity that might be usefully learned in formal educational contexts and professional development (p. 154). There are different rationales for teachers' and students' learning. The second section provides a background to oral storytelling and its place in current times (p. 154) and the in the third section I provide an introduction to how oral storytelling 'works' – and how a best to learn how to tell oral stories (p. 155).

Since I first wrote this book, I have developed two tutor packs on oral storytelling. They will be available for free downloading online, one from the ESCalate website (http://www.ESCalate.ac.uk – for use with any discipline students), and the other from http://www.CEMP.ac.uk specifically for media students. Both indclude video demonstrations of oral storytelling (Moon 2010a; 2010b).

A place for oral storytelling in education and professional development

There is no point in telling a story to others if those others are not engaged by the story. Storytelling implies the enlivening of a story to hold attention – to facilitate engagement. These qualities are central to the process of storytelling but they are also central to good teaching (Glanz, 1995; Martin and Darnley, 1996; Moon, 2001; Parkin, 2008). Related to this is the ability to communicate confidently without gazing at a handful of script. This is quite apart from managing the content of the story and its relationship to the learning processes. These are the basic reasons why it is helpful for those in teaching positions to learn to tell stories orally. Correspondingly in these days of concern for employability skills, storytelling is valuable for learners since most are expected at some stage in their undergraduate programmes to make an oral presentation because in their careers many will be required to present material or pitch ideas to others in formal situations. The practice of staid presentations of scripts read out in front-of-the-face presentations is common. There is often no teaching of how to present, so haphazard results are an outcome. If learners are taught to tell stories, they can learn to manage self-expression, posture and voice, and learn to speak without dependency on notes. That capacity is likely to serve them in other contexts in their careers as well.

So primarily I suggest that learning to tell oral stories is valuable as a set of communication capacities that aims for best practice in teaching and presenting. However, oral storytelling has other places in educational contexts. I list some of these. Forms of oral storytelling come into active work in politics (Levinson, 2008), business and management (Denning, 2001, 2004), religion, tourism (guiding tourists), various forms of training (Parkin, 1998), language learning (Heathfield, 2005), the arts and architecture, media subjects, work with children in a variety of contexts, care, social and community work (Gersie, 1991; Jennings, 1999, 2004), library studies, various therapies and, of course, performance studies. It is valuable as a parenting or grand-parenting skill. In addition there are leadership, confidence-building and public speaking schemes (e.g. Toastmasters, n.d.) in which the ability to present confidently is central. The confidence that can come with the ability to tell a story is related to personal development planning and student success programmes (META, 2005) and, of course, storytelling ability is a totally portable form of entertainment that can always be useful. Learning to tell stories could occur in student unions rather than within programmes, in association, for example, with student representative training programmes.

A background to oral storytelling

I add a few notes about the place of oral storytelling in case it might seem like an activity of the past or only for children. Storytelling is common to all civilisations (Hopen, 2006). Stories come under a variety of overlapping headings – wonder tales, fairy tales, tall tales, myths, legends, ghost stories, trickster stories, jokes and more.

They are portable entertainment and as people travelled they shared their stories; and because oral telling leaves stories flexible and open to interpretation and reinterpretation, they gained new form, meaning, names and the beginning of one story was furnished with the ending of another. Perhaps this is not quite as Iff, the floating gardener, describes it Rushdie (1990: 85, 86). The Plentimaw fish eat stories. These fish, says Iff, 'are "hunger artists" ... when they are hungry, they swallow stories ... and in their innards ... a little bit of one story joins on to an idea from another and hey presto when they spew the stories out they are not old tales but new ones'.

It might be imagined that strong images and storylines in stories are more stable than weak ones. Stories were told 'at the loom, in the field, with needle or adze or brush in hand', as well as in the market square and entertaining the nobles at the ball (Parkinson, n.d.). Stories were told as entertainment or in order to change minds (parables). At times, they have been collected, sometimes to serve a purpose – I said that the brothers Grimm collected stories to promote nationalism in Germany in the early to mid-nineteenth century. To bring that seriously up to date, it was announced at a folk festival in 2009 that the British National Party was using folk song to promote nationalism. Some more recent collections of traditional stories are those of Foss (1977), Marshall (1996), Riordan (1984), Bushnaq (1987), Carter (1991), McCaughrean (1999), Warner (1996), and Crossley-Holland (1987) (see Zipes, 2000 for further information). Collecting with the implied casting of the oral into print has not stopped the processes of reinterpretation, as the Disney Corporation has demonstrated (Grainger, 1997; Cassady, 1994).

Storytelling for adults and children has happened everywhere in the past, but still occurs, in its own ways widely despite the availability of printed media and entertainment through radio and television. There are different cultural forms of traditional storytelling (Nwobani, 2008; Pendry 2008; Shah, 2008; Jackson, 2008) and I have made many references to why story is still important. There are different ways in which storytelling manifests itself in the modern world formally and informally. In the UK, stories are told in pubs, in story groups, in folk clubs, at festivals, in schools, in care homes, in residential care for the elderly. There are storytelling performances in theatres, and cafés, at National Trust Properties (Schreiber, 2009), in street performances and ghost walks. Storytelling is used in celebrations and religions (sermons). Storytelling is a means, too, of giving comfort to displaced groups of people (Aylwin, 1994) and in after dinner speaking. The National Society for Storytelling supports storytelling in the UK (http://sfs.org.uk) and lists a substantial number of professional storytellers. In the United States there are a number of schools of storytelling on the internet. Further information about storytelling can be obtained from the websites of the George Ewart Evans Centre for Storytelling (http://storytelling. research.glam.ac.uk) as well as from the Society for Storytelling (www.sfs.org.uk).

Learning to tell stories orally

I am including in this section of this chapter much of the content of a workshop on oral storytelling that I run. Towards the end of the section there will be descriptions of other ways in which to run workshops. However, the main advice is to just go and try telling a story. It may turn out to be easier than it might seem! Driving along in a car or, for me, kayaking alone in an estuary is a good place in which to practice!

Some general points about learning to tell stories orally

First, storytelling is not a matter of learning stories word for word. Occasionally there are sets of words that are important in story because the story revolves around them, but that is relatively rare and there are, of course, the names of the characters to learn. If these are difficult, shorten them. It is the nature of oral stories that they are reinterpreted. When I am looking for stories, I find that some contain whole sections that do not carry forward the action of the story. Sometimes they add to the aesthetic qualities of the story, and I would tend to retain them, but sometimes they are bits of other stories that have become incorporated and are extraneous.

Selecting stories

Obviously stories are selected according to the audience for whom they are intended, but this may not mean that they cannot be drawn from children's books. Many traditional stories were told in the past to adults, but in Victorian times they were modified for children. That mainly meant taking out sex and extreme violence. In my experience an adult can get as 'lost' in a good story as children, and, likewise, young children can be enthralled by what are meant to be adult stories.

Finding stories and therefore finding the appropriate sources for stories is a matter of individual choice. The new storyteller has to find out what makes a 'good' story to tell. I can only say that the sorts of stories that appeal to me for telling are 'strong stories' (Chapter 2) with a beginning, middle and clear ending and some sort of plot or twist. Beyond that they have a touch of magic – again I can only use that word to describe the something that makes me want to share that story with others. It has a jewel-like quality. I can often look through whole books of stories, and find nothing with that quality. Clearly factors like length and complexity can be an issue too. Most times when I tell stories, they have to be short – sometimes only four minutes or more typically ten minutes – and length becomes a criterion for choice. Sometimes stories I tell relate to a theme. Recently I had to select a series of stories for a 'Medieval Fete' that celebrated the anniversary of the consecration of a church, and I tried to include stories with references to churches. Other times it is Halloween or Christmas – and so on.

There are some storytellers who will only use stories that they hear orally. I am less precious about storytelling and I find stories mostly in books. There is great delight in looking through a new book of stories for those that might be suitable. I seek books in libraries, occasionally new books in bookshops but also in charity and second-hand shops. There are some sources of good stories on the internet – but

I had to work hard to find stories that please there. I have said before that Geraldine McCaughrean's (1999) book of world myths and legend has been a wonderful source.

Styles of telling stories

There are different styles of storytelling. None is right or wrong. I did not set out to learn a style; a style just happened when I began to tell stories. Some storytellers act as if they are a conduit through which the story flows. The teller is still and the story comes out through the voice alone. In contrast, others move and the story comes out through voice and body. The movement flows with the voice – it is not that the teller says something and then mimes it. Another style is more conversational: the teller tells the story as a part of a conversation with the listeners. There may be singing or a musical instrument integrated with the story.

Learning a story

It is the learning of a story that mostly concerns potential tellers. It is not difficult, but again it is a matter of an individual finding her best way of learning. Some people can learn a story from reading it several times and learning from the words. A common method is to imagine the story as a series of scenes and, in effect, describe what is going on in each scene. Each description will lead on to the next scene and the teller works from these mental images of what is going on in the story. This seems to be closer to the nature of story since images incorporate the unspoken elements of story.

When I learn a story I read it through probably twice, then I summarise it on paper in a numbered sequence. Each 'number' is a scene or event in the story. My notes might take two sides of A5 paper. There is no point in writing the story again. As I write I am visualising the events of the story. I repeat in the top corner of the sheet any difficult names of people or places. I may underline various phrases from the written story that either I *must* use in order to make the story work or that I want to use because it helps the flow of the story. If there are difficult scenes, I sometimes roughly sketch them. I then tell the story to myself wherever there is undisturbed space to tell the story out loud. I need to get right 'inside' the story in my mind. This practice in telling the story is vital!

Since I have found that I tell a story through my whole body and move when I tell, I will sometimes tell short sequences of the story and see how I will move. I can only put it this way because moving as I tell is intuitive – movements just happen, but it is useful to know what might happen. I think that the feeling of the movement helps my remembering of the story. However, I have said that some people tell stories in this way, and some do not.

It can also be helpful to think more deeply about the characters in a story. Who are they, what are they feeling, what do they look like? What is their history? This is more important in a longer story, in which the personalities of the characters are more relevant.

I usually keep the notes about the story with a photocopy of the original story. Since I now have a large collection of stories, I have needed to order the stories and make a list of their titles. I do not always use the titles given – they are often simply made up by the person who wrote the story out the last time! I do not necessarily introduce a story with the title; I might say, 'This is a story from China' or some such words. I often write notes on an index card, which I would take to a storytelling session. This is particularly useful when there are difficult names of characters or places or sets of words that have to be said and the card is a last minute crib. Though I have rarely needed the card, it is comforting to know it is there.

In learning stories from the sequence of scenes, it is useful to bear in mind that stories tend to have underlying structures. They are often something like the following:

- introduction or opening word;
- an initial situation;
- a problem that has to be solved;
- the introduction of some sort of 'helpers', crucial to solving the problem;
- obstacles – there are often three in traditional stories;
- attempts to succeed – and there may be more than one try;
- success – achievement – transformation – resolution;
- and a final few words.

It is also worth thinking of the involvement of the senses in the telling of a story. Invoking vivid sight, touch, sound and smell or movement sensations enriches the experience for listeners. These can be added to a story.

Beginnings and endings

Endings and beginnings are really important. A weak ending leaves the listeners with frustration and negativity. I think that the beginning of a story should be designed according to the context of the storytelling. There are times to give a title and start in an organised manner and there are times to 'jump straight into' the story with no introduction. There are some traditional beginnings for stories, such as:

- Once upon a time ...
- Once upon a time and in a place that we may not know ...
- Snip snap my story's in ... (end on: Snip snap my story's out ...)
- It happened where north, south, east and west meet ...
- Once there was ... or: Once there was not ...
- I shall light the story fire, and the flame will burn brightly ... (end on: The flames of the story fire are dying now, but the story's embers will glow on for ever ...)

(This list is largely taken from or modified from Grainger, 1997.)

Some of these generate a nice atmosphere for story – and, of course, it is possible to develop beginnings and endings for the particular story. Sometimes I use a small gong to denote the beginning and the ending of a story. It defines the 'storytelling space' very clearly.

One reason for weak endings is to do with the quality of the story, but even with a good ending, the ending can still fail if the telling tails away or 'subsides'. The pacing may need to be modified to signal the ending – it might slow down or speed up to a climax. It can be helpful to use a formal ending as well, such as:

- ... and that is the end of my story.
- ... and so it was until this day – unless, that is, you know differently.
- My tale, now I have told it; in your heart, now hold it.
- A story, a story, let it come – and now it goes ...
- ... and that is the way it was, and that is the way it is – up to this time now.

(Again this list is modified from Grainger, 1997.)

Telling the story

In my experience – and this is likely to be the case in formal education – there is limited time for each story. I might use the same story for a 10- or a 20-minute spot. It is a matter of how it is told and the detail – it is important to judge time but looking at a watch halfway through a story is not a good idea!

Another issue is whether the teller sits or stands. Sometimes there is a storyteller's chair – even sometimes a special one. I stand if possible because it leaves me free to move. Some people will always sit, but there are occasions when the audience is seated on the ground (especially if they are children) and telling from a position looming above does not work. This is a matter of 'reading' the situation and working out how best to manage it.

As in any performance, there is a need for eye contact with the audience. Storytelling is about engaging the audience. There are times when, in a story, the teller is talking through one character to another, and then eye contact may be with the imagined other. With large audiences, the eye contact needs to be exaggerated – as do any gestures or movements.

Pacing and the use of pause are vital skills. The use of silence is very powerful. It can tell of events in the story as much as the words. That goes also for creating variety in presentation – using loud and soft voice, coming forward and moving back. Sometimes there is extraneous sound, like the ubiquitous mobile phone, and the skilled teller can link the phone call into the story: 'Oh yes, and the phone rang just at that moment. It was her father telling her ... ' or ' ... but it was just a call for someone else.' This will probably elicit a laugh even in a serious story. I find that the odd aside can be useful if said quickly with a forward gesture to denote that the teller is coming out of the story briefly (e.g. 'Wish I could find one like that'; 'Sounds rather nice, doesn't he?').

The use of props is a matter of judgement. I do not often use props, but just sometimes it can be useful when there is a single object. In one story I tell, there is a very round pebble. I sometimes say, 'It was a pebble like this' and hand it round. The pebble in the story is imbued with magic. I tell the story of willow pattern china also, and hand round broken pieces of the china with relevant pictures on it. In another story there are seals that slip out of their skins to become people. I often hold a black piece of silk when telling that story.

There are some obvious things that go wrong with storytelling and many of them are the same as those that can be wrong with teaching and presentations. Beyond having a poor story, some are:

- lack of 'presence';
- unclear or too quiet a voice;
- pace is too fast or too slow or there is too much repetition;
- disorganised telling – muddling the story sequence;
- body language not right;
- too much performance (irritating);
- apparent disengagement of the teller with her story;
- monotonous telling.

Most storytellers think that the worst that can happen is that they will forget the story. In my experience, this rarely happens. Remembering a story is not at all like remembering or forgetting something 'learned by heart'. My main concern with forgetting is to lose names. Mostly they just seem to appear as if helped by the flow of the story, but if there are foreign or unfamiliar names a list on the floor can help, even if it is not actually consulted. It is worth noting that the commonly promoted methods for memorising is through linking words into a story (Bower and Clark, 1969; Buzan, 2006). Occasionally I forget a detail that is important to the story, and then I will just say, quite casually, 'Oh, I forgot to tell you that ... ' I have never dried up. Storytelling is like a conversation with an audience and one finds one's way around difficult bits.

There are books and coaching schemes that help people to learn to tell stories, but in the end it is only by telling stories and watching others tell them that people can become proficient storytellers. Some sources for storytelling are Baker and Greene (1987), Wood and Richardson (1992), Cassady (1994), Grainger (1997), Parkin (1998) and Denning (2001). The Society for Storytelling in the UK holds a substantial library of books on story.

Formats for workshops on storytelling

Workshops need to have three main components. They must include some introduction to storytelling such as what I have said above. Second, they must involve participants in telling stories and, third, they should provide participants with the opportunity to listen to the storytelling of others who are learning to tell stories.

What can be done depends on the time available. Following the introduction of storytelling:

- Half the group are given a break and the other half are briefed and told a simple story. They are asked to think about how they would present it. The other half of the group come in and are paired off with those who have a story to tell and they listen. The groups are then reversed.
- The participants are reminded of a well-known folk or fairy story. They are divided into groups and each group is asked to divide the story into its various scenes and each person takes a 'scene'. They spend a short time thinking about how the scene 'works' and how they will present the scene and then they each tell their scene. It does not matter if there is conflict between different interpretations.
- (A longer workshop, e.g. a day with a group of 10.) The whole group is given a set of different short stories (or they could be made available online). There should be sufficient stories to allow choice. They each choose a story and are given time to learn it for presentation – at least an hour. Later, the participants reconvene and each in turn tells her story.

In terms of feedback to tellers, I do not think that in short workshops where people are having only one opportunity to tell it is appropriate to give any feedback. Tellers get enough information about what works and what does not work from their own telling and from listening to others. In the longer workshop, when the numbers are kept to around 10, a helpful method of giving feedback is, after each telling, to ask listeners to write on a piece of paper two or three of the best features of the telling and one thing that 'you could try differently next time'. The papers are given to the teller and it is up to her when or where she reads them.

Of course, what is required with anything like storytelling is practice, and a pleasant and entertaining way of practising is to set up a story circle. Participants meet regularly (e.g. once a month) and each tells a short story. There are a number of sources of story games to improve story skills, for example Parkinson (2004, 2005, 2007a) and the book list of the Society for Storytelling.

Thinkpoint

The storyteller buys his or her audience's suspension of disbelief at the cost of delivering a good story – the unbelievable must be made believable. The story is a dare, which he or she must pull off.

(Gabriel, 2000: 12)

Chapter 14

New ways with story

Introduction

Throughout the planning of this book, I had expected to research the subject matter for this chapter in different places from the other material and that has been the case. It has been on different shelves in the library, on different websites and there have been different people with whom to talk. That does say something about the growth in these technological approaches, as they appear to have grown anew from technological possibilities – not what was there before. I have not covered the material in any depth but have scanned it in order to relate the ideas to the rest of the book. Nor do I start to pretend expertise in the technological aspects of what I write here. At the back of my mind as I have looked at this material has been the question: where in this material are the commonalities with story as I have depicted it? Are we talking of a really new kind of meaning for story or not?

My brief research has suggested two 'new ways' to consider:

- digital storytelling (p. 162);
- interactive story, games and simulation (p. 164).

There are overlaps and terminology is confusing in this field. Books with the title 'digital storytelling' might be about games and interactive story and not what others have called 'digital storytelling' in higher education, and 'interactive story-telling' may also focus on games. Coming from the 'old way' of oral storytelling, I particularly notice a distinction between those who seem to see the 'new ways' as building on the strengths of traditional views of story and those who think that their new ways are brand new and will supersede story as we know it. I also note that we may have shifted from the teller–listener divide to something in between – because in interacting with the story, or creating a digital story, the participant becomes part of the creation process for the story.

'Digital storytelling'

By 'digital storytelling' I refer to the construction of short 'stories' by use of one or more programmes that combine photographs or other visual material with words in audio or text form. Music may be incorporated and the story may use video (Alexander and Levine, 2008). The stories usually endeavour to capture the essence of an experience so they tend to be broad-form story. Typically they last two to three minutes and the text consists of only 200–300 words, with a beginning, middle and end structure to distinguish them from 'simple reports' (Boase, 2008). The development of digital stories has been an activity in many settings, including higher education.

The values of digital story seem to flow from four aspects of the process:

- the use of the technology itself;
- the process of the construction of the story;
- the outcome for the maker;
- the use of the material by others and enhancement of other learning such collaborative working.

The first value – from the use of the technology itself – can facilitate the development of confidence. For some who have been asked to make digital stories, the use of computers and relevant software and digital cameras or recording machines, while relatively simple, is a new experience and the achievement of a completed story is important. This is illustrated in a project run in collaboration between Sheffield Hallam University Faculty of Health and Wellbeing and Pilgrim Projects Ltd, Cambridge, in the Patient Voices programme (Pilgrim Projects, n.d.). In this case, students were taught to facilitate the making of digital stories by health and social services users. The users commented on the confidence that they gained in making the stories (www.patientvoices.org.uk) and in the employment of technology.

Second, there is value in the thought processes that go into distilling the subject matter from other experiences and focusing on the story. This is a powerful form of reflection. Jenkins and Lonsdale (2007, 2008) have developed a framework derived from Moon (1999a) and McDrury and Alterio (2003) to enable a 'measurement' to be made of the reflective impact of the stories and the quality of learning that is likely to emanate from them. Jenkins and Lonsdale discuss pedagogic strategies that enhance the reflective outcomes of such student work.

The third value concerns the development of a pleasing product. There is a product when an essay has been written, but there may more value, for modern students, in a multimedia production, aspects of which will be close to areas of personal life (e.g. social networking, film viewing, etc.). Few, perhaps, would think of setting out to write a story, but when they have made a digital story they have written a kind of story and this is an empowering process (Skouge and Rao, 2009). My fourth point relates to the use of the digital stories to stimulate reflection in others who see the stories. The stories become a teaching resource for use with other students, as was the case in the Patient Voices project (previous page). Jenkins and Lonsdale also describe the development of digital stories in Leisure, Tourism and Hospitality subjects as a way of presenting critical incidents for discussion with students.

The last 'value' is a catch-all! Digital storytelling can be valuable because of the subject matter itself (e.g. exploring visual subjects such as architecture). Or the process may be used to facilitate the development of social contact and collaborative work skills in new students. The method was, for example, incorporated in induction. Students were sent out in groups with a camera to make a digital story relating to their experience of the town local to their university. Showing the 'stories' enabled them to introduce themselves to others and to engage in a group task from early on (Jenkins and Lonsdale, 2008). Also fitting into this catchall category, digital story has been used in a population context. The BBC Wales Capture Wales project enabled the public to become participants in the medium – not just consumers. The outcomes are still under review and discussion (Kidd, n.d.; Fyfe, 2007)

Clearly there are valuable ways of using digital stories in higher education. It seems fairly obvious that some digital stories are stories and many are more like statements of how things are. Perhaps the interesting question in the context of this book is what the technique adds to what we knew and could do before in terms of story. One difference is in its brevity. While it is not so different from the construction of a poster, there are relatively few activities that demand succinct presentation and this is clearly a capability required in work situations. Perhaps the use of digital story is also influenced by the pull of new technologies and a sense that we need to be keeping up with students, or is it to do with the notion that story-making becomes somehow more acceptable when digitised?

There are plenty of support materials for digital story-making on the internet, for example http://www.techsoup.org/learningcentre//training/archives/p10096. cfm; http://www.youtube.com/watch?v=LknwSi5wSx8; http://www.life-pilot. co.uk/creating%20digital%20story%20with%20moviemaker.pdf. Matthews-DeNatale (2008) provides some potential assessment criteria (though these should be selected in relation to the particular purpose fulfilled by the digital storytelling exercise). She also lists open sources for music and images and websites for digital storytelling in different topics.

'Interactive storytelling', games and simulation

I am taking these three topics under one heading because there are common issues. However, I ultimately focus on interactive storytelling because that has most relevance to story.

Games are situations set up in which entertainment is afforded by the provision of a task to be achieved or situation managed. The achievement will involve physical or psychological demands on the part of the player. There may be a story to be told about the game once it has been played, but in essence games are sets of circumstances with prescribed possibilities for their outcomes. There are many differences between whole story and whole game (Glassner, 2004: 108–38). In attempting to compare them Goldstone (2009) names the 'camp' of narratologists, basing game on traditional story ideas, and those with a gameplay focus, the ludologists; and Glassner (2004) describes them as 'uneasy bedpartners' (p. 208). However, games do seem to be advantaged by qualities of story. One could say that, for success, games seem to need to employ some of the qualities of good story. For example, Goldstone talks of the essential quality of engagement in game. This breaks down into the need for motivation to play, which is sustained to completion, and 'innovation', which might be translatable to the notion of surprise, which, of course, is important in traditional story.

I add simulation here because I have acknowledged earlier that simulation plays a role in story-making. Simulation software (such as Second Life) provides a method for storytelling and teaching (Aldrich, 2006; Littleton and Bayne, 2008). It is not telling a story as such, but the idea of it is closely related to the processes of story. I have several times mentioned the notion that the process of imagination in story reading is one of simulation (Oatley, 2008a). It would be interesting to understand what is happening when the work of the imagination is 'taken over' or 'done for it' by provision of detailed sensory imagery. It may be that the more that is given to the audience, the less the latter needs to be active, and, unlike those who argue for the gains from interactivity, perhaps there is a loss of actual learning opportunity.

Interactive story is a range of activities conducted through the medium of computer technology that involve some interaction between the story and the subject (listener/reader/viewer, etc.). Mostly I am talking about what has come to be called 'interactive storytelling' and games. This topic takes us more into activities that depend on technology for their achievement and, as such, this 'electronic creativity' (Murray, 2001) sharpens the question of whether we are looking here at something new and different in the quality of story, or just another different form of representation. Taking this a step further, it enables us to consider whether story is an activity of the brain, mind and body (i.e. the human) or a generalised output that is modified by its form of representation. If the former is the case, then these new technologies will give us new qualities of story. If the latter, it is only the representational details of story that differ and story is still story whatever the medium. A question that follows on is whether the new ways will supersede traditional ways with story such as books (Darnton, 2009, cited by Hess, 2009).

In this section I will not dwell on the actual technologies because they are constantly in a state of evolution (Biocca, 2002). Essentially the developments are in the interactivity of the audience or subject (I change my use of term here as seems appropriate) and interface and the manner in which new technology increasingly facilitates 'the work of the imagination ... to become real' because the [subject] can be a character, making the choices of the character (Murray, 2001). It allows the subject to see the world as if she is another character. For Murray, this implies that we are working with 'a serious medium of expression'. She says, 'Just as a novel tells stories that you couldn't tell if you only had the conventions of ancient Greek Tragedy', we are able to 'get at things about human life that we couldn't tell before'. While recognising the need to keep some limits of interactivity, she considers therefore that we are in new territory with regard to story (Murray, 1997). Biocca (2002) puts the views about story metaphorically. He sees 'older narrative structures' as 'train cars steaming down a linear predictable track', but in these new approaches the audience is the conductor, 'steering the train off the track and into a field of dreams' (p. 98).

The quality of involvement of the audience (ability to steer) has come to be called 'immersion'. Biocca (2002) refers to it as 'presence' or 'telepresence' – 'being inside the narrative space' (p. 101). In this respect we come back to the discussion of framing (Chapter 4) in terms of engagement and stepping into another reality. Traditional story is certainly potentially immersive in these ways, but the argument of the technologists is that the immersion experience is of a completely different order in interactive technologies.

Biocca (2002) suggests that there are different dimensions of the experience of immersion (p. 108): the involvement of the physical person – sensation, body, physiological events (e.g. heart rate), etc.; 'interface intelligence' – the responsiveness of the technological interface to the person; the fixity or ubiquity of access of the interface and interpersonal aspects of its functioning (how much the audience interact through the interactive medium). An assumption that seems to lie behind much of this consideration of immersion is that the more sophisticated the technology, the more realistic the experience is and hence the more satisfying it is to the audience. However, we have talked of the general capacity of stories to 'transport', to take the listener into other realities, to generate powerful emotion. A principle purpose of poetry and much short story writing is to stimulate powerful experience in the listener. We are back to the idea that making meaning is a constructive process for the individual (Chapter 3) and I could say that we can do the 'immersion' through listening to a simple story without necessarily the aid of technology.

I come back to the question: does interactivity fundamentally change the nature of story? Murray (1997) sees technology as making story different – enhancing the experience of story, increasing the 'palette' which enables us to 'switch from one person's view to another, from one cultural view to another, in which you can look at the same situation, go back into it, replay it, see how it would go differently'. Miller (2004) supports this view, contrasting the 'static' nature of traditional stories, with 'passive readers', with the active choice-making involvement of the new media. In an example, she comments, 'How do you ratchet up the spookiness of a scary story when you can't control when the player will see the shadowy figure outside the window' (p. 83). It seems to me that traditional story can do this very well and much use is made of the unspoken elements of story to achieve this. In interactive story there may be a tendency to ignore this central quality of story. It is interesting to note Glassner's (2004) comment that when audience is given the choice to experience or reduce tension in interactive story, they will tend to choose to reduce tension. He sees this as a problem for those who construct interactive stories. Glassner is one of those who see interactive media and games as enhancing some aspects of the representation of story, but not removing the need for a good underlying story which will unfold in a relatively linear sequence. One of the distinctions between those holding these different views on interactive and traditional story is the effort they have made to explore what story is. As was shown in the early chapters of this book, there is much more to story than the few words of explanation or theory given in many texts.

So far I have looked at the way in which different writers have considered interactive story and games, but what of the audience experience? I reiterated in Chapter 3 that it is the audience who construct the meaning and the personal experience of story. The writer/constructor of story can only guide the audience by manipulating external experience. She cannot make the audience experience something. What I am suggesting seems to be in accordance with the findings of Pope (2010), who explored the responses of audiences to interactive stories. Thirty-six computer-literate adult readers were given seven interactive stories to read and their reactions were monitored as they read, in a subsequent questionnaire and in focus groups. While two-thirds of the readers said that they would read an interactive story again, more would do it for technical interest rather than because they had had 'a great reading experience'. Around half of them found the plots confusing or they found lack of excitement and 'no sense of ending'. Pope (2010) says that his results indicate that the problem is in 'the lack of clear narrative structural markers' which blocked 'full enjoyment of the reading experience'. However, Pope does not dismiss the potential of interactive texts on the basis of these findings, but suggests a set of guidelines that enable the deficiencies to be overcome. Broadly his suggestions go along with those who would say that the starting point must be a good story. He also says that there must be a tight relationship between interactivity and the storyline so that 'control and choice for the reader should only be offered where they support navigation or are essential for the development of the narrative', and he suggests that interactivity should be limited to 'a level where it enhances and does not impede reading absorption' (Pope, 2010). He also addresses the design of the technology so that it does not interfere with the reader's reading (Sloane, 2000). The guidelines are being tested in the development of 'Genarrator' software that provides a simple template for writers of interactive story (Pope, n.d.). It could be that in the longer term there is more satisfaction to be gained from the experience of being a writer of interactive story than the audience for one.

In my brief perusal of the literature and conversations about interactive story, I have found that the more convincing accounts are written by those who stress the importance of an initial strong story at the heart of the development of interactivity. This seems to echo the conclusion of Glassner's (2004) comparison of game and story, in which he seems to suggest that when games do not work the problem is often to be found in the underlying story structure or in the unfolding of the storyline. But maybe I would say this, wouldn't I?

Concluding comment

In reviewing these technological representations of story and in being challenged to see them as making story something totally new and different, I have come closer to the idea that working with story is an inherent part of being human. Story seems to be a response of us as humans to a set of coherent and well-designed stimuli in some or other form of representation, be it technological, aural or whatever. What I am saying is not negative to the new ways with story. I am instead arguing with Pope and Glassner that the new ways are ways of representing story just as are books and novels, drama and radio and all the other forms of representation. The interactivity on the screen is a reflection of what we do in our heads in processing the complexities of living – which is, of course, far more complex than those 'realities' constructed on a screen. The principles of good story would seem to underlie the technologies that are satisfactory.

In my very brief perusal of the topic in this chapter, three things bother me in what I have read. The first is the cursory manner in which some writers describe the nature of story. Second, the same writers tend also to view the audience for traditional story as 'passive', as opposed to the 'activities' of their participants of 'interactive' story. Active and passive are value-laden words, particularly in educational contexts. Referring back to Chapter 3, it seems obvious to me that the audience for traditional story is anything but passive – and may just be more mentally active than those being fed meaning from an interactive screen. My third point is related. There is artificiality in the judgements made about the 'passivity' of the audience for traditional story. No-one would call a creative writer 'passive'. She is actively constructing a story. 'Interactivity' implies that a creative writing role (albeit limited) is being given to the audience. Even if interactivity simply means that she seeks further information about an aspect of the plot, of course she becomes more active. Writing a story and listening to it are totally different activities and not to be conflated.

So when Alexander and Levine (2008) argue that 'stories are now open-ended, branching, hyperlinked, cross-media, participatory, exploratory and unpredictable', I respond in two ways: first, yes they are because that is the way the brain works; and, second, I would say that those stories among this plethora of descriptions that are effective are those that are close in structure to the traditional story.

Thinkpoint

Story is what kids tell us, 'This happened, and then that happened, then this happened.' We've all heard them trail on with an endless tale with no structure. Plot echoes a situation or design to the universe – cause and effect, karma.

(Goldberg, 1990: 224)

Afterthoughts

So in the process of all this writing and researching, I have learned a great deal about story, but I know that there is much more to know ... When I have recently been asked to run workshops on story, I notice my reaction is first mild panic and then a sense still of 'What do I know about story that is worth putting over?' That may sound odd but I do recall that I have felt the same about other topics when I have just finished writing about them (reflection, critical thinking, etc.). And, of course, story is still a very diverse topic and I reflect that workshops are often easier to construct when one knows relatively little about a topic and not the-writing-of-a-book's-worth. I just hope that the reader can feel that she has made a worthwhile journey through this jungle of ideas and can emerge with some ideas of value to her. If it is a carpet bag of odds and ends, I hope that there is richness.

I want to mention one other area of thinking that I encountered towards the end of my writing. I have not reopened chapters to add it because it would take me into the details of contested knowledge in the science journals – and it has been hard enough to keep to the publisher's word limit. The material concerns fairly recent discoveries of 'mirror neurones' in the human brain. I came across this in a reference in *New Scientist* (Slack, 2007) and in Mar and Oatley (2008). Mirror neurones fire when the subject observes an action and again when she enacts it. This immediately seems to be an explanation for why yawning seems to be 'infectious', but as I have thought further about it, without going into the physiology I speculate that mirror neurone systems may hold the key to the manner in which we learn from story though vicarious experiencing when listening to story, and they may have implications for 'engagement'. They would seem also to have much to do with the unspoken aspects of story, allowing us to comprehend the actions of another without consciousness or the mediation of language and without actively following the actions ourselves. But further such explorations are for another day. A general introduction to this material is in Rizzolatti et al. (2009) and an overview is found on Wikipedia.

References

Adams, R. (1972), *Watership Down*, New York: Avon Books.

Akister, J. (2005), 'Using a patchwork text to assess family therapy students', *Journal of Family Therapy* 27: 276–279.

Aldrich, C. (2006), 'Second Life is not a teaching tool', The Learning Circuits Blog, http://learningcircuits.blogspot.com/2006/11/second-life-is-not-teaching-tool.html (accessed Nov. 2009).

Alexander, B. and Levine, A. (2008), 'Storytelling: emergence of a new genre', http://net.educause.edu/ir/library/pdf/ERMO865.pdf (accessed Nov. 2009).

Allen, R. (1997), *Fast Fiction*, Cincinnati: Story Press.

Alterio, M. (2004), 'Collaborative journaling as a professional development tool', *Journal of Further and Higher Education* 28(3): 41–51.

Alterio, M. and McDrury, J. (2003), 'Collaborative learning using reflective storytelling', in N. Zepke, D. Nugent and L. Leach (eds) *Reflection to Transformation*, Palmerston North: Dunmore Press Ltd.

Alvarez, J. and Merchan, C. (1992), 'The role of narrative fiction in the development of imagination for action', *International Studies of Management and Organisations* 22(3): 27–45.

Astington, J. (1990), 'Narrative and the child's theory of mind', in B. Britton and A. Pellegrini (eds) *Narrative Thoughts and Narrative Language*, Hillsdale, NJ: Lawrence Erlbaum Associates.

Atkinson, T. and Claxton, G. (2000), *The Intuitive Practitioner*, Milton-Keynes: Open University Press.

Ausubel, D. and Robinson, F. (1969), *School Learning*, London: Holt, Rhinehart and Winston.

Ayalon, O. (1991), 'Foreword', in A. Gersie, *Storymaking in Bereavement*, London: Jessica Kingsley.

Aylwin, T. (1994), *Traditional Storytelling and Education*, Greenwich: University of Greenwich.

Bailey, J. (1998), 'The supervisor's story: from expert to novice', in C. Johns and D. Freshwater (eds) *Transforming Nursing through Reflective Practice*, Oxford: Blackwell Science.

Baker, A. and Greene, E. (1987), *Storytelling: art and technique*, New York: Bowker.

Bartlett, C. (1997), 'Where is the storytelling in science?', in A. Kavanagh *The Power of the Story*, Proceedings of the University College of Cape Breton's First Annual Storytelling Symposium, Sydney, Nova Scotia; University College of Cape Breton Press.

Bartlett, F. (1932), *Remembering*, Cambridge: Cambridge University Press.

Baxter Magolda, M. (1992), *Knowing and Reasoning in College Students: Gender-related Patterns in Students' Intellectual Development*, San Francisco: Jossey-Bass.

——(1994), 'Post college experiences and epistemology', *Review of Higher Education* 18(1): 25–44.

——(1996), 'Epistemological development in graduate and professional education', *Review of Higher Education* 19(3): 283–304.

——(1999), *Creating Contexts for Learning and Self-authorship: constructive developmental pedagogy*, San Francisco: Jossey-Bass.

Bayliss, R. (1998), 'Pain narratives', in T. Greenhalgh and B. Hurwitz (eds) *Narrative Based Medicine*, London: BMJ Books.

BBC Radio 4 Appeal (2009), http://www.bbc.co.uk/radio4/religion/radio4apeal. shtml.

Beaty, E., Gibbs, G. and Morgan, A. (1997), 'Learning orientations and study contracts', in F. Marton, D. Hounsell and N. Entwistle (eds) *The Experience of Learning*, Edinburgh: Academic Press.

Belenky, M., Clinchy, B., Goldberger, R. and Tarule, J. (1986), *Women's Ways of Knowing*, New York: Basic Books.

Benjamin, W. (1968), 'The storyteller', in W. Benjamin, *Illuminations*, New York: Harcourt.

Bettelheim, B. (1976), *The Uses of Enchantment*, London: Thames and Hudson.

Biocca, F. (2002), 'The evolution of interactive media', in M. Green, J. Strange and T. Brock (eds) *Narrative Impact*, Mahwah, NJ: Lawrence Erlbaum Associates.

Bluck, S. (2001), 'Autobiographical Memories: a building block of life', in G. Kenyon, P. Clark and B. de Vries (eds) *Narrative Gerontology*, New York: Springer.

Bly, R. (1992), *Iron John*, Cambridge, MA: DaCapo Press.

Boal, A. (1995), *The Rainbow of Desire*, London: Routledge.

Boase, C. (2008), 'Digital storytelling for reflection and engagement: a study of the uses and potential of digital storytelling', Centre for Active Learning and Department of Education, University of Goucestershire.

Boje, D. (1991), 'The storytelling organisation: a study of performance in an office-supply firm', *Administrative Science Quarterly* 36(1): 7–17.

——(2002), *Narrative Methods for Organisational and Communication Research*, London: Sage.

Bolton, G. (1994), 'Stories at Work: fictional-critical writing as a means of professional development', *British Journal of Educational Research* 20(1): 55–68.

——(1999), *The Therapeutic Potential of Creative Writing – Writing Myself*, London: Jessica Kingsley.

Bowden, J. and Marton, F. (1998), *The University of Learning: beyond quality and competence in higher education learning*, London: Kogan Page.

Bower, G. and Clark, M. (1969), 'Narrative stories as mediators for serial learning', *Psychonometic Science* 14(4): 181–182.

Brookfield, S. (1987), *Developing Critical Thinking*, Milton Keynes: Society for Research into Higher Education and Open University Press.

——(1990), 'Using critical incidents to explore learners' assumptions', in J. Mezirow and Associates, *Fostering Critical Reflection in Adulthood*, San Francisco: Jossey-Bass.

——(1998), 'Critical thinking techniques', in M. Galbraith, *Adult Learning Methods*, Malabar: Krieger Publishing.

Brookfield, S. and Preskill, S. (1999), *Discussion as a Way of Teaching*, Buckingham: Society for Research into Higher Education and Open University Press.

Brown, L. (2003), 'Patchwork text – example two: perspectives on research and knowledge in professional practice', *Innovations in Education and Teaching International* 40(2): 174–179.

Bruner, J. (1986), *Actual Minds, Possible Worlds*, Cambridge, MA: Harvard University Press.

——(1990), *Acts of Meaning*, Cambridge, MA: Harvard University Press.

——(2002), *Making Stories: law, literature, life*, New York: Farrar, Straus and Giroux.

Burke, C. (1991), 'Tulips, tinfoil and teaching: journal of a freshman teacher', in C. Christensen, D. Garvin and A. Sweet (eds) *Education for Judgement*, Boston: Harvard University Press.

Bushnaq, I. (1987), *Arab Folktales*, Harmondsworth: Penguin.

Buzan, T. (2006), *Use Your Head*, Harlow: Pearson.

Cameron, J. (1994), *The Artist's Way*, London: Pan Books.

Campbell, J. with Moyers, B. (1988), *The Power of Myth*, New York: Doubleday.

Carey, S. and Smith, C. (1999), 'On understanding the nature of science knowledge', in R. McCormick and C. Praechter, *Learning and Knowledge*, London: Paul Chapman Publishing and Open University Press.

Carr, W. and Kemmis, S. (1986), *Becoming Critical*, London: Falmer Press.

Carter, A. (1991), *Virago Book of Fairy Stories*, London: Virago.

Carter, K. (1993), 'The place of story in the study of teaching and teacher education', *Educational Researcher* 22(1): 5–12.

Cassady, M. (1994), *The Art of Storytelling*, Colorado Springs: Meriwether.

Castaneda, C. (1970), *The Teachings of Don Juan: The Yaqui way of knowledge*, Harmondsworth: Penguin.

——(1971), *A Separate Reality*, Harmondsworth: Penguin.

Chan, E. and Chung, L. (2004), 'Teaching abstract concepts in contemporary nursing through spirituality', *Reflective Practice* 5(1): 125–134.

Clandinin, D. and Connelly, M. (1990), 'Narrative and story in practice and research', in D. Schon (ed.) *The Reflective Turn*, New York: Teachers' College Press, Columbia University.

——(1994), 'Personal experience methods', in N. Denzin and Y. Lincoln (eds) *Handbook of Qualitative Research*, London: Sage.

Clark, P. (2001), 'Narrative gerontology in clinical practice', in G. Kenyon, P. Clark and B., de Vries (eds) *Narrative Gerontology*, New York: Springer Publishing Company.

Clarke, L. and Nisker, J. (2007), *In Our Hands: on becoming a doctor*, Halifax, Nova Scotia: Pottersfield Press.

Claxton, G. (1999), *Wise Up: the challenge of lifelong learning*, London: Bloomsbury.

——(2000), 'The anatomy of intuition', in T. Atkinson and G. Claxton, *The Intuitive Practitioner*, Maidenhead: Open University Press.

Clough, P. (2002), *Narratives and Fiction in Educational Research*, Buckingham: Open University Press.

Coffield, F. (2000), *The Necessity of Informal Learning*, London: The Policy Press.

Coles, R. (1989), *The Call of Stories*, Boston: Houghton Mifflin.

Collingridge, V. (2009), *Making History*, BBC Radio 4, 7 April.

Connelly, M. and Clandinin, D. (1986), 'On narrative methods, personal philosophy and narrative unities in the story of teaching', *Journal of Research in Science Teaching* 23(4): 293–310.

——(1990), 'Stories of experience and narrative inquiry', *Educational Researcher* 19(4): 2–14.

Cook I. (1997), 'Participant observation', in R. Flowerdew and D. Martin, *Methods in Human Geography*, Edinburgh: Pearson Education.

Cooper, J. (1991), 'Telling our own stories', in C. Witherell and N. Noddings (eds) *Stories Lives Tell*, New York: Teachers' College Press, Columbia University.

Cornford, F. (1945), *The Republic of Plato*, London: Oxford University Press.

Cowan, J. (1998), *On Becoming an Innovative University Teacher*, Milton Keynes: Society for Research into Higher Education and Open University Press.

Cowling, W. (2001), 'Unitary appreciative inquiry', *Advanced Nursing Science* 23(4): 32–48.

——(2004), 'Pattern, participation, praxis and power in unitary appreciative inquiry', *Advances in Nursing Science* 27(3): 202–214.

Crace, J. (2008), 'Lost in transmission', *Guardian*, 15 April.

Crimmens, P. (1998), *Storymaking and Creative Groupwork with Older People*, London: Jessica Kingsley.

Crossley, M. (2002), 'Introducing narrative psychology', in C. Horrocks, K. Milnes, B. Robersts and D. Robinson, *Narrative, Memory and Life Transitions*, Huddersfield: University of Huddersfield Press.

Crossly-Holland, K. (1987), *British Folk Tales*, London: Orchard Books.

Cummings, S. and Brocklesby, J. (1997), 'Towards democratic myth and the management of organizational change in ancient Athens', *Journal of Organizational Change Management* 10(1): 71–95.

Damasio, A. (1999), *The Feeling of What Happens*, London: Heineman.

Daniels, H. (2001), *Vygotsky and Pedagogy*, London: Routledge Falmer.

Darnton, R. (2009), *The Case for Books: past, present and future*, Cambridge, MA: Perseus.

Dawson, J. (2003), 'Reflectivity, creativity and the space for silence', *Reflective Practice* 4(1): 33–39.

Day, J. (1991), 'The moral audience: on the narrative mediation of moral judgement', in M. Tappan and M. Packer (eds) *Narrative and Storytelling: implications for understanding moral judgement*, New Directions for Child Development No. 54 (Winter), San Francisco: Jossey-Bass.

de Rivera, J. and Sarbin, T. (1998), 'Introduction', in J. de Riviera and T. Sarbin (eds) *Believed-in Imaginings: the narrative construction of reality*, Washington, DC: American Psychological Association.

Denning, S. (2001), *The Springboard: how storytelling ignites action in knowledge-era organzations*, Boston: Butterworth Heinemann.

——(2004), *Squirrel Inc.: a fable of leadership through storytelling*, San Francisco: Jossey-Bass.

——(2008), 'The knowledge-based organization: using stories to embody and transfer knowledge' (audio and text), http://www.storytellingwithchildren.com/2008/01/12/steve-denning-the-knowledge-based-organization/.

Denny, T. (1978), 'In defense of storytelling as a first step in educational research', paper presented at International Reading Association Conference, Houston.

DeSalvo, L. (2000), *Writing as a Way of Healing*, Boston: Beacon Press.

Dittrich, L. (2001), *Ten Years of Medicine and the Arts*, Washington, DC: Association of American Colleges.

Djikic, M., Oatley, K., Zoeterman, S. and Peterson, J. (2009), 'On being moved by art: how reading fiction transforms the self', *Creativity Research Journal* 21(1): 24–29.
Donald, A. (1998), 'The words we live in', in T. Greenhalgh and B. Hurwitz (eds) *Narrative Based Medicine*, London: BMJ Books.
Donaldson, M. (1992), *Human Minds*, Harmondsworth: Penguin.
Dowling, J. (2007), Book reviews, *Storylines* (Summer).
Drake, S. and Elliot, A. (2005), 'Creating a new story to live by through collaborative reflection, concentric storying and using the old/new story framework', paper presented at the Senario-based Learning Conference, Institute for Reflective Practice, Gloucester, 2005.
Eisner, E. (1988), 'The primacy of experience and the politics of method', *Educational Researcher* 20: 15–20.
——(1991), 'Forms of understanding and the future of education', *Educational Researcher* 22: 5–11.
——(1997), *The Enlightened Eye*, Upper Saddle River, NJ: Prentice Hall.
Elbow, P. (1981), *Writing with Power*, New York: Oxford University Press.
Ellis, C. and Bochner, A. (1992), 'Telling and performing personal stories', in C. Ellis and M. Flaherty (eds) *Investigating Subjectivity*, London: Sage.
Engels, S. (1995), *Stories Children Tell*, New York: W.H. Freeman.
Estes, C, (1992), *Women Who Run with the Wolves*, London: Rider.
Festinger, L. (1957), *A Theory of Cognitive Dissonance*, Stanford, CA: Stanford University Press.
Field, J. (1952), *A Life of One's Own*, Harmondsworth: Penguin.
Fisher, J. (1996), *Stories for Thinking*, Oxford: Nash Pollock Publishing.
——(1999), *First Stories for Thinking*, Oxford: Nash Pollock Publishing.
Fisher, R. (n.d.), 'Stories for thinking', http://www.teachingthinking.net (accessed Nov. 2009).
Foss, M. (1977), *Folk Tales of the British Isles*, London: Macmillan.
Fowler, J. (1981), 'The ups and down in the life of Betty', *Nursing Times* 77(4): 146–150.
——(1985), 'A game of patients', *Nursing Times*, 16 October.
——(1987), 'Sister Vision's Dream – a leadership fable', *Nursing Times* 83(4): 37–38.
——(1995), 'Taking theory into practice', *Professional Nurse* (Jan.): 226–230.
——(2001), 'Evaluating practice development – research', in J. Dooher, A. Clark and J. Fowler (eds) *The Handbook of Practice Development*, Dinton, Wiltshire: Quay Books, Mark Allen Pub.
Fowler, J. and Dooher, J. (2001), 'Qualitative evaluation of clinical supervision', in T. Butterworth, J. Cutcliffe and B. Proctor (eds) *Themes in Clinical Supervision*, London: Routledge.
Fowler, J. and Rigby, P. (1994), 'Sculpting with people – an experiential learning experience', *Nurse Education Today* 14: 400–405.
Fowles, J. (1997), *The Magus*, London: Vintage.
Frank, A. (1996), *The Wounded Storyteller*, Chicago: University of Chicago Press.
Fulford, R. (1999), *The Triumph of Narrative*, Toronto: Ananasi.
Fuller, R. (1982), 'The story as the engram: is it fundamental to thinking?', *Journal of Mind and Behaviour* 3: 127–142.
Fyfe, H. (2007), 'Habits of the heart: storytelling and everyday life', paper given on 7 June 2007 at George Ewart Evans Centre for Storytelling, University of Glamorgan, Cardiff.
Gaardner, J. (1996), *Sophie's World*, London: Phoenix House.

Gabriel, Y. (2000), *Storytelling in Organizations*, Oxford: Oxford University Press.

Gardner, H. (1983), *Frames of Mind*, New York: Basic Books.

Gargiulo, T. (2006), 'The power of stories', *Journal for Quality and Participation* 29(1): 5–8.

Gauntlett, D. (2007), *Creative Explorations: new approaches to identities and audiences*, London: Routledge.

Geertz, C. (1973), 'Thick Description', in C. Geertz, *The Interpretation of Culture: selected essays*, New York: Basic Books.

Gerrig, R. (1993), *Experiencing Narrative Worlds*, New Haven, CT: Yale University Press.

Gersie, A. (1991), *Storymaking in Bereavement*, London: Jessica Kingsley.

——(1992), *Earthtales: storytelling in times of change*, London: Green Print.

——(1996), *Dramatic Approaches to Brief Therapy*, London: Jessica Kingsley.

Gersie, A. and King, N. (1990), *Storymaking in Education and Therapy*, London: Jessica Kingsley.

Ghaye, T. and Lillyman, S. (1997), *Learning Journals and Critical Incidents*, Dinton: Quay Books.

Gilbey, J. (2008), 'Fools! I will destroy you all', *Times Higher Education Supplement*, 18 June.

Giono, J., McCurdy, M. and Lipkis, A. (2005), *The Man Who Planted Trees*, White River Junction, VT: Chelsea Green Publishing.

Glanz, J. (1995), 'Storytelling to spark ideas', *College Teaching* 43(4): 39–140.

Glaskin, G. (1974), *Windows of the Mind*, Bridport, Dorset: Prism Press.

Glassner, A. (2004), *Interactive Storytelling: techniques for the 21st Century*, Nattick, MA: A.K. Peters Ltd.

Goffman, E. (1961), *Encounters: two studies in the sociology of interaction*, Indianapolis: Bobbs-Merrill.

Gold, J. and Holman, D. (2001), 'Let me tell you a story', *Career Development International* 6/7: 384–395.

Gold, J., Holman, D. and Thorpe, R. (2002), 'The role of argument analysis and story telling in facilitating critical thinking', *Management Learning* 33(3): 371–388.

Goldacre, B. (n.d.), Bad Science website, http://www.badscience.net/ (accessed Nov. 2009).

——(2008), *Bad Science*, London: Fourth Estate.

Goldberg, N. (1990), *Wild Mind*, London: Rider.

Goldstone, W. (2009), 'Storytelling and the games industry', http://www.willgoldst one.com/storytelling_and_games-willgoldstone.pdf (accessed Nov. 2009).

Goodson, I. and Sikes, P. (2001), *Life History Research in Educational Settings*, Buckingham: Open University Press.

Goodson, I. and Walker, R. (1995), 'Telling tales', in H. McEwan and K. Egan (eds) *Narrative in Teaching, Learning and Research*, New York: Teachers' College Press, Columbia University.

Gough, N. (1993), 'Environmental education, narrative complexity and postmodern science/fiction international', *Journal of Science Education* 15(5): 607–625.

Grainger, R. (1995), *Drama and Healing*, London: Jessica Kingsley.

Grainger, T. (1997), *Traditional Storytelling in the Primary School Classroom*, Leamington Spa: Scholastic Press.

Greene, M. (1990), 'Realizing literature's potential', in J. Mezirow and Associates, *Fostering Critical Reflection in Adulthood*, San Francisco: Jossey-Bass.

Greenhalgh, T. (1998), 'Narrative based medicine in an evidence based world', in T. Greenhalgh and B. Hurwitz (eds) *Narrative-Based Medicine*, London: BMJ Books.

Greenhalgh, T. and Collard, A. (2003), *Narrative-based Healthcare: sharing stories*, London: BMJ Books.

Greenhalgh, T. and Hurwitz, B. (eds) (1998), *Narrative Based Medicine*, London: BMJ Books.

Grove, P. and Steventon, G. (2008), 'Thinking outside the box: enhancing structured creative learning in Second Life', IPED Conference on Researching Academic Visions and Realities, Coventry University, September 2008.

Griffin, M. (2003), 'Using critical incidents to promote and assess reflective learning in preservice teachers', *Reflective Practice*, 4(2): 207–220.

Grimm, J. and Grimm, W. (n.d.), *Grimm's Fairy Tales*, London: Blackie.

Grumet, M. (1987), 'The politics of personal knowledge', *Curriculum Inquiry* 17(3): 319–335.

Gudmundsdottir, S. (1995), 'The narrative nature of pedagogical content knowledge', in H. McEwan and K. Egan, *Narrative in Teaching, Learning and Research*, New York: Teachers' College Press, Columbia University.

Guerin, B. and Miyazaki, Y. (2006), 'Analyzing rumors, gossip, and urban legends through their conversational properties', *Psychological Record* 56: 23–34.

Hammond, C. (2008), *Case Study*, BBC Radio 4, 7 May.

Hardie, K. (2007), 'On trial: tutor as a silent witness', Higher Education Academy UK Cenre for Legal Education, from Directions 7, http://www.ukcle.ac.uk/directions/previous/issue15/hardie.html (accessed 25 June 2009).

Hardy, B. (1977), 'Narrative as a primary act of mind', in M. Meek, A. Warlow and G. Barton, *The Cool Web*, London: Bodley Head.

Harrett, J. (2008), 'What's in a Story? Telling tales and written words: the same or different', presentation at the Atrium, Cardiff: George Ewart Evans Centre for Storytelling, University of Glamorgan.

Hart, T. (2001), *From Information to Transformation*, New York: Peter Lang Publishing.

Hastie, R. and Davies, R. (2001), *Rational Choice in an Uncertain World*, London: Sage.

Hawes, L. (1991), 'Organising narratives/codes/ethics', *Journal of Organisational Change* 4(3): 45–51.

Heath, C., Bell, C. and Sternberg, E. (2001), 'Emotional selection in memes', *Journal of Personality and Social Psychology* 81(6): 1028–1041.

Heathfield, D. (2005), *Spontaneous Speaking: drama activities for confidence and fluency*, Peaslake, Surrey: Delta Publishing.

Hertog, J. and McLeod, D. (2001), 'A multiperspectival approach to framing analysis: a field guide', in S. Reese, O. Gandy and A. Grant, *Framing Public Life*, Mahwah, NJ: Lawrence Erlbaum Associates.

Hess, A. (2009), 'The book of the week: Robert Darnton, *The Case for Books*', *Times Education*, 10 December: 46–47.

Hesse, H. (1974), *Siddhartha*, London: Picador.

Hines, R. (1988), 'Financial accounting: in communicating reality, we construct reality', *Accounting Organizations and Society* 13(3): 251–261.

Holbeck, B. (1989), 'The language of fairy tales', in R. Kvideland and H. Sehmsdorf (eds) *Nordic Folklore: recent studies*, Indiana: Indiana University Press.

Holmes, V. and Gregory, D. (1998), 'Writing poetry: a way of knowing nursing', *Journal of Advanced Nursing* 28(6): 1191–1194.

Hopen, D. (2006), 'Editor's notebook: the art and purpose of storytelling', *Journal for Quality and Participation* 29 (Spring): 3.

Hopkins, R. (2008), *The Transition Handbook*, White River Junction, VT: Chelsea Green Publishing.

Huberman, M. (1995), 'Working with life history narratives', in H. McEwan and K. Egan (eds) *Narrative in Teaching, Learning and Research*, New York: Teachers' College Press, Columbia University.

Huczynski, A. and, Buchanan, D. (2007), *Organizational Behaviour*, Sixth Edition, Harlow: Prentice Hall.

Hughes, E. (1967), *Poetry in the Making*, London: Faber and Faber.

Hunt, C. (1998), 'Writing with the voice of the child', in C. Hunt and F. Sampson (eds) *The Self on the Page*, London: Jessica Kingsley.

——(2000), *Therapeutic Dimensions of Autobiography*, London: Jessica Kingsley.

Hunt, C. and Sampson, F. (1998), *The Self on the Page*, London: Jessica Kingsley.

Illes, K. (2003). 'The patchwork text and business education: rethinking the importance of personal reflection and co-operative cultures', *Innovations in Education and Teaching International* 40(2): 209–215.

Institute of Reflective Practice (2005), Conference on 'Senario-Based Learning', Gloucester, UK.

Ireland, A. and Moon, J. (2008), *Making Groups Work: improving group work for media students through the principles of academic assertiveness*, Bournemouth: Centre for Excellence in Media Practice, Bournemouth University. (www.CEMP.ac.uk – accessed April 2010).

Jackson, M. (2008), 'For the benefit of all mankind', *Storylines* (Autumn): 4.

Jackson, P. (1995), 'On the place of narrative in teaching', in H. McEwan and K. Egan (eds) *Narrative in Teaching and Learning*, New York: Teachers' College Press, Columbia University.

Jenkins, M. and Londsdale, J. (2007), 'Evaluating the effectiveness of digital storytelling for student reflection', *Providing Choices for Learners and Learning*, Proceedings of ASCILITE Conference, Singapore, 2007, http://www.acilite.org.au/conferences/singapore 07/procs/jenkins.pdf.

——(2008), 'Podcasting and students' storytelling', in G. Salmon and P. Edinsingha (eds) *Podcasting for Learning in Universities*, Oxford: Oxford University Press.

Jennings, S. (1999) *Creative Storytelling with Adults at Risk*, London: Karmac.

——(2004), *Creative Storytelling with Children at Risk*, London: Karmac Books.

——(2008), *Creative Storytelling for Adults at Risk*, Oxford: Speechmark Publishing.

Jones, M. (1991), 'What if stories don't tally with the culture?', *Journal of Organizational Change* 4(3): 27–32.

Jordan, B. (1989), 'Cosmopolitical obstetrics: some insights from the training of traditional midwives', *Social Science Medicine* 28(9): 925–944.

Jung, C. (1977), *Memories, Dreams and Reflections*, Glasgow: Collins – Fount Paperbacks.

Kafka, F. (1997), *The Castle*, Harmondsworth: Penguin.

Kean, D. (2007), 'Storytellers who make up the skills gap', *Financial Times*, 20 February.

Kelly, G. (1955), *The Psychology of Personal Construct Theory*, New York: W.W. Norton.

Kember, D. (2001), 'Beliefs about knowledge and the process of teaching and learning as a factor in adjusting to study in higher education', *Studies in Higher Education* 26: 205–211.

Kenyon, G. and Randall, W. (2001), 'Narrative gerontology: an overview', in G. Kenyon, P. Clark and B. de Vries (eds) *Narrative Gerontology*, New York: Springer Publishing.

Kenyon, G., Clark, P. and de Vries, B. (2001), *Narrative Gerontology*, New York: Springer Publishing.

Kidd, J. (n.d.), 'Digital storytelling at the BBC: the reality of innovative audience participation', http://yle.fi/ripe/Papers/Kidd.pdf (accessed Nov. 2009).

King, P. and Kitchener, K. (1994), *Developing Reflective Judgement*, San Francisco: Jossey-Bass.

King, S. (2001), *On Writing*, London: Hodder and Stoughton.

Kirsch, I. (1998), 'Volition as a believed in imagining', in J. de Riviera and T. Sarbin (eds) *Believed-in Imaginings: the narrative construction of reality*, Washington, DC: American Psychological Association.

Kloss, R. (1994), 'Helping students through the Perry Scheme of intellectual development', *College Teaching* 42(4): 151–159.

Koch, T. (1998), 'Storytelling: is it really research?', *Journal of Advanced Nursing* 28: 1182–1190.

Kuhn, D. (1999), 'A developmental model of critical thinking', *Educational Researcher* 28(2): 16–26.

Lakoff, G. and Johnson, M. (1980), *Metaphors We Live By*, Chicago: University of Chicago Press.

Lamarque, P. (1990), 'Narrative and invention: the limits of fictionality', in C. Nash (ed.) *Narrative in Culture*, London: Routledge.

Laming, D. (2004), *Human Judgement*, London: Thomson.

Larsen, S. and Seilman, U. (1988), 'Personal meanings while reading literature', *Text* 8: 411–429.

Launer, J. (2002), *Narrative-based Primary Care*, Oxford: Radcliffe Medical Press.

Lauritzen, C. and Jaeger, M. (1997), *Integrating Learning through Story: the narrative curriculum*, New York: Delmar Publishing.

Lave, J. and Wenger, E. (1991), *Situated Learning: legitimate peripheral participation*, Cambridge: Cambridge University Press.

Lawton, G. (2007), 'Mind tricks: six ways to explore your brain', *New Scientist*, 22 September: 34–41.

Lanzara, G. (1990), 'Shifting stories: learning from a reflective experiment in a design process', in D. Schon (ed.) *The Reflective Turn*, New York: Teachers' College Press, Columbia University.

Lehrer, J. (2007), 'Blue monday, green thursday', *New Scientist*, 19 May.

Leman, P. (2007), 'The born conspiracy', *New Scientist*, 14 July.

Lesser, E. and Prusak, L. (2004), 'Storytelling', in E. Lesser and K. Prusak (eds) *Creating Value with Knowledge*, Oxford: Oxford University Press.

Levinson, H. (2008), 'What's the story, Gordon?', *Analysis*, BBC Radio 4, 20 February.

Lieberman, M. (2007), 'Social cognitive neuroscience: a review of core processes', *Annual Review of Psychology* 22: 415–450.

Lieblich, A. and Josselson, R. (1997), *Interpreting Evidence*, London: Sage.

Linden, J. (1999), 'The contribution of narrative to the process of supervising PhD students', *Studies in Higher Education* 24(3): 351–364.

Littleton, F. and Bayne, S. (2008), 'Virtual worlds in education', *ESCalate News* 10 (Spring).

Llosa, M. (1986), *The Green House*, New York: Farrar Straus and Giroux.

Lucas, U. (2008), 'Being pulled up short: creating moments of surprise and possibility in accounting education', *Critical Perspectives on Accounting* 19: 383–403.

——(2009), 'Reflection: a key personal agency for learning to be professional?', paper to support a presentation at the conference on Learning to be a Professional through a Life-wide Curriculum, University of Surrey, 31 March–1 April 2009.

Lucas, U. and Meyer, J. (2005), 'Towards a mapping of the student world: the identification of variation in students' conception of, and motivations to learn accounting', *British Accounting Review* 37(2): 177–204.

Lukinsky, J. (1990), 'Reflective withdrawal through journal writing', in J. Mezirow and Associates, *Fostering Reflective Learning in Adulthood*, San Francisco: Jossey-Bass.

McAllister, L., Higgs, J. and Smith, D. (2008), 'Facing and managing dilemmas as a clinical educator', *Higher Education Research and Development* 27(1): 1–13.

McAlpine, L. and Weston, C. (2002), 'Reflection: improving teaching and students' learning', in N. Hativa and N. Goodyear, *Teacher Thinking, Beliefs and Knowledge in Higher Education*, Dordrecht: Kluwer Academic Publishers.

McCaughrean, G. (1999), *Golden Myths and Legends of the World*, London: Dolphin Paperback.

McCloskey, D. (1990), 'Storytelling in economics', in C. Nash (ed.) *Narrative in Culture*, London: Routledge.

McDrury, J. and Alterio, M. (2003), *Learning through Storytelling in Higher Education*, London: Routledge.

McEwan, H. and Egan, K. (1995), 'Introduction', in H. McEwan and K. Egan (eds) *Narrative in Teaching, Learning and Research*, New York: Teachers' College Press, Columbia University.

McFague TeSelle, S. (1975), *Speaking in Parables*, Philadelphia: Fortress Press.

McKee, R. (1999), *Story*, London: Methuen.

McKeough, A. and Genereux, R. (2003), 'Transformation in narrative thought during adolescence', *Journal of Educational Psychology* 95: 537–552.

McLeod, J. (1997), *Narrative and Psychotherapy*, London: Sage.

McNamee, S. and Gergen, K. (1992), *Therapy as Social Construction*, London: Sage.

McNaughton, J. (1998), 'Anecdote in clinical practice', in T. Greenhalgh and B. Hurwitz (eds) *Narrative Based Medicine*, London: BMJ Books.

Maisch, M. (2003), 'Restructuring a Master's dissertation as a patchwork text', *Innovations in Education and Teaching International* 40(2): 194–200.

Mancuso, J. (1986), 'The acquisition and use of narrative grammar structure', in T. Sarbin (ed.) *Narrative Psychology*, Westport, CT: Praeger.

Mandler, J. (1984), *Scripts, Stories and Aspects of Schema Theory*, Hillsdale, NJ: Lawrence Erlbaum Associates.

Mandler, J. and DeForest, M. (1979), 'Is there more than one way to recall a story?', *Child Development* 50: 886–889.

Mansfield, S. and Bidwell, L. (2005), 'The use of creative writing techniques in developing students' use of reflexive journals', Staff development day, Dundee University, 27 June.

Mar, R. and Oatley, K. (2008), 'The function of fiction is the abstraction and simulation of social experience', *Perspectives on Psychological Science* 3 (3): 173–192.

Mar, R., Oatley, K., Hirsch, J. dela Paz, J. and Peterson, J. (2006), 'Bookworms versus nerd: exposure to fiction versus non-fiction, divergent associations with social ability and the simulation of fictional social worlds', *Journal of Research in Personality* 40: 694–712.

Mar, R.A., Djikic, M. and Oatley, K. (2008), 'Effects of reading on knowledge, social abilities and selfhood: theory and empirical studies', in S. Zyngier, M. Bortolussi, A. Chesnokova and J. Auracher (eds) *Directions in Empirical Studies in Literature: In Honor of Willie van Peer*, Amsterdam: Benjamins.

Marsh, E. and Fazio, L. (2006), 'Learning errors from fiction: difficulties in reducing reliance on fictional stories', *Memory and Cognition* 34(5): 1140–1149.

Marsh, E., Meade, M. and Roediger, H. III (2003), 'Learning facts from fiction', *Journal of Memory and Language* 49: 519–536.

Marshall, S. (1986), *English Folk Tales*, London: Phoenix.

Martin, G. (1981), *The Architecture of Experience*, Edinburgh: Edinburgh University Press.

Martin, S. and Darnley, L. (1996), *The Teaching Voice*, London: Whurr Publishers.

Marton, F. and Booth, S. (1997), *Learning and Awareness*, Hillsdale, NJ: Lawrence Erlbaum Associates.

Marton, F., Hounsell, D. and Entwistle, N. (1997), *The Experience of Learning*, Edinburgh: Scottish Academic Press.

Maslin-Ostrowski, P. and Ackerman, R. (1998), 'Case story', in M. Galbraith (ed.) *Adult Learning Methods*, Malabar, FL: Krieger Publishing Company.

Matthews-DeNatale, G. (2008), 'Digital storytelling: tips and resources', http://net.educause.edu/library/ir/pdf/ELOI8167B.pdf.

Mattingly, C. (1990), 'Narrative reflections on practical actions', in D. Schon (ed.) *The Reflective Turn*, New York: Teachers' College Press, Columbia University.

Meek, M., Warlow, A. and Barton, G. (1977), *The Cool Web*, Trowbridge: Bodley Head.

META (2005), 'Discussion day: session 1 handout', FTTL Project, University of Gloucestershire, 17 October 2005.

Meyers, C. (1986), *Teaching Students to Think Critically*, San Francisco: Jossey-Bass.

Mezirow, J. (1991), *Transformative Dimensions of Adult Learning*, San Francisco: Jossey-Bass.

Middleton, D. and Edwards, D. (1990), 'Conversational remembering: a social psychological approach', in D. Middleton and D. Edwards (eds) *Collective Remembering*, London: Sage.

Miller, C. (2004), *Digital Storytelling: a creator's guide to interactive entertainment*, Burlington, MA: Focal Press.

Milne, A. (1974), *The House at Pooh Corner*, London: Methuen.

Milner, M. (1957), *On Not Being Able to Paint*, London: Heinemann.

——(1987), *Eternity's Sunrise*, London: Virago.

Mitchell, R. and Charmaz, K. (1996), 'Telling tales, writing stories', *Journal of Contemporary Ethnography* 25(1): 144–166.

Moon, J. (1995), *A Handbook on the Development of Foundation Courses in Health Promotion*, Cardiff: Health Promotion Wales.

——(1999a), *Reflection in Learning and Professional Development*, London: Routledge Falmer.

——(1999b), *Learning Journals: a handbook for academics, students and professional development*, London: Routledge Falmer.

——(2001), *Short Courses and Workshops*, London: Routlege Falmer.

——(2002), *The Module and Programme Development Handbook*, London: Routledge Falmer.

——(2004), *A handbook of Reflective and Experiential Learning*, London: Routledge.

——(2006), *Learning Journals: a handbook for reflective practice and professional development*, London: Routledge.

——(2008a), *Critical Thinking: an exploration of theory and practice*, London: Routledge.

——(2008b), *Making Groups Work: improving group work through the principles of academic assertiveness in higher education and professional development*, Bristol: ESCalate, http://ESCalate.ac.uk/5413 (accessed Nov. 2009).

——(2009a), *Achieving Success through Academic Assertiveness: real life strategies for today's students*, New York: Routledge.

——(2009b), 'The use of graduated scenarios to facilitate the learning of difficult-to-describe concepts', *Art and Design in Higher Education* 8(1): 57–70.

——(2010a), *Oral Storytelling: a resource pack for use in education (any discipline)*, http://ESCalate.ac.uk (Summer 2010)

——(2010b), *Oral Storytelling: a resource pack for use in education (media students)*, http://CEMP.ac.uk (Summer 2010)

Moon, J. and Fowler, J. (2008), 'There is a story to be told: a framework for the conception of story in higher education and professional development', *Nurse Education Today* 28(2): 232–239.

Morgan, A. (1995), *Improving your Students' Learning*, London: Kogan Page.

Morpurgo, M. (2006), *Singing for Mrs Pettigrew: a story-maker's journey*, London: Walker Books.

Mortiboys, A. (2005), *Teaching with Emotional Intelligence*, London: Routledge.

Murdoch, I. (1989), *The Message to the Planet*, Harmondsworth: Penguin.

Murray, J. (1997), *Hamlet on the Holodeck*, New York: The Free Press.

——(2001), 'When stories come alive', *Women's Review of Books* 18(5): 11.

Neelands, J. (1992), *Learning through Imagined Experience*, London: Hodder and Stoughton.

Neissler, U. and Winograd, E. (1988), *Remembering Reconsidered*, Cambridge: Cambridge University Press.

Noddings, N. (1996), 'Stories and affect in teacher education', *Cambridge Journal of Education* 26(3): 435–447.

Nwobani, C. (2008), 'Chi Creation Griot Network', Society for Storytelling, *Storylines* (Autumn).

Nymark, S. (2000), *Organisational Storytelling*, Oslo: Foglaget Ankerhus.

Oakley, A. (1984), *Taking It Like a Woman*, London: Jonathan Cape.

——(1989), *The Men's Room*, London: Virago.

——(1992), *The Secret Lives of Eleanor Jenkinson*, London: HarperCollins.

Oatley, K. (1999), 'Why fiction may be twice as true as fact: fiction as cognitive and social simulation', *Review of General Psychology* 3(2): 101–117.

——(2008a), 'The mind's flight simulator', *Psychologist* 21(12): 1030–1032.

——(2008b), 'The science of fiction', *New Scientist*, 28 June.

Osis, M. and Stout, L. (2001), 'Using narrative therapy with older adults', in G. Kenyon, P. Clark and B. de Vries (eds) *Narrative Gerontology*, New York: Springer Publishing.

Ovens, P. (2003), 'Using patchwork text to develop a critical understanding of science', *Innovations in Education and Teaching International* 40(2): 133–143.

Packer, M. (1991), 'Interpeting stories, interpreting lives', in M. Tappan and M. Packer (eds) *Narrative and Storytelling: implications for understanding moral development*, San Francisco: Jossey-Bass.

Pagano, J. (1991), 'Moral fictions: the diemma of theory and practice', in C. Witherell and N. Noddings (eds) *Stories Lives Tell*, New York: Teachers' College Press, Columbia University.

Paley, V. (1995), 'Looking for magpie; another voice in the classroom', in H. McEwan and K. Egan (eds) *Narrative in Teaching and Learning*, New York: Teachers' College Press, Columbia University.

Parker, J. (2003), 'The patchwork text in teaching Greek tragedy', *Innovations in Education and Teaching International* 40(2); 180–193.

Parkin, D. (2008), 'Bringing life to the material', *ESCalate News* (Summer).

Parkin, M. (1998), *Tales for Trainers*, London: Kogan Page.

Parkinson, R. (2004), *Tall Tale Telling*, London: Imaginary Journeys.

——(2005), *Imagine On*, London: Imaginary Journeys.

——(2007a), *Yarn Spinning*, London: Imaginary Journeys.

——(2007b), *New Lamps from Old*, London: Imaginary Journeys.

——(2009), *Transforming Tales*, London: Jessica Kingsley.

——(n.d.), 'History of storytelling', http://www.uncommon-knowledge.co.uk/psychology_articles/historyofstorytelling.pdf.

Parks, T. (2008), 'Everything is connected', *Guardian*, Saturday 13 September.

Pendry, J. (2008), 'Many cultures, one community', *Storylines* (Summer).

Perry, W. (1970), *Forms of Intellectual and Academic Development in the College Years*, New York: Holt, Rhinehart and Winston.

——(1985), 'Different worlds in the same classroom', http://isites.harvard.edu/fs/html/ich.topic58474/perry.html (accessed Nov. 2009).

Phillips, N. (1995), 'Telling organizational tales: on the role of narrative fiction in the study of organizations', *Organizational Studies* 16(4), 625–649.

Piaget, J. (1971), *Biology and Knowledge*, Edinburgh: Edinburgh University Press.

Pierce, C. (1957), *Essays in the Philosophy of Science*, New York: The Liberal Arts Press.

Pilgrim Projects (n.d.), Pilgrim Projects patient voices website, http://research.shu.ac.uk/user-involvement/digitalstorytellingnewsletterweb2.pdf (accessed Nov 2009).

Pinar, W. (1975), 'Currere: toward reconceptualization', in W. Pinar (ed.) *Curriculum theorizing*, Berkeley, CA: McCutcham Publishing Corp.

Pirsig, R. (1974), *Zen and the Art of Motorcycle Maintenance*, London: Bodley Head.

Playback Theatre (n.d.), http://www.playbacktheatre.co.uk (accessed Nov. 2009).

Plummer, K. (1995), *Telling Sexual Stories*, London: Routledge.

Polkinghorne, D. (1988), *Narrative Knowing and the Human Sciences*, Albany, NY: University of New York Press.

Pollack, L. (2000), 'That's infotainment', *People Management* 6(25): 18–20.

Polyani, M. (1969), *Knowing and Being*, ed. M Greene, Chicago: University of Chicago Press.

Pope, J. (2010), 'Where do we go from here? Reader's responses to interactive fiction', *International Journal of Research into New Media Technologies* 16(1): 75–94.

——. (n.d.), Genarrator, http://genarrator.cemp.ac.uk/ (accessed Nov. 2009) and http://genarrator.blogspot.com/ (accessed Nov. 2009).

Postman, N. and Weingartner, C. (1969), *Teaching as a Subversive Activity*, New York: Dell.

Prentice, D., Gerrig, R. and Bailis, D. (1997), 'What readers bring to the processing of fictional texts', *Psychonomic Bulletin and Review* 4: 416–420.

Prochaska, J. and Velicer, W. (1997), 'The transtheoretical model of health behavior change', *Ameri can Journal of Health Promotion* 12: 38–48.

Progoff, I. (1975), *At a Journal Workshop*, New York: Dialogue House Library.

Rainer, T. (1978), *The New Diary*, North Ryde, NSW, Australia: Angus and Robertson.

Randall, W. (2001), 'Storied worlds: acquiring a narrative perspective on aging, identity and everyday life', in G. Kenyon, P. Clark and B. de Vries, 2001 (eds) *Narrative Gerontology*, New York: Springer Publishing.

Rappaport, J. (1993), 'Narrative studies, personal stories and identity transformation in the mutual help context', *Journal of Applied Behavioural Science* 29(2): 239–256.

Read, H. (1935), *The Green Child*, Harmondsworth: Penguin.

Redwine, M. (1989), 'The autobiography as a motivating factor for students', in S. Weil and I. McGill (eds) *Making Sense of Experiential Learning*, Buckingham: Society for Research in Higher Education and Open University Press.

Repede, E. (2008), 'All that holds: a story of nursing', *Journal of Holistic Nursing* 26: 226–232.

Rice, E. (1976), *Papa's Lemonade*, New York: Greenwillow Books.

Richardson, L. (2000), 'Writing: a method of inquiry', in N. Denzil and Y. Lincoln (eds) *Handbook of Qualitative Research*, London: Sage.

Richardson, R. (1996), *Fortunes and Fables*, Stoke on Trent: Trentham Books.

Ricoeur, P. (1984), *Time and Narrative*, Chicago: University of Chicago Press.

Riordan, J. (1984), *The Woman in the Moon*, London: Hutchinson.

Rizzolatti, G., Fabbri-Destro, M. and Cattaneo, L. (2009), 'Mirror neurones, their clinical relevance', *Nature Clinical Practice Neurology* 5(1): 24–34.

Robinson, J. and Hawpe, L, (1986), 'Narrative thinking as a heuristic process', in T. Sarbin (ed.) *Narrative Psychology*, London: Praeger.

Rollnick, S., Kinnersley, P. and Stott, N. (1993), 'Methods of helping patients with behaviour change', *British Medical Journal* 307: 188–190.

Roorbach, B. (1998), *Writing Life Stories*, Cincinnati: Story Press.

Rosen, M. (2009), *Word of Mouth*, BBC Radio 4, 14 April.

Rosenstein, B. (2002), 'The Sorcerer's Apprentice and the reflective practitioner', *Reflective Practice* 3(3): 255–261.

Rowland, G., Rowland, S. and Winter, R. (1990), 'Writing fiction as inquiry into practice', *Journal of Curriculum Studies* 22(3): 291–293.

Rowling, J.K. (2000), *Harry Potter and the Goblet of Fire*, London: Bloomsbury.

Rozin, P., Millman, L. and Nemeroff, C. (1986), 'Operation of the laws of sympathetic magic in disgust and other domains', *Journal of Personality and Social Psychology* 50: 703–712.

Rushdie, S. (1990), *Haroun and the Sea of Stories*, London: Granta.

Ryan, P. (2008), 'Narrative learning/learning narratives: storytelling, experiential learning and education', lecture given at George Ewart Evans Centre for Storytelling, University of Glamorgan, 29 May 2008.

Salisbury, J. (1994), 'Becoming qualified – an ethnography of a post-experience teacher training course', PhD thesis, University of Wales, Cardiff.

Sandford, J. (1966), '*Cathy Come Home*', film directed by Ken Loach London: BBC.

Sarbin, T. (1986), 'Introduction and overview', in T. Sarbin, *Narrative Psychology*, Westport, CT: Praeger.

Saunders, D., Brake, M., Griffiths, M. and Thornton, R. (2004), 'Access and science fiction', *Active Learning in Higher Education* 5(1): 27–42.

Savin-Baden, M. (2008), 'Problem-based learning in immersive educational worlds', IPED Conference on Researching Academic Visions and Realities, Coventry University, September 2008.

Savin-Baden, M., Toombs, C., White, D., Poulton, T., Kavid, K. and Woodham, D. (2009), 'Getting started in Second Life', http://www.jisc.ac.uk/news/stories/2009/08/secondlife/aspx (accessed Nov. 2009).

Saxe, R. and Wexler, A. (2005), 'Making sense of another mind: the role of the right tempero-parietal junction', *Neuropsychologia* 43: 1391–1399.

Schank, R. (1995), *Tell Me a Story*, Evanston, IL: North Western University Press.

Scheibe, K. (1986), 'Self-narratives and adventure', in T. Sarbin (ed.) *Narrative Psychology*, Westport, CT: Praeger.

——(1998), 'Replica, imitations and the question of authenticity', in J. de Riviera and T. Sarbin, *Believed-in Imaginings: the narrative construction of reality*, Washington, DC: American Psychological Association.

Schon, D. (1983), *The Reflective Practitioner*, San Francisco: Jossey-Bass.

——(1987), *Educating the Reflective Practitioner*, San Francisco: Jossey-Bass.

Schreiber, D. (2009), 'Sound of the City', *National Trust Magazine* (Spring).

Scoggins, J. and Winter, R. (1999), 'The patchwork text: a coursework format for education as critical understanding', *Teaching in Higher Education* 4(4): 485–499.

Seed, J., Macy, J., Fleming, P. and Naess, A. (1988), *Thinking Like a Mountain*, London: Heretic Books.

Seel, R. (2003), 'Story and conversation in organisations: a survey', http://www.new-paradigm.co.uk.

Seelye, J. (ed.) (2007), *The Swiss Family Robinson*, reprint of D. Goodwin's translation (1816) of Pastor J.D. Wyss's novel, Harmondsworth: Penguin. See Wikipedia entry (www.wikipedia.co.uk).

Selling, B. (1998), *Writing from Within*, Alameda, CA: Hunter House.

Send a Cow (2009), 'Send a Cow', BBC Radio 4 Appeal, 25 January.

Shah, T. (2008), *In Arabian Nights*, New York: Doubleday.

Shotter, J. (2001), 'Participative thinking: "seeing the face" and "hearing the voice" of social situations', *Career Development International* 6/7: 343–347.

Skouge, J. and Rao, K. (2009), 'Digital storytelling in teacher education: creating transformations through narrative', *Educational Perspectives* 42(1–2): 54–60.

Slack, G. (2007), 'Found: the source of human empathy', *New Scientist*, 10 November.

Slater, M. (2002), 'Entertainment education and the persuasive impact of narratives', in M. Green, J. Strange and T. Brock (eds) *Narrative Impact: social and cognitive foundations*, Mahwah, NJ: Lawrence Erlbaum Associates.

Sloane, S. (2000), *Digital Functions – storytelling in a material world*, Stamford, CT: Ablex Publishing.

Slovic, P. (2007), 'When compassion fails', *New Scientist*, 17 April: 18.

Smith, L. and Winter, R. (2003), 'Applied epistemology for community nurses: evaluating the impact of the patchwork text', *Innovations in Education and Teaching International* 40(2): 161–173.

Snowden, D. (2004), 'Narrative patterns – the perils and possibilities of using story in organisations', in E. Lesser and K. Prusak (eds) *Creating Value with Knowledge*, Oxford: Oxford University Press.

Sobel, D. (1995), *Longitude*, Markham, Ontario: Thomas Allan and Son.

Society for Storytelling (n.d.), Special interest group in Education website, http://sfs. org.uk/special_interest_groups/education_storytelling-skills/.

Solzhenitsyn, A, (1963), *A Day in the Life of Ivan Denisovich*, New York: Bantam.

Sparkes, A. (1998) 'Narratives of self as an occasion of conspiracy', *Sociology of Sport Online*, http://physed.otago.ac.nz/sosol/vlila3.htm (accessed March 2010).

——(2002), *Telling Tales in Sport and Physical Activity*, Leeds: Human Kinetics.

Spence, D. (1998), 'The mythic properties of popular explanation', in J. de Riviera and T. Sarbin (eds) *Believed-in Imaginings: the narrative construction of reality*, Washington, DC: American Psychological Association.

Squier, H. (1998), 'Teaching humanities in the undergraduate medical curriculum', in T. Greenhalgh and B. Hurwitz (eds) *Narrative Based Medicine*, London: BMJ Books.

Stein, N. and Policastro, M. (1984), 'The concept of story: a comparison between children's and teachers' viewpoints', in H. Mandl, N. Stein and T. Trabasso, *Learning and Comprehension of Text*, Hillsdale, NJ: Lawrence Erlbaum Associates.

Strange, J. and Leung, C. (1999), 'How anecdotal accounts in news and in fiction can influence judgements of a social problem's urgency, causes and cures', *Journal of Personality and Social Psychology* 25(4): 436–449.

Strong-Wilson, T. (2006), 'Bringing memory forward: a method for engaging teachers in reflective practice on narrative and memory', *Reflective Practice* 7(1): 101–113.

Swap, W., Leonard, D., Shields, M. and Abrams, L. (2004), 'Using mentoring and storytelling to transfer knowledge in the workplace', in E. Lesser and K. Prusak (eds) *Creating Value with Knowledge* Oxford: Oxford University Press.

Tappan, M. (1991), 'Narrative authorship and the development of moral authority', in M. Tappan and M. Packer (eds) *Narrative and Storytelling: implications for understanding moral development*, San Francisco: Jossey-Bass.

Taylor, S., Fisher, D. and Dufresne, R. (2002), 'The aesthetics of management storytelling', *Management Learning* 33(3): 313–330.

Temple, J. and Gillet, A. (1989), *Understanding Reading Problems*, Orlando, FL: Houghton Mifflin.

Thomas, T. and Killick, S. (2007), *Telling Tales: storytelling as emotional literacy*, Blackburn: Educational Printing Services, Ltd.

Tibble, L. (2008), 'Patchwork text: developing reflection and experiential learning through a structured approach to action learning', ISOTL Conference, 15–18 May, London.

Toastmasters (n.d.), www.toastmasters.org (accessed Nov. 2009).

Tomkins, A. (2008), 'Learning to learn: developing critical stories for interview situations', study guide developed in Meta Project (FDTL project, University of Goucestershire).

Tripp, D. (1993), *Critical Incidents in Teaching: developing professional judgement*, London: Routledge.

Turkle, S. (2007), 'The secret power of things we hold dear', *New Scientist*, 9 June.

Turner, L. (2008), 'The lesson: the new Doctor Who provides an opportunity to investigate science fiction', *Guardian*, 15 April.

Usher, R. and Soloman, N. (1999), 'Experiential learning and the shaping of subjectivity in the work-place', *Studies in the Education of Adults* 31(2): 155–163.

Vinden, P. (1998), 'Imagination and true belief: a cross-cultural perspective', in J. de Riviera and T. Sarbin (eds) *Believed-in Imaginings: the narrative construction of reality*, Washington, DC: American Psychological Association.

Warner, M. (1996), *Wonder Tales*, London: Vintage.

Wertner, P. and Trudel, P. (2006), 'A new theoretical perspective for understanding how coaches learn to coach', *Sport Psychologist* 20: 192–212.

West, H. and Pines, A. (1985), *Cognitive Structure and Conceptual Change*, New York: Academic Press.

Wheeler, S., Green, M. and Brock, T. (1999), 'Fictional narratives change beliefs: replications of Prentice, Gerrig and Bailis (1997) with mixed corroboration', *Psychonomic Bulletin and Review* 6(1): 136–141.

Whelan, K., Huber, J., Rose, C., Davies, A. and Clandinin, D. (2001), 'Telling and retelling our stories on the professional development landscape', *Teachers and Teaching: theory and practice* 7(2): 143–156.

White, H. (1981), 'The value of narrativity in the representation of reality', in W. Mitchell (ed.) *On Narrative*, Chicago: University of Chicago Press.

Williams, J.T. (1995), *Pooh and the Philosophers*, London: Methuen.

Wilson, J. (2005), *Clean Break*, London: Random House.

Wilson, M. (2006), 'Story-literacy and the failure of ideas: storytelling in higher education', paper given at the Value Added Tales Conference, Northern Centre for Storytelling, Grasmere, 7–8 June.

Wilkes, A. (1997), *Knowledge in Mind: individual and collective processes in cognition*, London: Psychology Press.

Winter, R. (1986), 'Fictional-critical writing: an approach to case-study research by practitioners', *Cambridge Journal of Education* 16(3): 175–182.

——(1991), 'Interviewers, interviewees and the exercise of power', *British Journal of Educational Research* 17(3): 251–262.

——(2000), 'How to: orchestrate cerebral cells', *Times Higher Education Supplement*, 4November.

——(2003a), 'Conceptualising the patchwork text: addressing problems of coursework assessment in higher education', *Innovations in Education and Teaching International* 40(2): 112–122.

——(2003b), 'Alternative to the essay', *Guardian*, Education Guardian, 10 June.

Winter, R., Buck, A. and Sobiechowska, P. (1999), *Professional Experience and the Investigative Imagination*, London: Routledge.

Witherell, C. and Noddings, N. (1991), 'Prologue: an invitation to our readers', in C. Witherell and N. Noddings (eds) *Stories Lives Tell*, New York: Teachers' College Press, Columbia University.

Wolf, M. (2007), *Proust and the Squid*, New York: HarperCollins.

Wood, A. and Richardson, R. (1992), *Inside Stories*, Stoke on Trent: Trentham Books.

Zander, M. (2007), 'Tell me a story: the power of narrative in the practice of teaching art', *Studies in Art Education* 48(2): 189–203.

Zeldin, T. (1998), *Conversation*, London: Harvill Press.

Zeller, N. (1995), 'Narrative rationality in educational research', in H. McEwan and K. Egan (eds) *Narrative in Teaching, Learning and Research*, New York: Teachers' College Press, Columbia University.

Zipes, J. (1997), *Why Fairy Stories Stick*, London: Routledge.

——(2000), *The Oxford Companion to Fairy Tales*, Oxford: Oxford University Press.

——(2006), *Fairy Tales and the Art of Subversion*, second edition, London: Routledge.

——(2007), *Why Fairy Tales Stick*, London: Routledge.

Zunshine, L. (2006), *Why We Read Fiction*, Columbus, OH: Ohio State University.

Index